Learning
Through Two Languages
Studies of Immersion
and Bilingual Education

Fred Genesee
McGill University

NEWBURY HOUSE PUBLISHERS, Cambridge
A division of Harper & Row, Publishers, Inc.
New York, Philadelphia, San Francisco, Washington, D.C.,
London, Mexico City, São Paulo, Singapore, Sydney

Library of Congress Cataloging-in-Publication Data

Genesee, Fred.
Learning through two languages.

Bibliography: p.
Includes index.
1. Education, Bilingual—Canada. 2. Education,
Bilingual—United States. 3. Concentrated study.
4. Concentrated study—Case studies. I. Title.
LC3734.G46 1987   371.97′00971   86-33283
ISBN 0-06-632260-X

TO THE MEMORY
OF MY MOTHER AND FATHER

Cover Design: Sally Carson Design
Text Art: Fine Line Illustrations, Inc.
Production: Kewal Sharma
Compositor: ComCom Division of Haddon Craftsmen, Inc.
Printer and Binder: McNaughton & Gunn

Learning Through Two Languages:
Studies of Immersion and Bilingual Education

NEWBURY HOUSE PUBLISHERS
A division of Harper & Row, Publishers, Inc.

Language Science
Language Teaching
Language Learning

CAMBRIDGE, MASSACHUSETTS

Printed in the U.S.A.

63 22606

First printing: April 1987

2 4 6 8 10 9 7 5 3

Contents

LIST OF TABLES

LIST OF FIGURES

Preface

This book is about bilingual education. The primary focus is on bilingual education for majority group, English-speaking students in Canada, or what is more commonly referred to as immersion (chapters one to seven). Immersion programs in the United States will also be reviewed (chapter eight). Briefly, immersion programs are a form of bilingual education designed for majority language students, that is, students who speak the dominant language of society upon entry to school. In immersion programs, a second language, along with the students' home language, is used to teach regular school subjects such as mathematics and science as well as language arts. A major objective of immersion programs is bilingual proficiency.

Because of their conceptual relationship to immersion programs, and because of their overall educational and sociopolitical significance, bilingual education programs for minority language children in the United States (hereafter referred to simply as "bilingual education") will be an additional focus of this book (chapters nine to eleven). In bilingual education programs, students receive academic instruction in their home language along with instruction in English as a Second Language. The main objective of bilingual education programs is to foster English language proficiency through first language development so that the students can participate successfully in all-English classes.

Bilingual education generally defined is neither a new nor a recent educational innovation. Chapter one will begin by putting contemporary immersion programs and U.S. bilingual education for minority language students into an historical perspective by examining some early forms of bilingual education. This brief review will reveal a remarkable diversity of program models. A number of writers have attempted to summarize this diversity by proposing typologies that describe the structural characteristics of various bilingual programs, their social impact, or their intended outcomes. Some of the major typologies will be reviewed in chapter one so that the ensuing discussions of immersion and bilingual education can be better understood from a broad perspective. Chapter one also contains a discussion of the historical background and the immediate social circumstances that led to the introduction of immersion programs in Canada.

A detailed description of alternative Canadian immersion programs along with their theoretical rationale is presented in chapter two. Chapter three then describes the basic research approaches, methods, and testing instruments used in empirical evaluations of immersion. This is followed by a review and discussion of the English language and academic results of immersion. The main focus of attention in this and the following chapter is early total immersion, since this was the initial form of immersion and since pedagogically it represents the most radical departure from regular English schooling. The second language testing results, French in most cases, are reviewed in chapter four. In addition to considering the second language results of the respective immersion alternatives, including early, delayed, and late, the results of comparative evaluations of alternative immersion options are discussed in some detail.

A number of special immersion programs have been developed and evaluated in Quebec. Although these programs are unique and have not been adopted on a wide scale by other school districts, they are interesting in their own right, and in their uniqueness they contribute to our knowledge of immersion programs in general and to our understanding of second language learning. Three such programs are described in chapter five: a *double immersion* program, in which two non-native languages, instead of the customary one, are used for basic academic instruction along with the students' home language; an *activity-centered* immersion program, which stresses individual student initiative and activity in the pursuit of academic goals as an incentive for second language learning; and a *"super immersion"* program which is, in fact, a regular French language school except that most of the students are English-speaking.

The popularity of immersion throughout Canada brought with it students with diverse learner characteristics that are often associated with academic difficulty and poor achievement. Studies have been undertaken by a number of researchers to investigate the suitability of immersion programs for students with characteristics that might otherwise place them at a disadvantage in regular school programs. Three characteristics in particular have received careful examination: general academic ability (or intelligence), first language ability, and socioeconomic status. The results of these investigations are discussed in chapter six. The effectiveness of immersion in monolingual communities, those that do not have target language residents, are considered as well. This is followed in chapter seven by a discussion of social-psychological studies of immersion, including, for example, studies of immersion students' attitudes toward themselves, target language speakers, the use of the target language, and second language learning.

The final chapter on immersion, chapter eight, examines the results of immersion programs in the United States. Although the U.S. programs have not gained the same popular support as have Canadian programs, they are of interest because they embody goals that are seldom found in the Canadian programs. As well, the results of the U.S. programs serve to establish the generalizability of the Canadian results.

The next three chapters examine the other side of bilingual education, namely, bilingual programs for minority language students. In contrast to immersion programs, bilingual programs for minority language students prescribe initial academic instruction through the medium of the students' home language prior to instruction through English. Chapter nine provides an historical account of the political and social factors that were instrumental in the development of U.S. bilingual programs, as well as a discussion of the theoretical underpinnings and extant evaluations of bilingual education. Discussion of educational programs for minority language students in the United States is continued in chapter ten by considering a number of sociocultural factors that are thought to influence the academic performance of minority language students. Three classes of factors are identified and examined: societal, intergroup, and pedagogical or classroom.

Despite its complementarity to bilingual education for minority language students, immersion programs for majority language students are all too often misunderstood and misapplied to issues concerning the education of limited-English proficient or non-English proficient students. In chapter eleven, three pedagogical features of immersion programs that are of potential relevance to educational programs for minority language students are identified and discussed.

Chapter twelve—*Conclusions*—points out that bilingual education programs for both majority language and minority language students raise important and fundamental issues about the nature of language proficiency and its relationship to academic performance and achievement. Our determined and concerted efforts to unravel the complexity of these relationships will advance our understanding of not only bilingual education but all education.

I wrote this book while in the Department of English as a Second Language of the University of Hawaii. The department provided a wonderful, stimulating place for the preparation of this manuscript. My warmest thanks to the members of the department whose discussions with me have greatly enriched the content of this book and my thinking about second language learning and teaching: Craig Chaudron, Dick Day, Mike Long, Ted Plaister, Jack Richards, Charlie Sato, and Richard Schmidt.

I am also thankful to colleagues who were kind and patient enough to comment on early drafts of this book: Maggie Bruck, David Dolson, Else Hamayan, Naomi Holobow, Dan Holt, Wally Lambert, Barry McLaughlin, and

Dick Tucker. I hope that I have done their serious and thoughtful comments justice.

Finally, I am grateful to the Social Sciences and Humanities Research Council of Canada, Ottawa, for its generous ongoing support of much of the research reported in this book and for the Leave Fellowship they granted me in partial support of the preparation of this book.

FRED GENESEE

CHAPTER 1

Bilingual Education in Historical Pespective

Immersion is a form of bilingual education in which students who speak the language of the majority of the population receive part of their instruction through the medium of a second language and part through their first language. Both the second language and the first language are used to teach regular school subjects, such as mathematics, science, or physical education, in addition to language arts. The same subjects are never taught using both languages concurrently or during the same academic year. Different subjects are taught through the medium of each language. Generally speaking, at least 50 percent of instruction during a given academic year must be provided through the second language for the program to be regarded as immersion. Programs in which one subject and language arts are taught through the second language are generally identified as enriched second language programs.

The practice of providing educational instruction in a language different from that which the students normally use is not new or recent. Mackey (1978) suggests that such instruction may date back as early as 3000 B.C. It was often adopted because there were so few languages with written forms that schooling beyond the territory of the written language was necessarily through the medium of a non-home language. Many of these educational programs provided instruction in only one language and therefore were bilingual only to the extent that students became bilingual because the language of the school differed from the language of the home and community. There is also evidence of true bilingual education, that is, schools in which instruction takes place in at least two languages, during ancient times. Tablets engraved with bilingual texts that apparently were used to teach children to read and write Sumerian and Eblaite have been found in modern-day Syria (Lewis, 1977). Lewis (1977) points out that extensive contact between different language communities in ancient times also necessitated bilingual schools for the education of multilingual scribes who could provide communication and record-keeping services. Use of a non-home language as the sole or major medium of educational instruction was common during the expansion of the Greek Empire and subsequently the Roman Empire (Lewis, 1977). Use of Greek in school was not required by imperial Greece but was, nevertheless, widespread and often desired in the colonies as a means of teaching non-Greek speaking children language skills that they would need if they were to have access to important administrative or political positions.

Among the Roman elite, instruction in Greek was not simply a matter of practicality, but rather was often regarded as the cornerstone of the Roman child's education. According to Lewis, "instruction in Greek was assumed to be at least as good a foundation of the child's intellectual development as his mother tongue could be. . . . and it was regarded as a satisfactory means of improving the child's control of his mother tongue" (1977, p. 62). Apparently, however, there was not universal support for bilingualism and bilingual education among Romans. Detractors criticized the quality of Greek being learned in Rome. There was also some concern that acquisition of two languages simultaneously could be an intellectual burden and that the students' skills in Latin, their home language, would suffer if instruction in it were delayed too long. It is interesting to note that the same concerns are expressed today.

Latin was used as the dominant school language throughout the extensive territories of the Roman Empire as a way of promoting unity among diverse ethnolinguistic "colonies." Indeed, Latin continued to be the dominant language of education in much of Western Europe until a few hundred years ago. With the rise of nationalism around the sixteenth century, Latin was slowly replaced by local "national" languages; e.g., English in England, French in France (Fishman, 1972). Even in these cases, however, the language of schooling continued to differ from the home language in that standard languages or dialects were used in school while nonstandard language varieties were used in the home.

Bilingual education in the United States dates back to the mid-nineteenth century when a number of German-English parochial schools were established by the German communities in Ohio and Missouri (Andersson & Boyer, 1970; Castellanos, 1983). The German-English Public School was established in 1837 in St. Louis a year before the first all-English public school opened in the city. Twenty-three years after its inauguration, the school continued to attract a student enrollment half the size of the public school. An early German-English bilingual education project in Cincinnati, Ohio, around the same time spawned similar projects in other cities, such as Indianapolis, Baltimore, and Milwaukee. It has been estimated that at least one million American children were educated in German and English during the period from 1880 to the end of the century.

The use of other non-English languages for educational instruction in private, parochial schools was not uncommon in the United States during the same period. For example, schooling through the medium of Spanish could be found in California, New Mexico, and Florida. Norwegian-medium schools could be found in the Dakota territory toward the end of the nineteenth century, while Italian, French, Spanish, and German could be found in San Francisco schools during the early part of the twentieth century. Most of these schools were established by recently arrived immigrant groups intent on preserving their heritage languages and cultures. More will be said of contemporary bilingual education in the United States in chapters nine, ten, and eleven.

It should be apparent from this brief historical review that bilingual education is not a recent phenomenon. Nor is it simple. A variety of models of bilingual education have been used. They vary with respect to their goals, the characteristics of the participating students, the sequencing and amount of instruction in the languages involved, and their pedagogical approaches, among other things. A number of typologies have been proposed to describe the diversity of contemporary bilingual education. By far the most comprehensive and detailed of these is that of Mackey (1972).

Mackey classifies programs in terms of the patterns of language use in 1) the home, 2) the curriculum, and 3) the community and nation in which the school is located, as well as in terms of 4) the status of the languages themselves. The home may be unilingual or bilingual and the language of instruction in school may be a home language or it may differ from the home language. Criterion 2 includes several distinctions. There may be single-medium or dual-medium bilingual schools. Single-medium schools are bilingual insofar as the home and the school language differ. The languages must be used to convey knowledge and not simply taught as subjects for the program to be considered bilingual. The goals of the school may be maintenance of both languages at an equal level, or transfer from one medium of instruction to another (e.g., from the home language to the national language). Moreover, the thrust of the program may be toward the language of a wider culture (acculturation); it may be toward that of a regional, national, or neo-national culture; or it may be toward language revival. Language change may be complete or gradual, and the distribution of the languages for curricular purposes may be equal or different. Mackey identifies ten different curricular patterns using combinations of these distinctions.

Criterion 3 is intended to take into account the contexts in which the languages are used. He identifies nine contexts that differ with respect to whether the languages used in the home, the school, the area, and the nation are the same or different. Considering the curricular patterns just described together with these contexts yields 90 basically different patterns of bilingual schooling. Finally, Mackey's typology considers the functions and status of the languages and their linguistic and cultural similarities or differences. While a comprehensive way of describing bilingual schools, the taxonomy is largely static and purely descriptive. It provides no indications regarding the social or pedagogical bases of the programs, nor their social or pedagogical implications or impact.

Viewed in terms of Mackey's typology, the Canadian immersion programs would be classified as dual-medium schools for children from mostly unilinguial homes in which one of the school languages is also a home language; the programs aim for maintenance bilingualism. Moreover, the home language, English, is used in the area and in the nation, and it has high status both locally and internationally.

Fishman and Lovas (1970) have proposed a typology that is not based on the characteristics of students or languages, as in the case of Mackey's taxonomy, but rather focuses on the sociolinguistic goals and outcomes of different bilingual programs. Fishman and Lovas distinguish programs with four different goals: 1) transitional bilingualism, 2) monoliterate bilingualism, 3) partial bilingualism, and 4) full bilingualism. Furthermore, they identify probable societal outcomes of each program type. In the North American context, each program type would take the following form. Transitional bilingual programs use the students' home language until such time that they can receive all instruction in English. Transitional bilingual education programs in the United States are of this type. Such programs make no provision for continued maintenance or development of the home language and as such promote language shift. Monoliterate bilingual programs foster aural-oral skills in the first language primarily for home and culturally relevant contexts. Literacy in the first language is not fostered. Full literacy along with aural-oral proficiency in English is the primary objective. Fishman and Lovas suggest that, notwithstanding short-run maintenance of oral skills in the first language, the likely long-run outcome of such programs is a shift away from the first language to English.

Partial bilingual programs aim for oral fluency and literacy in both languages, but literacy in the home language is restricted to ethnically or culturally relevant domains, while literacy in English is intended for all domains. Thus such programs espouse maintenance bilingualism but identify English with economic and technological spheres. Programs of full bilingualism aim to develop proficiency in both languages in all domains, that is, dual-language maintenance. The Canadian immersion programs are of this type. Fishman and Lovas regard this as the ideal form of bilingual education but suggest that its goal of full bilingualism is not realistic in a monolingual society.

Ferguson, Houghton, and Wells (1977) have also sought to summarize the diversity of bilingual education by identifying different program goals. The goals they identify are broader than those suggested by Fishman and Lovas and include goals

1. to assimilate individuals or groups into the mainstream of society,
2. to unify a multilingual society,
3. to enable people to communicate with the outside world,
4. to gain an economic advantage for individuals or groups,
5. to preserve ethnic or religious ties,
6. to reconcile different political or socially separate communities,
7. to spread and maintain the use of a colonial language,
8. to embellish or strengthen the education of elites,
9. to give equal status to languages of unequal prominence in society, and
10. to deepen understanding of language and culture.

As we will see shortly, the Canadian immersion programs were developed by English speaking parents in the province of Quebec so that their children could better learn French and thereby bridge the cultural and linguistic gap that separates English from French Canadians. It is not intended that children attending immersion programs become French. These programs then could be seen to be an example of goal 6. The Canadian immersion programs may also be regarded as an example of goal 4 insofar as they seek to maintain the socioeconomic advantages of the English community by providing English Canadian children with bilingual skills that are increasingly valued in the job market. In many, if not most, cases, bilingual education programs for minority language children in the United States seek explicitly or implicitly to assimilate non-English speaking children to the American way of life, and, therefore, they may be viewed as an example of goal 1.

Classification of a particular bilingual program according to one of these typologies does not preclude classifying it according to one of the others. Indeed, each typology complements the other and together they serve to identify the multiply important dimensions of bilingual education. This digression into historical and contemporary perspectives on bilingual education is intended to broaden understanding of the particular forms of bilingual education that will be considered in some detail in the remainder of this book. Let us turn now to the historical and sociocultural background of the Canadian immersion programs. The reader can judge for himself or herself what classification, or classifications, is most apt.

THE CANADIAN IMMERSION PROGRAMS IN HISTORICAL PERSPECTIVE

Like many parts of the New World, Canada was settled and governed by different European nations during its early development. The first colonization of Canada was undertaken by the French beginning with Jacques Cartier's landing in Canada in 1534. French control gave way to British control in 1763 when the British defeated the French at the Battle of the Plains of Abraham near Quebec City (Cook, Saywell, & Ricker, 1977). French Canadian culture was deeply rooted in North America at the time of the British Conquest, and thus the French were able to resist the efforts of the British to assimilate them.

The British North America Act of 1867 legally constituted the Canadian confederation, which at the time consisted of Ontario, Quebec, New Brunswick, and Nova Scotia. Analogous to the American Constitution, the BNA Act, as it is usually referred to, affirmed Canada's linguistic duality only in Quebec, where the use of both the French and English languages was required in the Parliament and courts of the province. It was not until 1969 with the passage of the Official Languages Act that both languages were actually accorded official status nationwide. According to the act,

> The English and French languages are the official languages of Canada for all purposes of the Parliament and Government of Canada, and possess and enjoy equality of status and equal rights and privileges as to their use in all the institutions of the Parliament and Government of Canada. (Section 2)

This means that Canadians have access to services provided by the federal parliament and government in English or in French anywhere in Canada. The Act does not require that all Canadians be bilingual, only government employees dispensing federal services. This type of bilingualism is referred to as "institutional bilingualism." The Act does not apply to services provided by Canada's ten provincial governments or the two territorial governments in the Yukon and the Northwest Territories. In fact, at the provincial level, only one province, New Brunswick, recognizes French and English as official languages. The remaining nine provinces are monolingual, with eight recognizing English and one, the province of Quebec, recognizing French as the official language.

Despite the lack of official status for both English and French in most of the provinces, certain provincial government services are now available in both languages in most provinces. There is an increasing move in this direction. The official language policies of the provincial governments tend to reflect their respective populations. Thus, the one officially bilingual province, New Brunswick, has a sizeable percentage of both French-speaking and English-speaking residents; Quebec, which recognizes French as the only official language, is inhabited predominantly by French-speaking Canadians; and the remaining eight provinces, which all recognize English as the official language, have predominantly English-speaking residents.

Despite the historical importance of the French and English cultures in Canada, the federal government recognizes neither as the official culture. In 1971, the federal government adopted an official policy of multiculturalism, whose mandate is

> to encourage and assist within the framework of Canada's official languages policy and in the spirit of existing human rights codes, the full realization of the multicultural nature of Canadian society through programs which promote the preservation and sharing of ethnocultural heritages and which facilitate mutual appreciation and understanding among all Canadians.

Notwithstanding regional differences in the presence of English and French, generally speaking, both languages are important features of Canadian life. Consequently, competence in both English and French is an important means of communication in Canadian political, cultural, and economic affairs, and bilingual competence is often associated with tangible and intangible rewards. The reward value associated with English-French bilingualism is enhanced by the international status and utility of both English and French, be it in the diplomatic, economic, or cultural sphere.

The Quiet Revolution

Despite its historical importance during the early colonization and subsequent development of Canada; despite its contemporary status as an official national language; despite its demographic significance as the native language of approximately 25 percent of the Canadian population; and despite even its international status as a major world language, French has until recently been the disadvantaged partner in the Canadian confederation. This has been true to a large extent even in the province of Quebec where the vast majority of the population speaks French as a native language (some 80 percent in a total population of 6,000,000); indeed, many Quebecers speak only French. Evidence of the inferior status of French can be found in at least three areas: 1) legislation; 2) patterns of language use; and 3) language attitudes.

Legislation and the French Language.   As has already been noted, French is recognized as an official language by only two of Canada's ten provinces (namely, Quebec and New Brunswick). While the eight "English provinces" do not presently recognize French as an official language, they do not forbid its use. The legislative picture has not always been so tolerant. In fact, the use of French, particularly in public schools, has actually been forbidden by law in several provinces at certain times since confederation in 1867. For example, in 1890 the Government of the Province of Manitoba revoked an earlier law requiring the use of French in the provincial parliament and permitting its use in public schools. Students caught using French in school by the authorities could be punished. The 1890 law has since been repealed, and political efforts are being made to restore French to its original status. According to the new Canadian Charter of Rights and Freedoms, passed in 1982, public education will be available in all provinces in both official languages, where numbers warrant.

Patterns of Language Use.   Widespread daily use of French, except in communication with official federal government agencies, is limited to the provinces of Quebec and New Brunswick and to other specific regions where there are sizeable French speaking communities (e.g., the Ontario-Quebec border, northern Alberta, and parts of northern Ontario). Even in these areas, however, English often predominates over French as the *lingua franca*. This is particularly true in public settings and in business and commerce. In an extensive study of the language of work in Quebec, Gendron (1972) noted that

> In the province of Quebec itself, French remains basically a marginal language, since non-French-speaking persons have little need of it and many French-speaking people use English as much as and sometimes more than their mother tongue for important work. This applies even though Quebec's French-speaking people constitute a vast majority both in the labor force and in the overall population. (p. 108)

This means in effect that in mixed conversation groups, English-speaking persons concede much less to French than French-speaking persons do to English. Thus, the burden of bilingualism is unequally distributed between French- and English-speaking people, both with regards to the level of competence needed in the other language and the language demands made on them during the course of a normal work day.

Language Attitudes.   Perhaps no other single piece of evidence attests to the disadvantaged or inferior status that the French language has had relative to the English language than the results of a study carried out by Lambert, Hodgson, Gardner, and Fillenbaum (1960). In what has become a classic study in the social psychology of language, Lambert and his colleagues asked groups of English and French Canadians in Montreal to listen and give their reactions to people speaking either French or English. Unknown to the listeners, they were actually hearing the same perfectly bilingual individuals on separate occasions, sometimes speaking French and sometimes English. Analyses of the listeners' reactions to the speakers indicated that they reacted much more favorably toward the English "guises" than toward the French "guises." In other words, the same speakers were perceived significantly differently when heard using each of their two languages—it was as if they were two different people. Furthermore, it was found that not only did English Canadians form more favorable impressions of the English guises than the French guises, evidence of in-group favoritism, but so did French Canadians. That is to say, even the French Canadian subjects perceived the speakers more favorably when they spoke in English than when they spoke in French, despite the fact that this meant denigrating members of their own ethnolinguistic group.

Subsequent research has substantiated these findings (d'Anglejan & Tucker, 1973) and indicated further that the tendency for French Canadians to denigrate members of their own group in this way is not manifest by children before the age of 12 but emerges around adolescence (Anisfeld & Lambert, 1964) and thus appears to be a socially learned phenomenon (see Day, 1982, for a review of developmental research on language attitudes). Lambert has interpreted these results to mean that language can act as an important symbol of ethnolinguistic group membership, and that members of ethnic minority groups may internalize the negative stereotypes of their group that members of the majority group often hold.

Discontent over these linguistic and cultural inequities had been developing for some time, particularly in Quebec. Early attempts by the French-speaking community to arrive at a more equitable relationship with the English community through negotiation were largely unsuccessful. Faced with a repeated lack of responsiveness on the part of the English community to their concerns, French-speaking Quebecers began to make vocal and public demands for change. This culminated in the early 1960s with concerted political, social, and, in some cases, militant actions to bring about change. There were, for example, demonstrations against public institutions that would not or could not communicate with French-speaking Quebecers in French. The social unrest manifested during this period has come to be called the Quiet Revolution.

Calls from some Quebec politicians for separation from the rest of Canada during the last 25 years can probably be attributed in large measure to the earlier intransigencies of the English community to recognize and respect the language rights of the French community (Arnopoulos & Clift, 1980). That is to say, separatism has emerged as a final solution to a sociolinguistic problem that could not be resolved through social cooperation. One of the most important pieces of legislation to be passed by the "separatist" Parti Quebecois government after coming to power in 1976 was a law (Bill 101) which defined and ensured in law the linguistic rights of the French-speaking citizens of Quebec (see Bourhis, 1985, for a review of these issues). Some analysts think that the 1978 referendum in Quebec, which sought support for the separation of the province from Canada, failed because of Bill 101—passage of this bill reassured the French population that their language and culture would be respected.

THE ST. LAMBERT EXPERIMENT: THE ENGLISH COMMUNITY REACTS TO THE QUIET REVOLUTION

At the same time that the French community in Quebec was expressing dissatisfaction with inequities in the language situation, there was growing concern among some English-speaking Quebecers as well. More specifically, there was an emerging awareness in the English community, precipitated by the events of the Quiet Revolution, that French was becoming an important language of communication in most spheres of life in Quebec and, therefore, that English alone would no longer assure social and economic success in the province. The coexistence of French and English Canadians has been characterized by Canadian novelist Hugh MacLennan (1945) as two solitudes, an apt metaphor in this and many other communities inhabited by people of different linguistic and cultural backgrounds. Faced with the growing importance of French as the main working language of Quebec and with an increasing dissatisfaction with the linguistic barriers that separated English and French Canadians, a concerned group of English-speaking parents in the small suburban community of St. Lambert, outside of Montreal, began to meet informally in the early 1960s to discuss the situation (Lambert & Tucker, 1972).

These parents felt that their lack of competence in French contributed to and indeed was attributable in part to the two solitudes which effectively prevented them from learning French informally from their French-speaking neighbors. Their inability to communicate in French, they felt, was also attributable to inadequate methods of second language instruction in the English schools. At that time, French was taught for relatively short periods each day (20–30 minutes) by teachers who were usually native English-speakers with proficiency in French as a Second Language that varied from excellent to poor. There was an emphasis on teaching vocabulary and grammar rules and on using pattern practice drills based on the then popular audiolingual approach. This approach was common to many second or foreign language teaching programs throughout North America which retain some of the same characteristics even to this day. Unlike second language instruction in other parts of North America, however, second language instruction in Quebec began in elementary school and continued systematically until the end of secondary school. This is still true, and it has become customary in varying degrees in the other provinces as well.

Despite 12 years of second language instruction, however, students graduating from the public schools of Quebec were inadequately prepared to deal with the demands of using French in diverse real-life situations. As one of the 12 St. Lambert parents who spearheaded interest in alternative methods of second language instruction pointed out:

> Children were graduating from English . . . schools in this province with little more knowledge of French than their parents had had, despite claims that the programs had been considerably improved over the years. Their knowledge was not perceptibly superior to that of graduates from the English provinces of Canada and was not sufficient to enable the students to communicate with their French-Canadian neighbors. The parents felt their children were being short-changed and should have the opportunity to become "bilingual" within the school system, since it was so difficult to achieve this skill outside school. (Melikoff, 1972, p. 219)

Most of the St. Lambert parents who participated in these discussions could attest to the failure of second language instruction using their own experiences as evidence.

In their search for better methods of second language instruction for their children, the St. Lambert Bilingual School Study Group, as they called themselves, sought the assistance and advice of experts within their community. In particular, they consulted with Dr. Wallace Lambert of the Psychology Department, McGill University, who had conducted research on social psychological and cognitive aspects of bilingualism, and with Dr. Wilder Penfield of the Montreal Neurological Institute, McGill, who had conducted research on brain mechanisms underlying language functions. The involvement of these two scholars was indeed fortunate. Not only did they give their moral support to the parents' project but their professional advice shaped second language education in Quebec and Canada in important ways.

The efforts of the St. Lambert group succeeded finally with the school district agreeing to set up an experimental kindergarten immersion class in September, 1965, some two years after their first meetings. Melikoff notes in her description of events leading up to 1965 that school officials did not accept the experimental class because of any conviction that it was a worthwhile educational experiment but rather because public pressure on them was too great to ignore. She characterized the school district's attitude as follows: "At no time would the Board undertake to accept the experiment for more than a year at a time . . ." (p. 233).

Despite a lack of official support from school authorities, parents were surprisingly enthusiastic—registration for the experimental kindergarten class "opened one spring day at 1 P.M., and by 1:05 P.M. the quota of 26 children was reached" (p. 266).

The process of community involvement just described has been repeated many times since the first immersion class opened in St. Lambert in 1965. The introduction of French immersion programs in most school districts elsewhere in Quebec and Canada has been instigated and promoted by local community groups, along with the assistance of individual school district officials and researchers. Official support for new programs has typically been lukewarm.

It is important to emphasize here that it was in the educational system, and in French immersion in particular, that the St. Lambert parents sought a response to the important sociolinguistic changes that were taking place around them. Moreover, it was through educational innovation that they also sought to bring about social change within their own communities. Improved French second language learning was not intended to be the sole goal of immersion. Rather it was intended to be an intermediate goal leading to improved relationships between English and French Quebecers and thus ultimately to a breaking down of the two solitudes.

SUMMARY

Bilingual education is not a new or recent phenomenon. It is likely that it has existed since the very beginnings of formal education. In many cases, it meant that students were educated through the medium of a second language and, therefore, became bilingual as a by-product. Of interest in this book are programs in North America where two or more languages are used for instructional purposes during part of the students' elementary or secondary education. In particular, we will review and discuss second language immersion programs for English-speaking students in Canada and the United States (chapters one to eight) and bilingual education programs for non-English speaking students in the United States (chapters nine to eleven).

The Canadian immersion programs were developed in the mid-1960s in response to particular sociolinguistic-political events in the province of Quebec and Canada, as just reviewed. Since that time they have evolved and expanded so that they take several different forms and can be found in all provinces of Canada and in several regions of the United States. In the next chapter, we will examine the psycholinguistic rationale behind immersion and its major pedagogical characteristics; we will also examine alternative forms of immersion in Canada.

CHAPTER

2

French Immersion: An Experiment in Bilingual Education

CANADA (handwritten in margin)

The alternative educational program that the St. Lambert parent group developed was an *early total immersion* program. In this program all curricular instruction, beginning in kindergarten and continuing through the primary elementary grades, was taught through French (see Figure 1 on page 21 for a schematic representation of the whole program). At first, French was to be used as the only medium of instruction until the end of the third grade; this was later altered so that only kindergarten and grade 1 children were taught entirely in French. When English was introduced into the curriculum, it was used to teach English language arts for approximately one hour per day. Instruction through English was subsequently expanded in successive grades to include other subjects, such as mathematics or science. By the sixth grade, or the end of elementary school, approximately 60 percent of the curriculum was taught in English and 40 percent in French. This was accomplished by teaching through English in the morning and through French in the afternoon of each day.

This basic pattern is characteristic of many current early total immersion programs, although there are, of course, variations among programs. For example, early immersion programs offered elsewhere delay the introduction of English until the third grade (see Genesee, 1978a), or even the fourth grade (Genesee & Lambert, 1983; Gray, 1981), or they limit the amount of exposure to English once it is introduced (Morrison, 1981). Some important variations will be discussed later in this chapter. Follow-up to the early immersion years is often provided at the secondary school level by offering a number of selected courses in French. These courses may be either language subjects or other subjects. The particular courses and number of such courses that students take at this level are a matter of individual student choice.

The goals of the St. Lambert immersion program as well as most other immersion programs are

1. to provide the participating students with functional competence in both written and spoken aspects of French;
2. to promote and maintain normal levels of English language development;

3. to ensure achievement in academic subjects commensurate with the students' academic ability and grade level; and
4. to instill in the students an understanding and appreciation of French Canadians, their language and culture, without detracting in any way from the students' identity with and appreciation for English-Canadian culture.

THEORETICAL RATIONALE

The St. Lambert parents' decision to offer intensive second language instruction during the early elementary grades in contrast to later grades was based on neuropsychological, psycholinguistic, and social psychological theories of the time. The work of Wilder Penfield at the Montreal Neurological Institute indicated that patients who suffered brain damage during infancy or childhood were much less likely to have permanent language impairment than patients who had suffered brain damage during adolescence or adulthood (Penfield & Roberts, 1959). These findings were substantiated by Lenneberg (1967), who, along with Penfield and Roberts, had argued that the human brain is more "plastic" and, consequently, better able to acquire languages prior to puberty. Beyond this state of development, it was argued, the physiological structures and cognitive processes of the brain become fixed and are less effective at learning new skills, including language. This evidence and this argument have since been called into question (Genesee, 1987; Krashen, 1974).

From a psycholinguistic perspective, as well, it is clear, even from everyday observation, that most children appear to acquire basic communication skills in their first language apparently effortlessly and without systematic instruction during the first six or seven years of life. Some linguists (e.g., Chomsky, 1972) and psycholinguists (e.g., McNeill, 1970) have explained the child's apparent facility at first language learning in terms of a specialized language learning capacity that is innate. Others have argued that this facility is not due to a language-specific ability but rather to general cognitive capacities that can be used in first language learning (Lenneberg, 1967; Slobin, 1973). Whatever the precise explanation, both groups of theorists believed that this capacity diminishes with age, thereby making language learning, first or second, increasingly difficult. Much anecdotal evidence indicates that indeed adults have considerable difficulty acquiring a second language and, in fact, often never achieve nativelike competence. Thus, it was argued that early immersion in a second language would facilitate a child's second language learning by taking advantage of his or her special neurolinguistic, psycholinguistic, and cognitive capacities to learn language.

The neuropsychological and psycholinguistic justifications for early immersion also received support from social psychology. Young children are generally thought to be better second language learners because they have fewer attitudes and prejudices that can interfere with learning. Older students, in contrast, may have had experiences or may have formed attitudes that can jeopardize learning, especially second language learning which is fraught with social and political significance. Indeed, research by Lambert using the matched-guise technique, as discussed earlier, found that young French Canadian children initially have positive attitudes toward their language and only later learn the negative stereotypes that are prevalent among adults. It was thought, therefore, that young English Canadian children would be more open to other languages and language groups in general and, thus, would be more open to learning French in particular (for a review of the development of racial attitudes in children, see Katz, 1976). This line of argument figured prominently in the thinking of the St. Lambert Study Group because of its long-range goal of effecting some degree of cross-cultural communication with French Canadians through improved second language proficiency.

Taken together, these three perspectives favored early intensive exposure to a second language, and so it was that the St. Lambert parents decided on early immersion beginning in kindergarten. The question of an optimal age for second language learning continues to be a controversial topic and more will be said about it in chapter four.

IMMERSION CLASSROOMS

Integrated Second Language Learning. The most distinctive feature of immersion programs is their use of the second language to teach regular academic subjects, such as mathematics and science, in addition to language arts. Immersion teachers teach regular school subjects in French much as they would if their students were native speakers of the language. Formal instruction in French grammar takes place during French language arts classes. A study by Ireland, Gunnell, and Santerre (1980) on language teaching strategies in immersion programs indicated that, in fact, there was little explicit teaching of French grammar during the first or second year of the programs in the schools they investigated, but that there was an increasing emphasis on teaching grammar in the upper elementary grades. Informal observation of French language arts instruction in early immersion programs suggests further that, when instruction in French grammar does occur, it is more typical of a native language approach than a second language approach. For example, one does not observe lessons on verb declensions, gender, and the like, as one often sees in French-as-a-second language (FSL) classes. At the same time, the French language arts materials used in immersion classes are often developed specially by local school boards since the corresponding native language materials are too advanced for immersion students.

In terms of second language learning, generally speaking, immersion programs are designed to create the same kinds of conditions that are thought to occur during first language acquisition; namely, there is an emphasis on creating a desire in the students to learn the language in order to engage in meaningful and interesting communication (Macnamara, 1973; Terrell, 1981). Thus, second language learning in immersion is often incidental to learning about mathematics, the sciences, the community, and one another. This contrasts with more traditional methods in which emphasis is on the conscious learning of the elements and rules of the second language for their own sake. Immersion programs are also designed to allow the students to apply their "natural language learning" abilities to learn the language. It has been hypothesized that language learning in children is a systematic process that reflects the child's active cognitive attempts to formulate linguistic rules that correspond to adult competence in the language—a process referred to as creative construction (Dulay & Burt, 1978a; Slobin, 1973). According to this conceptualization, opportunities to communicate in the language are necessary and advantageous for learning, and errors are a normal and important part of the learning process. The use of the second language in immersion programs for normal routine communication in the classroom permits the students to progress according to their own individual rates and styles, again in much the same way that first language learners do (Bloom, Hood, & Lightbown, 1974; Nelson, 1981).

Speaking and Listening Skills.   Since the students are not native speakers, there is an emphasis during the initial phase of immersion on the development of oral language and listening comprehension skills. Teachers make use of the children's personal experiences, of teaching strategies that entail repetition, such as games and songs, and of the common, concrete activities characteristic of kindergarten and grade 1 classes to develop basic oral and listening skills (Richards, 1985). A central feature of language learning at this stage is that it occurs through interaction with meaningful content (Lapkin & Cummins, 1984).

It is not uncommon during this early stage of immersion for the students to address their comments to one another and to the teacher in English. This might be regarded as a type of silent period in the second language during which comprehension skills are developed and consolidated before production of oral language begins. This sequence of aural-oral language development is characteristic of first language acquisition and is advocated by second language educators as well (Terrell, 1981). Moreover, this strategy of permitting the students to use English does not force them to use French before they are ready, with the potentially negative consequence of inhibiting their initial attempts at French.

Attempts by the children to use French in the classroom are encouraged by the teacher. Moreover, the teachers are discouraged from overcorrecting the children's use of the language. Research on first language acquisition has indicated that parents are more likely to correct their children's language for factual inaccuracies than for linguistic inaccuracies (Brown, Cazden, & Bellugi, 1970). Besides, excessive correction of second language errors is likely to inhibit learners from using the second language. By grade 1 most of the students are using French in the classroom. At this time the teacher begins to insist that all of them use French whenever they talk to the teacher or to one another. Since most children have acquired considerable proficiency in the language by this time, this rule is not difficult to enforce.

Reading and Writing Skills.   The development of oral and listening comprehension skills is a preliminary to teaching reading and writing skills in French. Although there is little systematic information on the strategies used to teach reading in French immersion programs, it is probably reasonable to assume that they are eclectic, ranging from language experience to phonics approaches. Reservations have been expressed about using an exclusively phonics approach to teach both French and English reading, especially if these take place simultaneously or close in time, for fear of inducing negative transfer between the two languages. A study by Pycock (1977) examined the English reading comprehension and writing skills of third-grade immersion students in St. Lambert, some of whom had learned to read English in grade 2 using a phonics approach and some using a language experience approach. Both groups of students had learned to read French from grade 1 using a phonics approach. It was found that the language experience group had higher reading comprehension scores and wrote longer compositions with fewer spelling errors and more adjective clauses than the phonics group. These findings suggest that there is some validity to the concern over teaching reading in both English and French using similar methods. Moreover, as we will see later, simultaneous instruction in reading English and French, as occurs in early partial immersion programs, is often reported to result in interference between the two languages, possibly because of negative transfer.

Academic Instruction.   The introduction of subject matter instruction through French tends to coincide with its introduction in a regular English curriculum, although there may be an initial delay during which basic oral and listening comprehension skills are developed, as discussed earlier. Students in immersion programs are expected to cover and master the same academic material at the end of each school year as students in the English program, and they do. There are no official or uniform policies regarding which subjects should be taught in French and which should be taught in English. Conventional wisdom favors subjects such as history, geography, and social studies for second language instruction since it is thought that they are more verbal and thus lend themselves to discussion and second language learning better than subjects such as mathematics and science. In fact, there is no empirical evidence that sheds light on this important issue. In lieu of such evidence, it is likely that any subject will be an effective vehicle for second language learning to the extent that the instructor uses it to promote extensive language use.

There is usually an attempt to maintain continuity of subjects being taught in each language from one grade to the next so that the students are not handicapped by a lack of terminology. Pragmatic considerations, such as the availability of appropriate teaching personnel, materials, equipment, and other resources, often figure in decisions regarding language of instruction. These considerations are particularly salient in the higher elementary grades and in secondary school when it is generally necessary to employ subject specialists.

It is important to point out here that, although the immersion programs are generally regarded as special language programs, they are also fundamentally academic. That is to say, their primary objective is normal academic development. Indeed, the success of the programs, to be discussed in chapters three and four, has been determined in large part by the fact that the participating students attain high levels of functional proficiency in a second language *at no cost to their academic or English language development.* It is likely that the programs would not enjoy the popularity they do, had there been any evidence of less-than-normal academic achievement among immersion students.

Language Territories.   A distinctive feature of the Canadian early immersion programs, and one that differs significantly from many American bilingual education programs for minority language children, is the use of monolingual language models. The French teachers in immersion programs present themselves to the students as monolingual French speakers even though in most cases these teachers are very proficient in English. Many early immersion students, in fact, learn of their French teachers' bilingual abilities only in later grades when they overhear them using English with an English teacher. The classrooms in which French and English instruction are presented are kept as separate as possible. This means that the children usually change classrooms for the French and English parts of the school day once English is introduced into the curriculum. An explicit rule that students must use French in the French classroom and with the French teachers is established. Rules requiring the use of English with the English teachers and in the English classrooms are not necessary, since the students are naturally prepared to use English whenever possible.

These two strategies—the use of monolingual second language teacher models and the establishment of "French territories" within the school—are adopted and observed conscientiously in order to facilitate the students' second language learning by encouraging, indeed, requiring, the students to use French. Otherwise, there would be a tendency for them to use English, their stronger language. The use of monolingual French models is recommended also to satisfy some of the sociocultural goals of the program. Monolingual teacher models provide English children in immersion with extended experiences with French-speaking Canadians, with whom they might otherwise have little contact. Language-use surveys have found that even immersion students in the bilingual city of Montreal have very little day-to-day contact with French-speaking people outside school (Genesee, 1978b; 1981a). Thus, immersion students are expected to come to respect and appreciate French Canadians and their culture through their school experiences. French culture is also part of the immersion experience because of the French Canadian cultural content of some of the textbooks used in the program.

The potentially negative implications that these policies might be expected to have on the participating students' atttitudes toward and knowledge of English

Canadian culture and language are effectively eliminated in a number of ways. As mentioned previously, the students are not forced to use French or to set aside English during the first year or so of the program or during extra-class activities, such as recess. The use of English-speaking teaching personnel during a substantial part of the later elementary school grades ensures a positive and significant presence for English. The overall administrative structure within which immersion takes place is English, including many English-speaking administrators (e.g., principals) and support staff (e.g., secretaries), thereby ensuring a respect for English. The students are exposed to many positive English Canadian models in their homes, in the community, and in the media. Consequently, the support for the French language and culture that characterizes immersion is never achieved at the expense of the children's home language and culture. Lambert (1980a) has referred to this type of bilingual education as "additive."

It is still rare in Canada to find teachers trained specially for immersion even though the program has been in existence for some 20 years now (Lapkin & Cummins, 1984). Some school districts provide special in-service training in lieu of or in addition to formal course requirements. Of course, immersion teachers are required to have native or native like competence in the language of instruction they will be using. Bilingual competence is not necessarily required, although it is customary.

Pedagogical and Sociocultural Characteristics of Immersion.   It should be apparent from this overview of early immersion that certain sociocultural conditions as well as specific pedagogical approaches constitute an integral part of the programs. Although all of these conditions and approaches have been reviewed in the preceding pages, the most important ones warrant summarizing here. The principal pedagogical approaches include the following:

1. The students are permitted to use their home language in school and in the classroom at least during the initial part of the program.
2. Teachers strongly encourage students who attempt to communicate in the second language. Conversely, teachers do not overcorrect the grammatical and structural errors the students make when using the second language.
3. Each language is used for regular curricular instruction in addition to language arts instruction. The same curricular material is never taught concurrently in both languages.
4. The second language teachers in immersion programs act as monolingual models (i.e., the French teachers use only French). This approach is important so that the socioculturally weaker language will be strengthened.

The main sociocultural conditions embodied in immersion are as follows:

1. The participating children speak the majority group language.
2. Educational, teaching, and administrative personnel working in immer-

sion programs value and support, directly or indirectly, the children's home language and culture.

3. The participating children similarly value their home language and culture and do not wish to forsake either.
4. The children and school personnel regard the acquisition of the second language as a positive addition to the child's repertoire of skills.
5. The children's parents wish to maintain the home language and culture while valuing their children's acquisition of the second language.

ALTERNATIVE FORMS OF IMMERSION

Since the St. Lambert experiment began in 1965, immersion has expanded dramatically. Immersion programs are now available in several different forms and in a variety of languages. The number of students enrolled in immersion has increased from approximately 17,763 in 1976 to 102,168 in 1982 (Stern, 1984), and immersion programs can be found in all Canadian provinces and the territories.

Participation in immersion programs is voluntary, and to date the majority of programs in Canada serve children from middle class socioeconomic backgrounds. In chapter eight, we will review the results of a preliminary evaluation of an early partial French immersion program in Cincinnati, Ohio, that has been designed for black students and students from working class backgrounds (Holobow, Genesee, Lambert, Met, & Gastright, 1987). This program has been offered in Cincinnati as a means of achieving ethnically and socioeconomically balanced classes using immersion as a magnet to attract students from diverse backgrounds to the same schools.

Early, Delayed, and Late Immersion.   The alternative forms of immersion currently available differ primarily with respect to the grade level(s) during which the second language is used as a major medium of curricular instruction. Differentiations are often made between early, delayed, and late immersion. A secondary basis of differentiation is made according to the amount of instruction provided in the second language (namely, total vs. partial), and/or the number of years during which the second language is used as a major medium of instruction. Excluded from this rough taxonomy are (1) second language programs in which the second language is used for teaching language arts and only one non-language subject, and (2) programs in which the second language is never used to teach at least 50 percent of the curriculum during any school year. These latter types of programs would generally be regarded as enriched second language programs.

Heritage Language Immersion.   In addition to its role in promoting Canada's two official languages, immersion programs have been used in interesting ways to revitalize and develop heritage languages. In western Canada, for example, immersion programs in Ukrainian and English have been developed for

English-speaking children whose parents are of Ukrainian descent (see Muller, Penner, Blowers, Jones, & Mosychuk, 1975; and Lamont, Penner, Blowers, Mosychuk, & Jones, 1976, for reports). An interesting heritage language immersion program has recently been developed in a small Mohawk community outside Montreal. Faced with the gradual erosion and potential total loss of their ancestral language over successive generations, the members of this community have embarked upon a program of early total immersion in Mohawk for their children who speak only English otherwise. Another feature of some interest in this project is the possibility that a French immersion component will be added in later grades. If this occurs, then this program will serve the dual role of revitalizing a heritage language while promoting proficiency in an additional second language of some local relevance to the students.

Double Immersion.   Trilingual or double immersion programs, in Hebrew, French, and English have been in existence for some years now in Montreal; these programs have been evaluated systematically and thoroughly by the McGill research group, and the results of their evaluations will be reviewed later (see chapter five).

Activity-centered Immersion.   One final form of immersion that will be described is an individualized, activity-centered program. Except for general pedagogical approaches described earlier, we know relatively little about the actual instructional practices used in immersion classrooms. This activity-centered program is of some interest because of what it tells us about possible methodological approaches that can maximize second language learning in immersion.

Let us begin our description of alternative immersion programs with early immersion.

Early Immersion Alternatives

There are two main types of early immersion—total and partial. The early total immersion program has already been described in the section on the St. Lambert experiment and is schematically represented in Figure 1. The early partial immersion program differs in that less than 100 percent of curricular instruction during the primary grades (i.e., K, 1, 2, and 3) is presented through the second language. The most common formula is 50 percent French and 50 percent English. The amount of French instruction in early partial immersion programs tends to remain constant throughout the elementary grades, in contrast to total immersion programs in which the French component decreases. Another difference between these two types of immersion is the sequencing of literacy instruction. In total immersion programs, literacy training in the native language occurs after literacy training in the second language has begun. In partial immer-

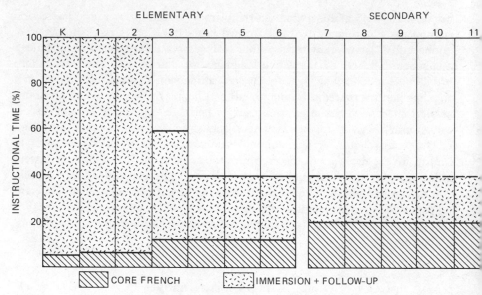

Figure 1 Schematic Summary of an Early Total French Immersion Program

sion programs, literacy training tends to occur in both languages simultaneously from grade 1 on.

Among early total immersion alternatives, the main variation involves the grade level at which English instruction is introduced. It may be in the second grade, as in St. Lambert (Lambert & Tucker, 1972); in grade 3 (Genesee, 1978a); or in grade 4 (Genesee & Lambert, 1983; Gray, 1981). Another variation among early total immersion options is the amount of instruction presented through English once it is introduced into the curriculum. In some cases, English exposure increases quickly (for example, from 20 percent in grade 3 to 60 percent in grade 5; see Genesee, 1978a), and in other cases it increases very slowly (for example, remaining stable at 20 percent during grades 3, 4, and 5; Morrison, 1981).

In general then, variations among early immersion options entail differences in exposure to the second language, with partial immersion and the early introduction of English language instruction resulting in less time being spent in the second language than total immersion or later introduction of English instruction. These variations allow us to examine the importance of exposure time as a factor in second language learning.

Delayed Immersion Alternatives

Immersion programs that postpone use of the second language as a major medium of instruction until the middle elementary grades (i.e., grade 4 or 5) are classified here as delayed. Usually these programs offer a core second language course of 20 to 45 minutes a day in the primary grades prior to the immersion component, which may be of one or two years duration (Cziko, Holobow, & Lambert, 1977). This may then be followed by partial immersion until the end of elementary school during which language arts and other subjects are taught through the second language. In delayed immersion options, training in first language literacy precedes training in second language literacy. The partial immersion alternative has often been used in heritage language programs, as described briefly earlier. In the Ukrainian-English immersion program, for example, half the school day is spent in Ukrainian and half the day is spent in English. In the first year of the program, the subjects taught in Ukrainian were oral language arts, social studies, music, art, and physical education. The subjects taught in English were language arts, mathematics, and science. Differential use of the heritage language for culturally relevant subjects while English is used for academic subjects is characteristic of many heritage language programs in Canada.

Late Immersion Alternatives

Late immersion programs postpone intensive use of the second language until the end of elementary school or the beginning of secondary school; see Figure 2. In one-year late immersion programs, all or most of the curriculum, except English language arts, is taught through the second language for one year (Genesee, Polich, & Stanley, 1977). In two-year late immersion programs this schedule is repeated for two consecutive years (Genesee, 1981b). Late immersion programs may be preceded by core second language instruction throughout the elementary grades, or they may be preceded by special preparatory second language courses one or two years immediately prior to immersion (Swain, 1978). The curriculum in late immersion programs is usually the same as that in a regular program. In other words, the students are expected to cover and master the same academic material during the course of the year as students in a regular all-English program; and they do. A transition period during the first couple of months is required in order to provide the students with the language skills they require for effective learning of subject matter. This transition is usually achieved easily and quickly in the case of late immersion preceded by core French from kindergarten, but tends to take longer if the students have had only preparatory French courses immediately prior to immersion (Swain, 1978).

Most late immersion alternatives—one-year or two-year, and with or without prior core French instruction from the primary grades—are followed in the higher grades by advanced second language arts courses and, in some cases, by selected non-language courses, such as geography or math, that are taught through French. For historical reasons, in Quebec there are French and English schools. Consequently, there exist equivalent curricula and materials in French and in English. This means that, at the secondary school level, im-

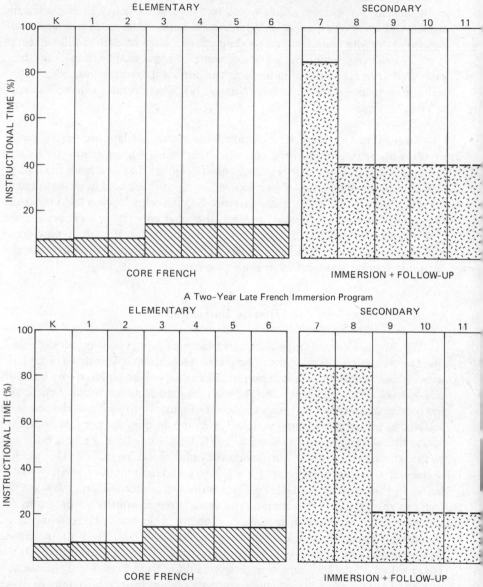

Figure 2 Schematic Summaries of Late French Immersion Programs

mersion students can choose to take certain courses in French or in English, and that they can write examinations in English or in French in fulfillment of their high school diploma. For example, an immersion student in the final year of secondary school in Quebec could choose to write leaving examinations in chemistry, mathematics, physics, geography, history, typing, and art in French or in English. The French exams would be designed for native French-speaking students in the French schools. Which examinations the student chooses will depend upon whether the corresponding courses were offered as follow-up options in his/her school. The results of some of these examinations have been examined in order to assess immersion students' achievement in academic subjects taken in French (Genesee, 1976a, 1977a). These results will be discussed in chapter three.

Immersion Centers.   An additional variant of the late immersion option involves the setting of the program. Most late immersion programs are located in schools that also offer the regular English program. In these cases the immersion classes are often situated in a separate wing of the school in order to create a French ambience in what is an otherwise English school. Some late immersion programs, however, are housed in centers that offer only late immersion; in these cases all communication in the school is conducted in French. Follow-up is provided in a regular secondary school with the immersion option. There are also early total immersion centers in some districts.

Double Immersion

By far the most common alternative forms of immersion, as just described, involve the use of a single second language. Genesee and Lambert (1983) have investigated variations in immersion for English-speaking children in which two non-native languages (French and Hebrew) are used as major media of curricular instruction during the elementary grades (see Figure 3). French and Hebrew were selected as immersion languages in the programs in question because both have sociocultural significance for the participants. On the one hand, French, being one of the official languages of Canada and the only official language of Quebec, has social and economic relevance to these children and their families on a day-to-day basis. In this regard, the Hebrew-French double immersion programs are the same as the St. Lambert program and other French immersion programs for majority language children in Canada. On the other hand, Hebrew is valued because of its religious and cultural significance and because of its increasing non-sectarian importance as a national language of Israel. In this respect, the Hebrew-French double immersion programs differ from French-only immersion in being heritage language or language revitalization programs. The underlying principles of both components are nevertheless the same. These programs will be described in some detail in chapter five because they represent interesting models of multilingual/multicultural education of possible interest to ethnolinguistic groups that are interested in revitalizing heritage languages and at the same time wish to acquire competence in an additional second language of some local or national relevance.

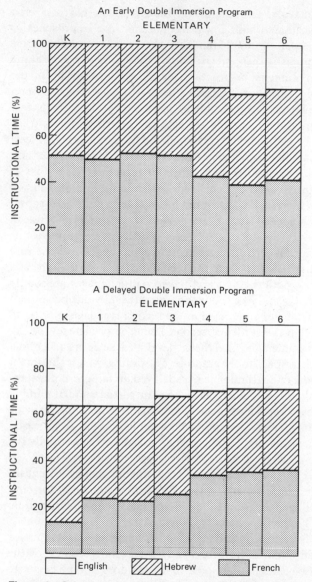

Figure 3 Schematic Summaries of Double Immersion Programs

SUMMARY

At the time of their development, the Canadian immersion programs were a major pedagogical innovation—they were designed to reflect what were thought to be the essential conditions for first language acquisition, namely, communicative use of the target language in meaningful, interactive situations. Since that time, there has been a substantial shift toward communicative approaches to second language teaching (see, for example, Krashen, 1981). The most distinctive feature of immersion programs is their integration of second language teaching with academic instruction. Immersion programs emphasize acquisition of the second language in order to perform academic tasks—to this extent, second language learning in immersion is incidental to learning cognitive skills and acquiring knowledge. Immersion programs are also characterized by exclusive use of the target language by instructional personnel and by the students, at least after some preliminary phase during which the students are allowed to use their home language freely with one another and with their teachers.

The first immersion program to be instituted was an *early* total immersion program. Early immersion in French was favored for psycholinguistic, neuropsychological, and social-psychological reasons. Early total immersion programs can be divided into three phases: 1) a monolingual phase (usually kindergarten to the second or third grade), when all curricular instruction is presented in the second language; 2) a bilingual phase (usually from the second or third grade to the end of elementary school), when both the first and the second languages are jointly used for curricular instruction; and 3) a follow-up phase (usually during secondary school), when selected courses are offered in the second language in order to maintain and further develop the students' second language proficiency.

Alternative forms of immersion have been developed since its inception. They differ primarily with respect to 1) grade levels, during which the target language is the main medium of instruction (early, delayed, or late); 2) percentage of instructional time spent in the target language (total or partial); and 3) number of years of immersion instruction. There are also immersion options that provide instruction in two non-native languages and in heritage languages. In all cases, the psycholinguistic rationale and the pedagogical approaches are essentially the same.

Proponents of second language immersion programs for majority English-speaking Canadian children have generally questioned their suitability for children from minority ethnolinguistic groups that do not enjoy the same individual or collective status that English speakers in North America enjoy (Lambert, 1980b; Tucker, 1980). In fact, even in Canada, English immersion programs for French-speaking Canadian children have been advised against because of the threat that such a form of education might pose to the children's home language and culture. This threat exists even in Quebec where French is spoken by the majority of Quebecers, because French is in a minority status demographically with respect to the rest of Canada and North America. The French language suffers some of the social psychological stigma associated with many minority languages, as indicated in the earlier discussion of language attitudes. The relevance of immersion for educating minority language children will be discussed in chapter eleven. In the next chapter, we will examine the English language and academic consequences of immersion for majority group, English-speaking Canadian students.

3

Research Findings: English Language and Academic Outcomes

In this chapter, we will review research findings pertinent to two pedagogical and linguistic questions posed by immersion programs. Simply put, they are:

1. What effect will participation in immersion have on the students' native language development?
2. Will the students' academic achievement suffer as a result of being taught academic subjects through a second language?

The findings pertinent to each question will be summarized in separate sections. Within each section, discussion will focus on research carried out in conjunction with evaluations of early immersion programs since they have generated the most research. Research carried out in the other program alternatives will then be considered.

Before examining the research findings, however, research methods used in the program evaluations will be described.

RESEARCH DESIGN

Typically, research on immersion programs has been of the classic between-groups design—the performance of students in immersion programs (hereafter referred to as IM) has been compared to that of comparable students in other programs. The minimum comparison in all evaluations has included English-speaking students in regular English programs (hereafter referred to as EC for English Control). Inclusion of this comparison group permits an assessment of IM students' English language development, academic achievement, cognitive or intellectual development, and second language achievement relative to that of students attending regular English-medium schools with a French-as-a-second language (FSL) component. In a number of evaluations an additional comparison group has been French-speaking students attending regular French-medium schools (hereafter referred to as FC). The latter group has usually been included in evaluations carried out in bilingual regions of the country where French-speaking students are readily available and, more importantly, where it is deemed important to evaluate IM students' French proficiency using native French speakers as a comparison.

It has also been typical for most evaluations of immersion programs to be longitudinal in nature; that is to say, the performance of the IM students has been monitored annually over a number of years. In the case of early immersion, it has been common practice for the research to span the students' entire elementary and secondary schooling, some 12 or 13 years. This is an important design feature, since it permits the investigator to observe any changes in student performance that might occur, for better or for worse, with continued attendance in the program. Troike (1978) has criticized national evaluations of bilingual education for minority language children in the United States for failing to assess its long-term impact; this will be discussed in more detail in chapter nine. We will see shortly that, had the immersion programs not been evaluated longitudinally, the initial results might have been interpreted negatively resulting in the programs being abandoned.

An additional design feature of many of the immersion evaluation projects has been the use of follow-up groups. Thus, the performance of the first or pilot group of students to be in the program has been compared to that of other groups who entered the program at a later date. In some cases more than one follow-up group has been evaluated; for example, in their evaluation of the Hebrew-French double immersion program, Genesee and Lambert (1980, 1983) included two follow-up groups, or cohorts as they are sometimes called. Use of follow-up groups, especially in the case of new programs, allows the investigator to assess the generalizability of findings collected during the first year or two of the new program against findings collected after the program has stabilized. It is possible that findings during the introductory years of a new program will be unreliable either because they are unusually good, owing to "halo effects," or because they are unusually poor, owing to problems in the new program that have not been worked out by the time of the first evaluation. It may also be that the first groups of students to enroll in the program are not representative of later groups; for example, because the first groups are more select.

There have been a number of major longitudinal evaluations of immersion programs in different parts of the country—in St. Lambert (Lambert & Tucker, 1972); in Montreal itself (Genesee, 1978a); in Ontario (Swain & Lapkin, 1982); in New Brunswick (Gray, 1980), and in British Columbia (Shapson & Day, 1983). Consequently, it is possible to assess the effectiveness of immersion in different settings, some where there are sizeable populations of target language speakers, such as in Montreal and Ottawa, Ontario, and some where there are virtually no target language speakers, such as in British Columbia and Toronto. In total, then, there are three generalizability checks possible when examining the reliability of the Canadian immersion evaluation results: 1) longitudinal generalizability, 2) cohort-to-cohort generalizability, and 3) setting-to-setting generalizability. As a result, it is unlikely that unique results from any one evaluation will go unnoticed and be inappropriately generalized. This degree of overlap is rare in educational research, and it increases one's confidence in the research results.

The Students

For purposes of evaluation, the IM and EC samples have been selected to be comparable with respect to general socioeconomic characteristics and academic ability. Comparability with respect to socioeconomic background has been assessed impressionistically and has been achieved by 1) selecting IM and EC students from the same schools, if the schools provide both types of programs, or 2) selecting students from socioeconomically comparable schools, if the programs are not housed in the same schools. For the most part, the research has been conducted with students from middle class to upper-middle class families, since these types of students make up the majority of the immersion group. The suitability of immersion for children from lower socioeconomic families will be considered in chapters six and eight.

Comparability with respect to general academic ability has been achieved using *a priori* selection procedures or *a posteriori* statistical adjustments. In the Montreal research, pre-selected stratified samples of IM and EC students who were average, above average, or below average according to their performance on standardized IQ tests were examined (Genesee, 1976b). This selection procedure has the advantage of not only equating the samples on IQ but also of permitting the researcher to systematically investigate the performance of students with different levels of ability. When *a priori* selection of comparable groups has not been possible, representative samples of students from each type of program have been selected, and their performance on language and achievement tests has been analyzed subsequently using analysis of covariance techniques to adjust for any possible differences in ability between the groups (Swain & Lapkin, 1982). Analysis of covariance is a statistical procedure that allows one to examine differences in performance between groups on certain tests while adjusting for any initial differences between them on another test.

While both procedures (i.e., *a priori* selection and covariance) are legitimate and generally acceptable means for achieving comparability of groups, neither is entirely satisfactory if the groups were not naturally equivalent at the outset. Neither procedure can eliminate differences in educational treatment that the groups might have received in the classroom were they not naturally equivalent. By way of illustration, imagine that the students in the classes from which the IM sample was selected tended to be average or above average in ability with relatively few below-average students, while students in the classes from which the EC sample was selected tended to be more equally distributed at all levels of ability. To the extent that this were true, then it might be expected that the IM classes would be given advanced level instruction while the EC classes would be given average levels of instruction consistent with their full range of student abilities. Since neither analysis of covariance or even an *a priori* stratified selection procedure alters the compositions of the IM and EC classrooms, then neither controls for the possibility of differential educational treatment. This state of affairs is inevitable whenever an educational alternative is optional. It follows, therefore, that such differences are an inherent and normal feature of the programs under evaluation and that the findings that result from these evaluations reflect real outcomes of the programs.

When selecting a control group against which to compare the performance of the IM students, ideally one would select students from the regular English program who are identical to the IM students in all respects, except for the fact that they are enrolled in a different school program. This is possible when more students than can be accepted to the immersion program have applied for admission. In this case, interested students can be assigned randomly to either the immersion program or the regular school program. In fact, this was done in St. Lambert. However, it has not been possible in other settings. Since attendance in immersion programs is optional, it is subject to selection biases. That is to say, students with particular personal, intellectual, or familial characteristics may choose immersion over the regular program, while students with other characteristics may remain in the regular program. The mere fact of choosing immersion as an alternative to regular schooling may implicate different levels or types of motivation, whether the decision to enroll in immersion is made by the students themselves, as tends to be the case for late immersion, or by the parents, as in the case of early immersion. To the extent that the IM and EC students have different characteristics, then the evaluation samples cannot be truly equivalent. As Swain and Lapkin (1982) point out, the issue is complicated by the fact that these types of selective characteristics cannot always be identified easily, and even if they could they cannot always be quantified or measured easily. One would need to be able to measure potentially distinguishing characteristics in order to ensure that the groups to be compared are indeed equivalent with respect to the relevant characteristics. Moreover, even if the relevant characteristic can be identified and measured, it may not actually be present in both groups and therefore cannot be controlled; motivation is an example of a factor that might not be present in the same form or to the same extent in both groups.

As in the case of the possibility of differential educational treatment, differences in student characteristics are inevitable in educational alternatives that are optional. Therefore, such characteristics constitute inherent characteristics of the students under evaluation. From the point of view of research, this means that we cannot claim to evaluate how well students who are in the immersion program would do were they in the regular program; such a comparison would require that the groups be identical except for program participation. However, we can evaluate how well students in immersion programs do compared to otherwise comparable students in the regular program. The possibility of selective participation also means that we cannot claim that any findings we report would be obtained in programs that were compulsory; our findings can be generalized only to programs that are similarly optional. Indeed, most researchers working in immersion would probably agree that the optional nature of the programs is an important feature of them and one that accounts, in part at least, for their success.

Evaluation Instruments

In this section, discussion will be limited to tests used to evaluate language and academic achievement. Needless to say, a wide variety of evaluation instruments have been used for these purposes. In the domain of language evaluation, the tests can be classified roughly into two categories—proficiency and psycholinguistic. The tests of language proficiency, generally speaking, evaluate language skills as they are traditionally identified, taught, and tested in schools. This category includes tests of vocabulary, spelling, writing, reading, and the oral communication skills of speaking and listening comprehension. Many of the tests of English language proficiency used in evaluations of immersion programs have in fact been standardized tests that are available commercially; e.g., *Metropolitan Achievement Tests* or the *Canadian Test of Basic Skills*. These are the same kinds of tests that are used widely by school districts for systemwide assessments of student performance. There are a number of advantages associated with using these tests. First, because they are widely used in schools they are generally familiar to and understood by teachers, administrators, and parents. This means that they have considerable "face validity" in the school and community. Moreover, such tests have been carefully designed and developed to be valid and reliable measures of common school-related language skills. The ready availability of psychometrically sound tests of language facilitates the task of the evaluator. Standardized tests are useful also because they provide a variety of norms, such as grade equivalent or percentile scores, that can be used as additional bases for interpreting evaluation results.

A few comments concerning standardized test scores are warranted here. Standardized test scores or norms are useful for interpreting performance on a test when no other basis of interpretation, such as the performance of a control group, is available. In fact, when comparison group results are not available, standardized or normed scores are essential because raw scores on standardized tests are meaningless otherwise. However, the performance of local comparison groups is a more meaningful and valid way of interpreting test scores, precisely because they are local. Thus, strictly speaking, the use of a control group, as is customary in the case of immersion evaluation research, eliminates the need to use normed scores.

Standardized scores have the statistical disadvantage that they tend to reduce differences in the test scores of individuals from different groups. When one is interested in determining if there are differences between two groups of students (e.g., IM and EC) and how significant such differences are, then this is not a desirable characteristic because it reduces the very differences one is looking for. This does not prevent one from using standardized scores when using a between-groups research design, but it means that statistical analyses of the test results should be performed using raw scores. This has been the practice, in fact, in the immersion research.

There are far fewer standardized French language tests than English language tests, and this has made the selection of French tests generally more difficult. The French tests that have been used in immersion program evaluations were selected to be culturally and linguistically appropriate for Canadian students. They were selected to emphasize general communication skills rather than skills in subcomponents of the language; tests of reading focused on comprehension rather than on phoneme-grapheme decoding skills, for example. Moreover, the French tests were selected to reflect native levels and types of proficiency; this was particularly true in the Montreal and New Brunswick evaluations where French Control groups were included in the evaluations. Reading, writing, listening comprehension, and oral production or speaking were the main French language skills evaluated.

A variety of psycholinguistic measures have been used to assess IM students' English and French language development. Generally speaking, these tests differ from the proficiency measures insofar as they attempt to examine the way that IM students process, store, and analyze language, in contrast to the proficiency measures which assess how well they can use language for normal academic and social purposes. For example, psycholinguistic measures might examine the nature of IM students' system of grammar, including its complexity and native or non-native features, whereas proficiency tests related to grammar would merely assess the students' grammatical correctness when speaking or writing. Details of specific psycholinguistic measures and their purposes will be provided in the following sections, where appropriate.

The evaluation of academic performance has also relied heavily on existing standardized achievement tests. Achievement in mathematics has been evaluated by most evaluators, and achievement in science and social studies less frequently. Since mathematics curricula tend to be more uniform from school to school and class to class, use of standardized tests of mathematics achievement poses relatively few problems. Use of standardized achievement tests in science and social studies and in other subject areas is somewhat more problematic because of the considerable variation that exists in teaching these subjects, even in the same district. This means that the content of a standardized achievement test in science or social studies may be appropriate for testing one group of students but not another. Thus, performance on such tests can be ambiguous to the extent that it is sometimes difficult to know whether poor scores by a group reflects truly poor mastery of the relevant material or whether it means that the material was simply never taught in class.

Student performance on a number of locally developed achievement tests will also be reported. As noted earlier, public education in Quebec consists of dual language systems with separate French and English schools. At the high school level, therefore, there are parallel courses in English and French, and there are parallel examinations required for completing a high school diploma. IM students can choose to write some of these examinations in French if they have taken the corresponding courses in French, and indeed some students do this. Genesee (1976a, 1977a) collected and analyzed the results of immersion students on a number of these examinations: geography, history, mathematics, physics, chemistry, typing, and art. These examinations have the advantage of being locally developed, and therefore they have considerable content validity, which is often lacking in standardized achievement tests that are developed for national use. They have the additional advantage that they pertain to more subject areas than are assessed by standardized tests of academic achievement. To date, these comparisons have been carried out using the results of late immersion students only.

Testing Procedures

It is not possible to describe in any simple way the complete testing procedures used in all immersion program evaluations, but a few generalizations may give the reader a reasonably accurate indication of the most common practices. Much of the testing, and particularly the proficiency and academic achievement testing, has been carried out with intact class groups or subgroups. In some cases the testing has been carried out by classroom teachers themselves, and in other cases trained, independent examiners did the testing, assisted by classroom teachers where and when necessary. The advantage of using independent, trained testers is that it ensures that testing procedures and the general treatment of the students will be uniform and unbiased. It might be argued that if the examinees are not familiar with the examiner, they will not perform at their maximum level. To the extent that this does occur, all groups are likely to respond similarly. Trained examiners are skilled at tailoring their interaction with different groups of students while at the same time respecting standardized procedures. Teachers, on the other hand, may be prone either to follow the standardized procedures and instructions rigidly or to alter them in ways that lower the validity of the test results. The use of independent examiners has the added practical advantage of not requiring extra work of the teachers. For the most part, English tests have been administered by native English-speaking examiners and French tests by native French-speaking examiners.

One major exception to group testing, as just outlined, has been the evaluation of oral production or speaking skills. This has often been carried out using a one-to-one interview between a trained interviewer and an individual student. In Montreal, for example, the interview was usually initiated by having the students describe a sequence of cartoon pictures; this was followed by an open-ended conversation that was designed to elicit maximum verbal output from each interviewee and encourage them to use a variety of linguistic forms (e.g., present, past, and future tense verb forms). The Montreal interviewers presented themselves as monolingual French speakers, many of whom in fact were bilingual. This procedure, which is highly plausible in the Montreal setting, was followed to ensure or at least encourage the students to use French as much as possible in their interviews. The interviews were tape-recorded and evaluated later by independent evaluators who were "blind" with respect to the group membership of the interviewees.

In some evaluations, especially in the case of early immersion, baseline testing was carried out at the beginning of the program (i.e., early kindergarten) in order to assess the comparability of the IM and EC samples at the outset, prior to participation in the program. Baseline testing usually included measures of verbal ability (often the *Peabody Picture Vocabulary Test*) and of general reasoning ability (often *Raven's Progressive Matrices*). Language proficiency and academic achievement tests were administered subsequently at the end of each school year in order to assess end-of-year performance. Typically, the performance of the different groups was compared using analysis of variance or analysis of covariance techniques, as described earlier. Important variations in these general testing procedures will be identified in the following sections.

ENGLISH LANGUAGE RESULTS

English language testing during the primary grades of early total immersion, prior to the introduction of English language arts instruction, has indicated that IM students score significantly lower than EC students on tests that require literacy in English, such as reading comprehension, spelling, and written vocabulary (Genesee, 1983; Lambert & Tucker, 1972; Swain & Lapkin, 1982). A lag in English literacy skills at this time is not surprising in view of the students' lack of formal training in these skills. What is more surprising is the level of literacy that the IM students actually demonstrate despite formal training. Table 1 summarizes the percentile scores of grade 1, 2, and 3 IM and EC students as reported by Polich (1974), working in Montreal, and by Shapson and Kaufman (1977), working in Vancouver. In both cases, English language arts instruction was not introduced into the curriculum until grade 3. It is evident from these results that, although the IM students scored lower than the EC students, they scored at the 35th percentile or higher on the various subtests of the Metropolitan Achievement Tests administered in grade 1. They showed noticeable improvement in grade 2, at which time they scored around the 45th percentile or higher. By grade 3, they had reached or were approaching parity with the EC students, with the exception of spelling. Numerous researchers have reported that IM students lag in the acquisition of English spelling until the end of grade 4 or 5. No long-term problems with spelling have been reported in the research.

Although deficits in English literacy have been found during the primary

Table 1   SUMMARY OF GRADES 1, 2, AND 3 ENGLISH LANGUAGE TEST RESULTS FOR AN EARLY TOTAL IMMERSION PROGRAM (IN PERCENTILE FORM)

Montreal (from Polich, 1974)

	Grade 1		Grade 2		Grade 3	
	IM	EC	IM	EC	IM	EC
Metropolitan Achievement Test						
Word knowledge	40	(75)	60	(75)	75	NA
Reading	35	(75)	45	(75)	55	NA
Word discrimination	40	(75)	65	(75)	65	NA

British Columbia (from Shapson & Kaufman, 1977)

	Grade 1		Grade 2		Grade 3	
	IM	EC	IM	EC	IM	EC
Metropolitan Achievement Test						
Word knowledge	36	70	44	76	52	64
Word analysis	40	80	50	80	NA	NA
Reading	48	74	44	68	66	60
Spelling	NA	NA	24	74	48	66

NA = not administered
Note: The scores for the Montreal EC group are reported as averages across all subtests.

grades of the total immersion program, there has been no evidence that IM students fall behind EC students in non-literacy skills, such as listening comprehension, oral production, or oral vocabulary skills. To the contrary, Genesee, Tucker, and Lambert (1975) found that early total IM students performed better than EC students on an interpersonal communication task that assessed their sensitivity to a listener's informational needs. More specifically, when asked to describe how to play a game to a child who could not see the game because he/she was blindfolded, IM students were more likely than non-immersion students to take the listener's handicap into account. They did this by describing the materials that made up the game (i.e., a die, a marker, a board, etc.) before describing the rules of the game. Without knowing the actual parts of the game, the rules are relatively meaningless. The non-immersion students' descriptions to the blindfolded listeners ressembled their descriptions to the listeners who were not blindfolded and could see the game in front of them. Genesee attributed the sensitivity demonstrated by the IM students to the immersion experience, wherein the normal assumptions about communicating in one's native language are not operative, and therefore one becomes more aware of and responsive to the parameters of interpersonal communication.

Lambert and Tucker (1972) examined the speaking skills of grade 1 and 2 St. Lambert early IM students in a different way. They used a story creation task in which each student was presented with a set of comic-strip type pictures and asked to make up a story based on the pictures. Their stories were tape-recorded and subsequently analyzed in detail for number of a) adjectives, b) nouns, c) different nouns, d) verbs, e) different verbs, and f) grammatical errors. The stories of the IM students were found to be equivalent to those of the EC students in all of the above respects. Thus, notwithstanding the emphasis on French as the main medium of instruction in early immersion classrooms, the IM students' use of English for oral communication was characterized by the same pattern of features as EC students'.

Assessments of the St. Lambert IM students' listening comprehension skills have also shown them to be comparable to those of EC students (Lambert & Tucker, 1972). Here the students listened to short stories and answered a number of multiple-choice questions on each one. It should not be surprising, perhaps, that IM students develop the same level of proficiency in interpersonal communication as children educated in English if one considers that the experiences fundamental to the development of these skills are probably found outside school, not in school. Indeed, children can be said to be communicatively proficient in oral language at the time they enter school. Moreover, to the extent that interpersonal communication among IM students themselves continues to take place in English even in school, then one would not expect significant negative effects to result from the immersion experience.

Testing after English language arts instruction has been introduced into the curriculum has indicated that at the end of one year IM students reach parity with EC students in those aspects of English that they tended to score lower on previously, including reading comprehension, vocabulary, and grammatical knowledge. As already noted, the one exception to this has been spelling.

Comprehensive and detailed evaluations of IM students' writing skills have also been carried out (see Genesee & Stanley, 1976; Lapkin, 1982; and Swain, 1975). Genesee and Stanley examined the writing skills of grade 4 and 6 early total IM students in Montreal in comparison with those of comparable EC students. Each student was asked to write a composition (narrative) based on one of three topic sentences provided by the examiner. The scripts written by the students were subsequently assessed by experienced grade 4 and 6 teachers who were unfamiliar with the students participating in the evaluation. The teachers were also "blind" with respect to the students' program. Two teachers independently graded each script according to: spelling, vocabulary, punctuation, sentence accuracy, sentence complexity and variety, organization, originality, and overall. The scales and criteria for evaluation were devised by senior English consultants working for Quebec's largest English language school system. With two minor exceptions, there were no significant differences between the IM students' scripts and those of the EC students (see Table 2).

Swain evaluated the writing skills of grade 3 early total IM students attending immersion schools in the Ottawa area. In contrast to Genesee's evaluation procedure, which relied on teachers' judgments of different aspects of the students' writing, Swain's evaluation consisted of detailed linguistic analyses performed by a trained linguist. The analyses examined vocabulary, technical skills (including spelling, punctuation, and capitalization), grammatical skills (includ-

Table 2 SUMMARY OF GRADES 4 AND 6 ENGLISH LANGUAGE TEST RESULTS FOR AN EARLY TOTAL IMMERSION PROGRAM

	Grade 4			Grade 6		
	IM	EC	F Ratio	IM	EC	F Ratio
Spelling	3.00	3.46	7.80*	3.54	3.51	0.01
Sentence accuracy	2.61	2.42	2.35	2.95	3.32	1.91
Sentence complexity	2.53	2.36	2.05	2.93	3.23	1.61
Organization	2.66	2.43	2.17	2.79	3.15	1.00
Originality	2.20	2.01	4.77*	2.25	2.47	0.62
Overall	2.57	2.37	2.96	2.91	3.28	1.26
Punctuation						
Appropriate	83%	61%		73%	83%	
Inappropriate	17	39		27	17	
Length						
Appropriate	70	49		46	67	
Inappropriate	30	51		54	33	
Vocabulary						
Superior	11	7		13	6	
Average	84	80		79	67	
Below average	5	13		8	27	

$*p < .05$ $**p < .01$ $***p < .001$
Note: Entries in the top half of the table are reported as means (max value = 5; min value = 1). Entries below are reported as percentage of total (max value = 100; min value = 0).

ing sentence types and grammatical errors), and creativity. The analyses indicated that in comparison with EC students, the IM students

1. used as much variety in their choice of English vocabulary, including nouns, verbs, adjectives, and adverbs;
2. made fewer morphological errors in their use of nouns, verbs, adjectives, adverbs, prepositions, and pronouns;
3. were less likely to misuse vocabulary;
4. made comparable numbers of punctuation, capitalization, and spelling errors;
5. wrote fewer simple and compound sentences and proportionately more complex and compound-complex sentences;
6. made the same number of syntactic errors; and
7. were at least as creative as the EC students.

Swain's results are consistent with Genesee's teacher-based results, and they corroborate Lambert and Tucker's linguistic analyses of IM students' oral language skills.

A lag in English literacy followed by parity within one year of having English language arts instruction characterizes the performance of students in all varieties of early total immersion, regardless of whether English language instruction begins in grade 2, grade 3, or even grade 4. In fact, Genesee, Holobow, Lambert, Cleghorn, and Walling (1985) found that even English-speaking students attending French-medium schools in Montreal achieved the same level of proficiency in English within one year. In the particular schools under evaluation, all curricular instruction was in French until grade 4, at which time two and a half hours of English language arts were provided per week. Even in comparison with early total immersion, this is indeed a drastic outback in English. These schools, in fact, could be classified as "super immersion" in that most of the participating students were English speaking. Systematic observations of a number of the classes indicated that the teaching styles of the teachers working in them were similar in some important respects to the teaching styles of immersion teachers. These findings are noteworthy in that they suggest that English language instruction can be delayed and reduced even more than is customary in most immersion programs without threatening the students' English language proficiency. We are continuing to monitor the progress of students in these French medium schools.

The rapid progress that IM students make in acquiring English literacy skills has often been attributed to transfer of skills from French to English. Anecdotally, it has been observed in the Montreal testing that sometimes IM students who are asked to do a reading test in English before being taught to read in English will attempt to process the English text as if it were French. For example, when asked to read aloud, the students would use French phonological rules to decode English words—English words come out sounding like French words. These attempts yielded approximations to English that were sufficiently close to prime the readers to the correct English form.

We know very little about the transfer of skills from one language to another (cf. Hakuta, 1986). We do not know in the case of reading, for example, precisely what is transferred, nor whether "transfer" is an accurate description of the psycholinguistic process that accounts for this phenomenon. It seems quite likely that there are certain processes that are basic to reading and that once learned can be applied to reading any, or almost any, language. At the same time, there may be reading skills that are language specific and that therefore must be learned for each language. One might expect the language-specific skills (those that are not easily transferable from language to language) to include the more technical aspects of language, such as spelling patterns or syntactic rules, whereas the transferable skills may be more in the nature of cognitive processes, such as the use of one's knowledge of the syntactic transitional probabilities of a language in reading. If this were indeed the case, one would expect less transfer of skills between languages that are structurally different from one another, such as English and Hebrew, than between languages that are relatively similar.

There is some empirical evidence for this hypothesis. In evaluations of the Hebrew-French double immersion program in Montreal (Genesee & Lambert, 1983), it was found that English and French reading scores were more highly correlated ($r = .74$) than English and Hebrew reading scores ($r = .42$). Hebrew differs greatly from English; for example, in terms of its syntax, orthography, and directionality. Cowan and Sarmed (1976) have similarly found that native Persian-speaking children who were educated in an English immersion program did not transfer from English to Persian to the same extent that English-speaking children in French immersion programs usually do from French to English. Like Hebrew, the Persian language differs significantly from English in terms of its syntax, orthography, and directionality, going from right to left.

In a related vein, Cummins (1981) has proposed that there are aspects of language development that are common to different languages and there are aspects that are more language specific. He has referred to those skills that are transferable as cognitive, academic language proficiency (CALP) or context-reduced, cognitively demanding communication skills. He distingusihes these types of skills from what he refers to as basic, interpersonal communication skills (BICS) or context-embedded, cognitively undemanding communication skills. Cummins goes on to explain that "... context-embedded communication derives from interpersonal involvement in a shared reality which obviates the need for explicit linguistic elaboration of the message." Face-to-face communication of an essentially social nature would fall within this category. "Context-reduced communication, on the other hand, derives from the fact that this shared reality cannot be assumed, and thus linguisitc messages must be elaborated precisely and explicitly so that risk of misinterpretation is minimized" (Cummins, 1984, pp. 12–13). Reading academic texts would fall within this definition. According to Cummins's model of linguistic interdependence, one would expect there to be a relationship between a bilingual individual's literacy skills in his/her two languages, whereas interpersonal communication skills in the two languages would not be expected to be related. The validity of this distinction and its developmental basis have been the subject of much controversy (see Rivera, 1984, for a complete description of Cummins's model along with critiques of it by other researchers). We will discuss Cummins's model in greater detail in chapter nine.

Alternative Early Immersion Programs

It might be expected that immersion alternatives that provide more English language instruction, either by teaching only 50 percent of the curriculum in French and the remaining 50 percent in English (as in early partial immersion programs) or by delaying the use of French as a major medium of instruction (as in delayed immersion) would result in higher levels of English language proficiency than early total immersion programs. The evidence does not support this expectation. No differences have been found in English language achievement between early partial IM students and early total IM students in grades 3 and 4 despite the fact that the partial IM students had received up to 50 percent of their instruction in English from kindergarten (Edwards, McCarrey, & Fu, 1980; Swain & Lapkin, 1982). Swain and Lapkin have reported that a group of early partial IM students in Ontario actually scored lower than a comparison group of EC students during the primary grades; similar findings have not been reported by other researchers so we cannot be sure how common this outcome is. Comparisons between delayed IM and early total IM students have also failed to find differences between the groups on tests of English language achievement (Cziko, 1975).

Thus, there is no evidence that increased use of English during the primary elementary grades as a result of either partial or delayed use of French as a medium of instruction yields greater proficiency in English than that achieved in early total immersion programs. At the same time, the reduced use of French in these alternatives usually results in reduced French language proficiency, to be discussed in the next chapter.

Late Immersion

English lanuguage testing of late immersion students indicates that the participating students experience no setbacks in their English language development as a result of immersion (Genesee, Polich, & Stanley, 1977). It should be remembered that English language arts continue to be taught in late immersion programs, so that the reduction in English instruction is much less in these programs than in early total immersion programs.

ACADEMIC ACHIEVEMENT

When immersion programs were first introduced into the public shool system, there was considerable concern among parents and educators alike that students would have difficulty assimilating academic material if it were taught through a second language. These concerns were fueled to a certain extent by the results of earlier research on the academic and lingusitic development of bilingual children (see Cummins, 1976, and Diaz, 1983, for reviews of this early research). For the most part, this research reported that bilingual children experienced linguistic and academic deficits when compared with monolinguals. As Cummins (1981) has pointed out, however, many of these studies were carried out in "subtractive bilingual" settings; that is, settings in which circumstances required that the individuals learn a second language because the language of school was different from the language of the home. Bilingualism in these settings is often associated with incomplete development of the school language and/or the home language, especially those aspects of language concerned with literacy and academic achievement. From an academic point of view, this in turn often leads to poor academic achievement because the students lack the requisite language skills to carry out school work. There were also important methodological weaknesses in the research; for example, in some cases the students' academic achievement was assessed using their weaker language, and translation-equivalent tests were used instead of properly developed target language tests.

In contrast to these early findings, research conducted since the 1960s has tended to find cognitive and linguistic advantages among bilinguals in comparison with monolinguals. Recent research tends to differ from the earlier research in that for the most part, it has been conducted in "additive bilingual" settings; that is, settings in which a second language is being learned by choice and consequently the first language is not threatened by acquisition of the second language (e.g., Diaz, 1983; Peal & Lambert, 1962). Thus, recent research has generally examined bilinguals with nativelike or high levels of proficiency in both their languages. As well, the methological shortcomings of earlier research were rectified.

Cummins (1976) has suggested that the apparent discrepancy in these sets of findings, notwithstanding methodological differences and weaknesses, can be reconciled. He proposes that there are language proficiency *thresholds* associated with positive and negative cognitive effects. In particular, there is a lower threshold of language proficiency that is necessary to avoid the negative academic and linguistic effects reported in the early research and a yet higher threshold required to experience the positive cognitive effects reported in the more recent research. Language proficiency that falls between these two levels will result in neither positive nor negative cognitive effects. Language proficiency that falls short of the lower threshold is said to result in negative cognitive effects because the students' interaction with the educational environment is impoverished. Language proficiency that falls above the higher threshold is said to result in cognitive advantages because the learner develops a better understanding of the relationship between language and meaning. According to Cummins's conceptualization, the Canadian immersion programs represent an additive bilingual setting where nativelike or at least high levels of proficiency in both languages are likely. Thus, academic or cognitive deficits are not likely to be found as a result of participation in these programs.

The academic progress of IM students has been assessed using different types of achievement tests: standardized, locally devised, and provincial. Virtually all full-scale evaluations of immersion programs in Canada include standardized achievement testing in mathematics. Standardized achievement testing of mathematics has been supplemented by standardized achievement testing of science in the higher elementary grades and in secondary school in the Tornonto and Ottawa evaluations (see Swain & Lapkin, 1982, for example). Locally devised achievement tests of geography and history, along with math and science, have been used in the Ottawa area (Barik, Swain, & Gaudino, 1975). Finally, the results of provincial examinations in a variety of subjects are available for IM students from Quebec; as noted earlier, these examinations are written by Quebec high school students in fulfillment of their high school diploma (Genesee, 1976a, 1977a).

The results of mathematics testing in early total immersion programs indicate that IM students score as well as EC students on English math tests, including computations and concepts subtests. This has been found to be true even during the primary grades when all math instruction is provided in French only.

One exception to this pattern has been arithmetic problem solving, where the early IM students sometimes score lower than EC students. This lag is not found when the IM students are examined in French, suggesting that it probably reflects difficulty in reading English rather than a real difficulty in doing mathematical problems *per se*. In fact, once English reading is introduced into the immersion program, and often prior, this lag disappears. No such lag is demonstrated by delayed or late IM students who have had math and reading instruction in English before having math instruction in French. IM students have also been found to score as well as, and in some cases higher than, FC students on math tests given in French (see Genesee, 1983). Thus, despite the legendary tendency for people to count and do calculations in their first language, teaching IM students math in French poses no apparent problems.

With respect to achievement in science, Swain (1978) reports that early total IM students in Ontario scored as well as EC students on standardized science tests. One-year late IM students in Ontario, however, did not fare so well—they were found to score significantly lower than EC students at the end of the first year of the program, but they caught up by the end of the second year. The late IM students who participated in this evaluation were in grade 8 and had not had French language instruction until one year prior to immersion, at which time they were given 20 minutes a day during the first eight months and 60 minutes a day during the last two months of the year. Swain suggests that limited exposure to the second language prior to receiving instruction in other academic subjects through the language may retard mastery of the material somewhat because the students lack sufficient competence in French to benefit fully from academic instruction. This type of lag has never been reported in Quebec where late IM students get FSL instruction for 20 to 40 minutes a day from kindergarten. Finally, the results of locally devised achievement tests in geography, history, math, and science confirm the results of standardized testing—no differences between IM and EC students at grades 9 and 10 have been found.

Genesee (1976a, 1977a) has analyzed the results of Montreal IM students on Quebec Ministry of Education Secondary School Leaving Examinations in physics, chemistry, and history. The analyses were limited to one-year late IM students. The performance of the IM students was compared to that of EC students using the same samples of students who comprised his evaluation groups. The IM students had written the exams in French while the EC students had written the corresponding exams in English. It was possible to equate the samples of students for IQ using analysis of covariance procedures since IQ scores were available for both groups. With these adjustments made, it was found that the one-year late IM students scored as well as their EC peers on all three examinations. Parenthetically, it was also found that the IM students scored as well as or better than the EC students on examinations related to English language arts, such as literature. The latter results confirm the standardized testing results.

The performance of the late IM students was also compared to that of FC students attending French-medium schools throughout the province of Quebec. These comparisons were based on the average performance of the FC students in the province as a whole. It was not possible to select subgroups of comparable FC students. The use of provincewide averages on the one hand and the average of a small group of IM students from the city of Montreal on the other means that there were probably large differences between the FC and IM samples with respect to socioeconomic, intellectual, and geographic factors. In particular, the students comprising the IM sample were probably on the average more advantaged socioeconomically and academically and were probably from a more urban setting than the FC students. On these grounds, one would expect the IM students to score higher than the provincial average. This in fact was found on comparisons using history, geography, mathematics, typing, and art. While not conclusive, these results are useful to the extent that they indicate that the IM students were achieving as expected.

SUMMARY

The results of standardized testing in English indicate that early total IM students often experience a lag in literacy-based language skills such as reading, spelling, and written vocabulary during that phase of the program when all instruction is given in English. At the same time, they demonstrate no problems with the interpersonal communication skills of speaking and listening comprehension. They reach parity with control students in all-English programs usually within one year of receiving English language arts instruction. One exception to this is spelling, which sometimes takes an additional year or two. Students in alternative immersion programs—partial, delayed, and late—demonstrate no lags in English language development.

The results of standardized testing in mathematics and science indicate that early IM students and late IM students with core French instruction throughout the elementary grades experience no lags in achievement as a result of receiving academic instruction in French. These results are confirmed by locally devised achievement tests in geography, history, math, and science. There is some evidence that late IM students with limited prior exposure to French experience temporary "underachievement" in some academic subjects, but that this is rectified relatively quickly. The results of Quebec Ministry of Education Examinations indicate that one-year late IM students achieve as well as their English-taught peers in regular subjects and in English language arts subjects at the end of secondary school. It has also been found from the Ministry results that IM students score higher than the provincial average for French students on a variety of examinations written in French, as would be expected of a select group of students. In chapter six we will examine the English language and academic achievement of students with different learner characteristics, including low ability, language disabled, and low socioeconomic students.

Research Findings: French Language Achievement

As noted in the preceding chapter, the French language assessment instruments include tests of language proficiency such as speaking, listening, reading, and writing as well as tests of linguistic competence such as grammar. The proficiency tests can be further subdivided into tests of language comprehension (i.e., reading and listening comprehension) and tests of language production (i.e., writing and speaking). Assessment of IM students' French language achievement involves three types of comparisons: 1) IM students versus EC students taking core FSL instruction; 2) IM students versus FC students in regular French-medium schools; and 3) IM students in one type of immersion program versus IM students in another type of immersion program (e.g., early vs. late). Core FSL instruction is generally limited to 30 to 60 minutes per day and focuses on teaching and learning language as a subject; no regular content is taught using the language.

Comparisons of the performance of IM students, be they in an early, delayed, or late alternative, with that of EC students indicate that the former are significantly superior to the latter on all types of French language tests. This is not unexpected in view of the IM students' much greater exposure to French. The more revealing and interesting comparisons are those involving FC students. Here the results are much more complex. The following descriptions characterize the most common patterns of results. There are undoubtedly local exceptions to these generalizations; only exceptions that serve to illustrate more general implications or issues will be discussed here.

EARLY IMMERSION

Reading and Listening Comprehension

It has been found that IM students are most likely to perform as well as FC students on tests of comprehension, including both reading and listening. This is particularly true of the performance of early IM students. In Table 3, for example,

Table 3 SUMMARY OF GRADES 4, 5, AND 6 FRENCH LANGUAGE TEST RESULTS FOR AN EARLY TOTAL FRENCH IMMERSION PROGRAM (GENESEE, 1978a)

	Grade 4				Grade 5				Grade 6			
	Max	Immersion	English Control	French Control	Max	Immersion	English Control	French Control	Max	Immersion	English Control	French Control
1. Test de Lecture California:												
Vocabulaire	52	38.17	30.83	42.55 ***	28	20.21	12.09	24.90 ***		NA	NA	NA
Compréhension	21	14.78	9.54	15.54 ***	30	21.33	13.92	22.47 ***		NA	NA	NA
Test de lecture silencieuse		NA	NA	NA		NA	NA	NA	49	22.46	11.73	30.93 ***
2. Test de rendement en Français	9	4.36	1.33	6.56 ***	9	3.47	1.63	6.70 ***	9	3.25	1.79	5.70 ***
3. Listening comprehension	37	30.30	16.61	30.94 ***	17	14.62	7.21	15.87 ***	16	10.98	6.16	11.89 ***
4. Speaking skills:												
Comprehension	5	4.97	3.32	5.00 **	5	4.92	3.67	5.00 ***	5	4.50	3.18	5.00 ***
Pronunciation	5	4.03	3.17	4.92 **	5	4.00	2.01	5.00 ***	5	4.01	3.40	5.00 ***
Grammar	5	4.49	2.64	4.91 **	5	4.00	2.02	5.00 ***	5	4.13	3.39	4.88 ***
Vocabulary	5	4.81	2.36	5.00 **	5	3.59	1.74	5.00 ***	5	3.92	2.69	4.99 ***
Communicativeness	5	4.61	3.12	4.94 **	5	3.65	2.53	5.00 ***	5	3.74	2.79	4.96 ***

NA = not administered

$*p < .05$ $**p < .01$ $***p < .001$

Note: Mean scores joined by a solid line differ significantly from one another according to the Newman-Keuls Multiple Comparison procedure.

which is taken from Genesee's longitudinal evaluation of early total IM students in Montreal, it can be seen that the early IM students in grades 4 and 5 scored as well as comparable FC students on the Comprehension subtest of the *Test de Lecture California* (California Reading Test), and their comprehension skills during an individual oral interview with a native French speaker were judged to be as good as those of FC students who were interviewed using the same procedures (Genesee, 1978a). It can also be seen from Table 3 that the early IM students in grades 4, 5, and 6 scored as well as FC students on a group-administered test of listening comprehension. Lambert and Tucker (1972) and Swain and Lapkin (1982) have reported similar results for students in the St. Lambert immersion program and for students in immersion programs in Ottawa, respectively.

It is important to point out here that IM students do not always perform at the same level as FC students on comprehension tests; this is evident from Table 3 in the case of the grade 6 IM students for both reading comprehension (see Test de Lecture Silencieuse results) and listening comprehension (see Speaking Skills: Comprehension subscore). Other evaluators have similarly failed to find comparable performance for IM and FC students on some comprehension tests (e.g., Foidart, 1981).

It is also important to note here that these findings pertain to comprehension of school-type language; that is to say, the careful, standard variety of French that is most commonly used in school. Whether IM students would demonstrate the same proficiency with less standard, more colloquial forms of French, as would be found in out-of-school settings, is an open question. Indeed, in language usage surveys conducted in Montreal (Genesee, 1978b, 1981a), IM students expressed concern that they had difficulty understanding and using French in some extracurricular settings because French Canadians speak too fast and use words and expressions that they are not familiar with. This is an understandable gap in their language proficiency. Exposure to a second language in a school setting alone will not provide learners with the full range of language varieties and styles that they are likely to encounter and need outside of school.

Speaking and Writing

In general, IM students are less likely to demonstrate nativelike levels of proficiency on tests that assess productive language skills, such as speaking and writing, or on tests that assess their knowledge of discrete elements and grammatical rules of the second language. Referring to Table 3 again, it can be seen that the IM students were rated significantly lower than FC students on most of the subskills of the oral production evaluation, and they were rated lower on the scales that pertain to productive aspects of speaking (i.e., pronunciation, grammar, vocabulary) than on the comprehension subscale.

IM students' less than nativelike competence in French is attested to by a number of linguistic analyses that have been carried out on their spoken and written language (Harley, in press; Harley & Swain, 1984; Spilka, 1976). Harley and Swain (1984) carried out detailed analyses of grade 5 early IM students' use of verbs during a 20-minute interview with a native French-speaking adult. The analyses were carried out on written transcriptions of the interviews. They found that, although the IM students used approximately the same proportion of verbs and almost the same variety of verbs in their interviews as did the FC comparison students, the IM students' verb systems were less complex and redundant than those of the FC students. They noted that where French has a more complex system than English, the immersion children opted for a simpler pattern that approximates English. In particular, the IM students tended to lack verb forms that were not important for conveying meaning in the classroom setting or for which grammatically less complex alternatives were available. At the same time, they also noted that, notwithstanding their simplified verb system, the IM students were always understood by their adult interlocutors. Harley (in press) similarly found that IM students' use of prepositions in writing differed from native speaker usage. More specifically, she found that IM students showed a systematic tendency to rely more heavily on prepositions to express the spatial notion of direction than did native speakers, a tendency, she suggests, that reflects the nature of the students' first language, English.

Spilka (1976) carried out error analyses of the spoken language of grade 4, 5, and 6 early IM students in St Lambert. She noted that they "cannot be mistaken for . . . native speakers of French" (p. 17). More specifically, she found that the IM students were less likely to use cleft sentences, topicalization, and sentential objects than native speakers, but they tended to employ many relative clauses and favored anteposition of adverbial phrases, reflecting English usage. Spilka concluded:

> The model after which Experimentals (i.e., immersion students) in this sample tended to pattern themselves was adult usage in Standard French (presumably that of the teacher); . . . French linguistic maturity was clearly lagging in Experimentals, yet this was seldom a barrier to communication; only one sentence in the entire sample (of 3086) could not be deciphered. (p. 31)

Taken together, the Harley, Swain, and Spilka findings suggest that IM students' production grammar is shaped in important ways by 1) their first language grammar system, 2) the communication demands made on them in immersion classrooms, and 3) the type of native speaker models they have available.

Functional Proficiency

Notwithstanding their linguistic weaknesses, early total IM students generally demonstrate very high levels of functional proficiency in French. For example, grade 4, 5, and 6 early IM students in Montreal scored in the 3 to 4 stanine range on the *Test de Rendement en Français*. In percentile terms, this means that the IM students scored between the 11th and 40th percentiles. This test is standardized on native French-speaking students and is used by the largest French school district in the province of Quebec in much the same way that the Canadian Test of Basic Skills or the Metropolitan Achievement Tests might be used by English language school districts elsewhere in Canada or the United States (see Table 3). The scores of the grade 5 and 6 IM students are probably underestimates of their end-of-year proficiency, since the test was administered in December of the school year instead of June in order to correspond with the date of testing for the standardization group. Gray (1981) also noted that early total IM students in New Brunswick demonstrated high levels of proficiency in French when compared to native French-speaking students. More specifically, she noted that grade 6 early total IM students generally scored slightly more than one year behind FC students on tests of French language achievement, including the Test de Rendement en Français, reading tests, and writing tests.

The functional proficiency attained by students in early immersion programs is perhaps best illustrated by their oral proficiency. The oral communication skills of IM students have been assessed by a number of investigators using a variety of techniques. As part of the Montreal and St. Lambert evaluations, samples of IM students were routinely interviewed individually by native French-speaking interviewers using an open-ended format, described in chapter two. The conversations between the interviewers and the students were tape-recorded and subsequently evaluated by other native French-speaking evaluators who were "blind" with respect to the program the students were participating in. Samples of FC students were similarly interviewed, recorded, and evaluated in order to provide a frame of reference with which to better evaluate the early IM students. The IM students thus evaluated have generally been rated between 3.5 and 5.0 on a 5-point scale, with 5 being nativelike (see Table 3).

Bruck, Lambert, and Tucker (1976) examined the communication skills of the St. Lambert early total IM students using more objective, analytic procedures. They asked students in grades 5 and 6 of the program to retell a story they had just seen in a silent film to someone who had not seen it. Bruck then carried out analyses of 1) the organization of the students' oral renditions of the stories, including the percentage of stories that had an introduction, no ending, or a poor ending; and also of 2) the amount and kinds of information transmitted, including the number of episodes, details, and subdetails that were recounted by each student. The IM students' stories were compared to those of native French-speaking students of the same age. For the most part, the IM students' stories were the same as the French students', and in particular the IM students recounted the same amount and kinds of information as the French students. These findings corroborate the relatively high subjective ratings that are typically assigned to IM students during face-to-face conversations, as described in the preceding paragraph.

In yet another study, Szamosi, Swain, and Lapkin (1979) recorded the conversations of a small sample of grade 2 IM students who individually spent some time playing with native French-speaking children of the same age who were attending a French school in Toronto. The play sessions occurred once a week for two months and took place in the French-speaking children's homes. Detailed analyses of the conversations of a pair of students were performed to see how well the IM student could function in French in a natural context. It was found that "the immersion students functioned with ease and naturalness and could joke, ask for clarifications, issue orders, respond appropriately to the French-speaking playmate . . ." (in Lapkin, 1983, p. 7).

LATE IMMERSION

Evaluations of late IM students' French language proficiency have tended to find the same pattern of results as in the case of early total IM students; namely, they score consistently better than EC students on all measures of French, and they are more likely to attain native levels of proficiency in comprehension skills and less than native levels in production skills or in their mastery of discrete aspects of French, be they phonological, lexical, or syntactic (see Genesee, 1981b, and Genesee, Polich, & Stanley, 1977, for examples). These findings are illustrated in Table 4, which summarizes Genesee's grade 9 results for one-year and two-year late IM students in Montreal. It can be seen from Table 4 that both late IM groups scored in the average stanine range on the *Test de Rendement en Français* and they both scored as well as a group of FC students on a test of reading comprehension *(Test de Comprehension de L'ecrit)*. Their comprehension skills during an oral interview were rated very high—4.78 for the one-year group and 4.95 for the two-year group (maximum score is 5), although neither group performed as well as the FC students on a standardized test of French listening comprehension *(Test de Comprehension Auditive)*. In contrast, both IM groups made more total errors as well as more specific errors on a dictation test than the FC group, and they were generally rated significantly lower than a sample of FC students on the separate scales of the oral evaluation, the one exception being comprehension, as already noted. The written compositions of the late IM students were also rated significantly lower overall than those of FC students.

Late IM students, like early IM students, achieve a high level of functional proficiency in French as evidenced by their average stanine scores on the *Test de Rendement en Français* and by their performance on the Quebec Departmental Leaving Examinations, as discussed in the preceding chapter. The functional proficiency of the late IM students is also attested to by their performance on the *Public Service Commission Test,* a test used by the Public Service Commission of the Canadian federal government to assess the French language proficiency of its employees for appropriate placement in jobs requiring competence in French. There are three levels to the test—A, B, and C, with C being the highest level of proficiency. There are four subtests: speaking, listening, reading, and writing.

Table 4 SUMMARY OF GRADE 9 FRENCH LANGUAGE TEST RESULTS FOR AN EARLY TOTAL FRENCH IMMERSION PROGRAM

Tests	French Control	Early Immersion	Grade 7/8 Immersion	Grade 7 Immersion	English Control	F Ratio
1. Test de rendement en français (9)	NA	5.47	5.31	4.73	2.02	69.52***
2. Test de compréhension de l'écrit (20)	16.05	16.97	17.71	15.61	8.98	56.99***
3. La dictée	7.69	10.58	11.63	20.54	38.72	79.74***
4. Test de compréhension auditive (17)	14.12	13.20	11.16	9.75	5.85	56.42***
5. Composition (5)	4.40	2.59	2.13	2.53	1.23	86.45***
6. Production orale						
Comprehension (5)	5.00	4.96	4.98	4.92	4.32	7.70***
Pronunciation (5)	5.00	3.98	4.12	3.84	2.85	62.92***
Grammar (5)	4.94	3.70	4.01	3.39	2.00	75.19***
Vocabulary (5)	5.00	3.44	3.78	3.16	1.98	67.96***
Communicativeness (5)	5.00	3.69	3.81	3.18	2.13	58.97***

NA = not administered

*$p < .05$ **$p < .01$ ***$p < .001$

Note: Maximum test scores are presented in parentheses. Mean scores joined by a solid line do *not* differ significantly from one another according to the Newman-Keuls Multiple Comparison procedure. French control results on oral production tests were not analyzed statistically.

Morrison (1981) administered levels A and B to groups of late IM students in the Ottawa area. The students were in grade 12 at the time of the testing. The majority of the students reached the B level of proficiency in all four skill areas, with more students achieving this level in reading, writing, and listening and fewer achieving it in speaking (see Table 5). Complete descriptions of Level B proficiency are given in Table 5.

Immersion Centers versus Dual-Track Schools

Before comparing the effectiveness of alternative forms of immersion, let us consider the effectiveness of immersion in different school settings. A number of investigators have assessed the results of immersion programs in schools that offer only the immersion program (immersion centers) in comparison to programs in schools that offer both immersion and a regular English program (dual-track schools). Immersion centers provide a more enriched French language setting in that virtually all communication in the school takes place in French. In dual-track schools, all communication in immersion classrooms and to IM students in the hallways is in French, at least insofar as communication between adults and the students is concerned, while communication outside the immersion classroom is usually in English. Thus, it would probably be expected that the French proficiency of IM students attending immersion centers would be higher than that of students attending dual-track schools.

In the case of early total immersion programs, this comparison has been made by Lapkin, Andrew, Harley, Swain, and Kamin (1981) working in schools in Ottawa and by Foidart (1981) working in schools in Manitoba. Lapkin et al. assessed the proficiency of grade 5 IM students and Foidart assessed the proficiency of grade 3, 6, and 9 students. As expected, it was found that students in the immersion centers scored significantly higher than students in dual-track schools on a variety of measures, including tests of listening comprehension, oral production, reading, and French language arts.

The same comparisons have been made by Genesee for one-year late immersion programs in Montreal (Genesee, Morin, & Allister, 1974). He examined the proficiency of grade 7 students and once again found the students in the immersion centers had achieved higher levels of proficiency than students in dual-track schools. Genesee's evaluation also included tests of listening comprehension, speaking, reading, and language arts. Genesee's results are limited to the first year of the late immersion program since no follow-up evaluation of center versus dual-track students was possible in subsequent grades. Unlike early immersion centers where early IM students take all of their classes together at all grade levels, late immersion centers are restricted to the year or years during which French is the major medium of instruction (e.g., grade 7 in the case of a one-year late immersion program beginning in grade 7). This means that in subsequent grades late IM students who have been in centers are often mixed with late IM

Table 5   NUMBER OF LATE IMMERSION STUDENTS RANKED AT DIFFERENT LEVELS OF THE PUBLIC SERVICE COMMISSION'S LANGUAGE KNOWLEDGE EXAMINATION

	Speaking		Listening		Reading		Writing	
	A	B	A	B	A	B	A	B
Ottawa grade 6 entry	26	7	6	30	9	26	8	27
Carleton grade 7 entry	6	11	1	16	2	15	0	17

Descriptions of Level B Proficiency

Reading Comprehension This level implies the capacity to read and to understand connected passages containing a variety of sentence types, turns of phrase, and current expressions, but it is unlikely that regional variants will be familiar to the individual at this level. Memoranda and letters are the kinds of text where comprehension will be optimal. The general meaning and the major points of articles and reports on general and work-related topics will be well understood, although nuances or specific details may frequently be missed. The time taken by the second language reader to comprehend a particular text may be moderately longer than for the average first language reader performing the same task.

Written Expression This level implies the ability to use a variety of sentence types (simple, compound, or complex) to express general ideas and opinions of nonspecialized and nontechnical topics. Errors in grammar and spelling will be minor but may not be infrequent. Memoranda and letters will be the kind of text usually mastered at this level, but these will definitely require revision for extra-office distribution. Nuances of style and regional variants will generally be absent, and sentences may be awkwardly connected. The time taken to compose a text at this level will be relatively longer when compared to the time taken by the average first language writer.

Aural Comprehension This level implies the capacity to understand continuous speech made up of a variety of sentence types and delivered at a normal speaking rate. The main points and general line of reasoning at meetings, in oral presentations, and in discussion groups will be understood at this level, although nuances of speech and specific details of the discussion may frequently be missed. The same difficulties could arise in situations involving communication through the media (radio, telephone, etc.) but would be less likely to occur in interviews. In all situations, an individual at this level could experience difficulty in understanding regional words, expression, and pronunciation. Background noise or a particularly fast speaking rate may have the same effect. General and work-related vocabulary will normally be better understood than more specialized vocabularly.

Oral Expression This level implies the capacity to take part in a variety of verbal exchanges using the different kinds of sentence types described above. The individual at this level would function optimally in a one-to-one interview, but should also be able to contribute to meetings and discussion groups. One would be able to convey the essentials of his/her line of reasoning. There would likely be difficulty in expressing nuances or in using specific vocabulary, idioms, and regional variants in their appropriate contexts. Grammar and pronunciation will most often show strong mother tongue interference but will only occasionally result in misunderstanding. Hesitations of moderate length may be relatively frequent on general or work-related topics and would increase as one attempts to speak in detail on any specific subject matter.

students who have been in dual-track schools. As a result, it becomes difficult to identify students who have been in center programs versus dual-track programs.

The evidence to date then suggests that immersion centers are more effective school settings for French language learning than schools that offer English medium education along with immersion. Immersion centers have the added advantage that they are easier to administer. Dual-track schools require two sets of teachers—one for immersion and one for the regular program. They also require two sets of school books, library books, and syllabuses at all grade levels. In contrast, immersion centers are relatively streamlined since they do not require such duality. Associated with the administrative complications of a dual teaching stream are potential ethnolinguistic problems that can arise when teachers representing different language groups that are in conflict outside school are sharing the same educational space (Cleghorn & Genesee, 1984). This issue will be discussed in more detail in chapter seven.

EARLY, DELAYED, OR LATE?

The development of alternative forms of immersion has led naturally to the question of their relative merits and advantages. More specifically, considerable interest as well as controversy has been generated over the relative effectiveness of each alternative in promoting second language proficiency. Indeed, since none of the major alternatives (early, delayed, or late) or any of their variants (e.g., partial vs. total) have been shown to result in negative effects to the students' English language development or academic achievement, evidence for differential effectiveness among the alternatives has been sought in the domain of second language achievement. The ensuing discussion then will focus on comparisons based on second language outcomes.

It is important to emphasize here that any conclusions that might be drawn concerning the relative advantages of one alternative over another with respect to second language learning do not necessarily imply that that alternative is the most desirable in all respects. There are a number of factors to consider when assessing the relative merits of alternative forms of immersion for a given community. For example, in bilingual settings such as Montreal or Ottawa, the presence of large numbers of target language speakers in the community, along with the evident social and practical benefits associated with knowing French, would be important factors to consider when examining the relative merits of early versus late immersion. Parents in such communities may feel that learning French is too important to delay until the middle of elementary school or the beginning of secondary school, as is the case in delayed and late immersion programs. Conversely, in relatively monolingual communities where the immediate practical benefits of learning French are modest at best and perhaps nonexistent, then a late or delayed immersion alternative might be considered more suitable, other things being equal. In communities where there is some interest in promoting second language learning in school, but at the same time parents are somewhat apprehensive about the effects of total immersion in French on their children's academic and English language development, notwithstanding the existence of all the research findings reviewed in the preceding chapter, a partial immersion option might be more desirable since it might be less threatening to all concerned. Thus, the ultimate decision as to which program is best for particular students in specific communities must be based not only on a consideration of each program's second language outcomes, to be discussed in this section, but also on other educational and community factors. Viewed from this perspective, then, there is no one best alternative; the goals and aspirations of the parents, children, and educators involved must be matched with the characteristics and likely outcomes of available alternatives.

The following review and discussion will focus on comparisons between 1) early total versus early partial immersion, 2) early versus delayed immersion, and 3) early versus late, including comparisons of one-year and two-year late immersion options.

Early Total versus Early Partial Immersion

Three investigations comparing early total and early partial immersion alternatives have been carried out—two in Ontario (see Swain & Lapkin, 1982; and Edwards, McCarrey, & Fu, 1980) and one in Quebec (see Genesee, 1981c). All three evaluations have found that overall early partial IM students perform less well than early total IM students on a variety of French language tests, including reading, writing, listening comprehension, and grammar. Genesee's evaluation also included assessments of the students' oral production skills—no significant differences were found between early total and early partial IM students at either grade 5 or grade 6 on any of these assessments.

Results from Ontario have indicated that grade 4 and 5 partial IM students scored in the bottom quartile on a reading test normed on early total IM students. Genesee found that his partial IM students scored in the below-average stanine range ($M = 3.37$) on a test of overall French language achievement normed on native French-speaking students while his total IM students scored one stanine higher—in the average stanine range ($M = 4.31$). These findings have been corroborated by Edwards and his colleagues working in Ottawa. The advantages demonstrated by the total IM students in grades 4, 5, and 6 have been found to persist until grade 8 (Swain & Lapkin, 1982).

Early versus Delayed Immersion

Systematic evaluations of early versus delayed immersion alternatives have been carried out by Cziko working in Montreal (see Cziko, 1975; Cziko, Holobow, & Lambert, 1977; and Cziko, Holobow, Lambert, & Tucker, 1977) and by

Lapkin working in Ontario (see Lapkin & Cummins, 1984; and Lapkin, Swain, Kamin, & Hanna, 1982, p. 45). In his evaluations, Cziko monitored the development of pilot and follow-up groups of delayed IM students in grades 4 through 6. He compared their achievement to that of early total IM students and English control students. He found that, although there were isolated cases when the delayed IM students scored as well as the early IM students (e.g., the grade 4 pilot and follow-up groups on the French reading comprehension test), the early IM students generally performed significantly higher than the delayed IM students on most tests.

Lapkin's results have been more mixed. In an evaluation of delayed versus early immersion programs in Toronto, Lapkin and Swain reported that grade 6 early IM students scored significantly better than delayed IM students on a test of listening comprehension, but that there were no significant differences between the groups on tests of reading, speaking, or writing. The delayed IM students' performance was particularly impressive in view of the fact that they had accumulated only 2,560 hours of French instruction in contrast to over 4,000 hours for the early IM students. In another evaluation, Lapkin and Cummins (1984) reported that grade 7 delayed IM students scored less well than grade 6 early IM students, who had participated in the Lapkin and Swain evaluation, on listening and reading tests; no other comparisons were carried out.

Taken together, these findings do not indicate an unequivocal or consistent advantage for early immersion over delayed immersion. In fact, they indicate that delayed IM students can make impressive progress in French in a relatively short period of time. Possible explanations for older students being faster second language learners will be discussed in more detail in the next section. Unfortunately, no long-term follow-up of delayed IM students in secondary school has been undertaken, so we do not know how durable their second language skills are when they pursue less intensive French language studies. Cziko, Holobow, Lambert, and Tucker (1977) report that delayed IM students did not sustain their advantage in French at the same level when they returned to a regular English curriculum with enriched French language arts instruction. Evidence reviewed in the next section suggests that the follow-up to immersion may be very important in sustaining and advancing the students' second language proficiency.

Early Total Immersion versus Late Immersion

A number of independent comparative evaluations of early versus late immersion alternatives have been carried out in Montreal (see Adiv, 1980a; Cziko, Holobow, & Lambert, 1977; and Genesee, 1981b), in Ottawa (Morrison, 1981), and in Toronto (Lapkin, Swain, Kamin, & Hanna, 1982). Comparisons between early total immersion and one-year late immersion have generally found that early IM students achieve higher levels of proficiency in French than do one-year late IM students. These findings are based on tests of reading, listening comprehension, oral production, grammar, and writing, and have been found for late immersion whether preceded by core FSL instruction from kindergarten or by preparatory FSL instruction immediately prior to entering immersion. The evaluations by Genesee and Adiv working in Montreal have assessed the progress of students in these two alternatives until the end of secondary school. Their findings have been somewhat inconsistent. Genesee found that the differential in favor of early IM students was most marked at the end of grades 7 and 8, immediately following the immersion year, but that it decreased noticeably in grade 9. Consistent with Genesee's grade 9 results, Adiv (1980a) also found relatively few differences in French proficiency between early and one-year late IM students in grade 10. However, a follow-up evaluation one year later, in grade 11, revealed consistent differences in favor of the early IM students once again.

Notwithstanding the possibility that these fluctuations are due to the use of a cross-sectional design and therefore reflect the performance of different students at each grade level, they illustrate the potential importance of the follow-up program in determining the participating students' long-term proficiency in French. More evaluations of follow-up programs in different school districts are clearly needed to ascertain the reliability of the findings reported here before we can discuss with any confidence the ultimate proficiency levels achievable in these two alternatives.

Turning now to comparisons between early immersion and two-year late immersion programs, there are two sets of pertinent studies—those carried out by Genesee (1981b) and Adiv (1980a) in Montreal and those carried out by Morrison (1981) in Ottawa. Genesee and Adiv assessed the French proficiency of early IM and two-year late IM students over four consecutive years until the end of secondary school. They consistently failed to find significant differences between samples of students drawn from these two types of programs. Their test battery included tests of listening comprehension, oral production, reading comprehension, dictation, and writing. That the two-year late IM students in Montreal achieved parity with the early immersion students despite the fact that the former had had considerably less cumulative exposure to French than the latter at the time of the evaluations (1,400 hours for the late IM students in comparison with 5,000 hours for the early IM students) implies relatively faster learning on the part of the older students.

Because the early IM students in Genesee's evaluations had received considerably more exposure to French in school than the late IM students by the time of testing, it is not possible from these data to isolate the effect of age *per se*. However, the *Test de Rendement en Français* provides a suitable basis for comparing groups of students at different ages since it has been standardized at most grade levels and is administered routinely at all grade levels as part of the Montreal evaluations. If one takes into account FSL instruction during kindergarten to grade 6, the two-year late IM students had had almost the same amount of exposure to French at the end of grade 8 as the early IM students had had at the end of grade 2, namely two and a half years. When a *post hoc* comparison is made between grade 2 early IM students (see Polich, 1974) and grade 8 two-year late IM students, it is found that, whereas the latter scored in the average stanine range (i.e., 5) on the grade 8 test, the former scored in the below-average range on the grade 2 test.

These results corroborate findings from other studies of short-term second language learning in conventional instructional programs in demonstrating that young children are not necessarily more effective learners than older children (Asher & Price, 1967; Burstall, 1974; Fathman, 1975; Price, 1978; Stern, 1963) and, in fact, younger learners usually make slower progress. Thus, there seems to be an advantage to late instruction in a second language; this advantage probably derives from the learning efficiency of older students. Older students may be more efficient because they are more mature cognitively and therefore are better able to abstract, classify, generalize, and consciously attend to language *qua* language. These cognitive skills may be particularly well suited to the task of second language learning in school where language is often taught and used in an abstract, decontextualized manner (Cummins, 1981). Younger students may use unconscious, automatic kinds of learning strategies and therefore may be at a relative disadvantage in such contexts. Indeed, general observation indicates that older students tend to learn faster than younger students in most cognitive domains. Rosansky (1975) has made the contrasting argument— namely, that second language learning is "blocked" in the case of older learners by cognitive factors and, in particular, by the development of formal operations as defined by Piaget. However, as already noted, the evidence does not indicate that older learners are in fact "blocked."

Analysis of the evaluations of the two-year late immersion versus early immersion programs in Ottawa by Morrison and her colleagues reveals that the picture is not so simple (Morrison, 1981). In contrast to the Montreal results, the Ottawa results indicate that students who had participated in an early total immersion program outperformed students who had participated in a two-year late immersion program on most measures of second language proficiency. Comparison of the Montreal and Ottawa programs reveals one likely basis for the apparent discrepancy between these two sets of results. The Ottawa early immersion program provides much more French than does the Montreal program. The amount of French exposure in the Ottawa program by grade level is kindergarten to grade 1: 100 percent; grades 2 to 5: 80 percent; grades 6 to 8: 50 percent. In the Montreal program, the amount of exposure to French is as follows: kindergarten to grade 2: 100 percent; grade 3: 80 percent; grade 4: 60 percent; grades 5 to 8: 40 percent. The late immersion programs in both cities are quite comparable —kindergarten to grade 6: 30–45 minutes per day of FSL; grades 7 and 8: 80 percent French immersion. Thus, one possible explanation for the advantage of the Ottawa early immersion program lies in the additional exposure to French that it provides relative to the Montreal program.

The findings just reviewed suggest that time makes a difference in second language learning. The results of a number of other immersion evaluations support this suggestion; for example, the finding that early total immersion programs generally yield higher levels of proficiency than early partial immersion programs is consistent with this suggestion. The results of other investigators also support this possibility. Carroll (1975), in an international study of the teaching of French as a foreign language in eight countries, found that, among a number of different predictors, length of French instruction was the most important predictor of second language learning. Burstall (1974) found that students who had been introduced to French instruction in the primary grades (at age eight) as part of an experimental second language program in Britain acquired greater proficiency than did same-aged students who had received less instruction in French. Research by Lapkin, Swain, Kamin, and Hanna (1982) indicates that it is not simply amount of second language exposure that matters, but rather intensity of exposure. They report that a group of grade 8 one-year late IM students were less proficient than another group of grade 8 late IM students who had received more concentrated exposure to French, whereas they were more proficient than students in an extended core French program, which by the time of the evaluation had amounted to more than twice as many hours as the late IM program, but it was extended over several years.

A corollary advantage associated with starting second language instruction in school early is the opportunity it affords for extended use of the second language outside school. Extracurricular use of the language is tantamount to extending the learning experience. This type of exposure is likely to be particularly important since it has been found that individuals who begin second language learning in childhood in natural settings generally achieve higher levels of proficiency in the long term than those who begin in adolescence or adulthood (Asher & Garcia, 1969; Oyama, 1976, 1978; Selinger, Krashen, & Ladefoged, 1975). The possibility of improving second language learning through out-of-school use is likely to be particularly important in bilingual communities where real opportunities to use the language exist. Needless to say, the possibility of out-of-school second language use is available to learners who begin the study of a second language in the later grades as well as to those who begin in the early grades, but the late starters will have a shortened time frame within which to take advantage of this possibility.

The significance of amount of exposure for second language learning is not always so clear-cut, however. As we have already seen, the results of yet other immersion evaluations indicate that amount of exposure is not always correlated with level of second language achievement. Genesee's comparison of the Montreal two-year late IM studens with early IM students attests to this. To illustrate this point further, Shapson and Day (1982) found no significant differences between three variants of late immersion that differed with respect to the amount of instruction time in French and the students' exposure to French prior to immersion. Students who had had no previous French language instruction prior to entering immersion and students who had received less French during their one-year late immersion program (60 percent versus 90 percent) demonstrated the same level of proficiency on tests of listening comprehension and language arts as did students who had had more previous exposure and more exposure in immersion. Unfortunately, the range of assessment instruments was limited so that we do not know whether the researchers' findings are generalizable to a complete range of language skills, including speaking, reading, and writing.

Aside from the general question of the importance of time as a factor in second language learning, an important question that arises from the Montreal results is why the considerable additional exposure to and instruction in French that the early IM students had had relative to the late IM students did not result in measurably higher levels of proficiency. It has been suggested that less time is needed by older learners to achieve the same or nearly the same levels of second language proficiency that younger learners achieve over a longer time period because of cognitive factors. At the same time, the nature of the language learning environment itself is probably an important factor. On the one hand, one might expect extended exposure to French in an immersion program, or in any second language learning environment for that matter, to stimulate continuous development of the second language if the learners' linguistic or communicative needs in that environment are expanded progressively. If, on the other hand, there is a finite set of language skills required to function effectively in most immersion programs, and if this repertoire of requisite skills is needed relatively early in the program, then one would expect IM students to reach a plateau in their linguistic development relatively early. In other words, continuous growth in the second language will occur only if there are increased demands made on the learners' language system.

There are, in fact, surprisingly little systematic, objective data on the linguistic and communicative characteristics of early immersion classes. For example, we do not know the nature of immersion teacher talk and whether it changes from the lower grades to the higher grades. More specifically, we do not know what language functions or communicative behaviors are used or needed in immersion classes at different grade levels. Nevertheless, a study by Adiv (1980b) provides some support for the present speculation concerning a plateau in language development. She carried out detailed analyses of early IM students' use of 17 specific linguistic structures (e.g., prepositions, object pronouns, adjectives) and found that the students did not demonstrate mastery (i.e., 90 percent correct use in obligatory contexts) of most of the structures by the end of grade 3. These findings then suggest that there may be a plateau in second language learning around grade 3.

Although purely speculative, this line of thinking raises some interesting questions if pursued just a bit further. The possibility of such an early plateau must be reconciled with the finding that IM students from successively higher grades maintain their standing on achievement tests relative to their respective norming groups. This is indicative of some form of growth. To illustrate this point, consider grade 6 early IM students who score in the average stanine range on a test normed on grade 6 French-speaking students—they can be said to demonstrate growth when compared to grade 3 early IM students who score in the average stanine range on the grade 3 version of the test. It may be, however, that there is no fundamental growth in linguistic competence underlying perform-ance on these two tests; rather the grade 6 students may simply be demonstrating that they are able to apply the linguistic skills they have acquired earlier in new ways or in the service of new tasks. What is called for is an analysis of the underlying language functions required to successfully perform the grade 3 and grade 6 tests. Similarly, what is needed are detailed investigations of the language learning environment of immersion classes, including a focus on the language teacher and his/her language behaviors and on the linguistic characteristics of pedagogical materials. Such studies are needed in order to determine what kinds of functional communication demands are being made on the language learner. To date, most immersion research has focused on the language learner. Clearly, however, language learning is an interactive process.

SUMMARY

In this chapter we have reviewed the second language learning outcomes of alternative immersion programs, focusing on early total immersion and late immersion. Interpretation of the results was facilitated by distinctions between language proficiency and linguistic competence and between production and comprehension. In general, it has been found that IM students in all alternatives are more likely to demonstrate nativelike levels of proficiency in second language comprehension than in second language production, be it in reading and writing or in listening and speaking. IM students demonstrate high levels of functional language proficiency in reading and writing, and they are effective communicators in both oral and written language, even though there are often linguistic errors in their phonology, vocabulary, and grammar. Their evident linguistic deficien-cies do not appear to be a serious impediment to their effective functional use of French for academic or interpersonal purposes.

At present, it is difficult to provide a comprehensive or detailed description of IM students' second language system owing to the paucity of studies on this aspect of their language development; research by Harley and her colleagues at the Ontario Institute for Studies in Education is a notable exception. Two general characterizations of their language do appear to be emerging, however. First, from a discrete, structuralist perspective, their language system is less complex and less redundant than that of native speakers, although it is nonetheless com-municatively functional and effective. Second, IM students' language system is distinctively non-idiomatic; that is to say, IM students' use of lexical and syntactic forms deviates from native usage in ways that cannot necessarily be labeled incorrect but which are simply uncommon or highly unlikely in the case of a native speaker. This characteristic of IM students' French has been noted by Harley in her study of prepositions and by Spilka in her analysis of IM students' spoken language. It was also noted by Genesee, Holobow, Lambert, Cleghorn, and Walling (1985) in analyses of the writing skills of English-speaking students attending French-medium schools in Montreal. They noted that, although the written compositions of these students were generally graded the same as those of native French-speaking students when evaluated using error analysis techniques, they were nevertheless clearly distinctive from the French students' compositions because of the occurrence of non-native forms. These forms were not easily identified by linguistic analyses because they were often grammatically correct, albeit non-idiomatic.

It must be acknowledged that examination of IM students' use of French outside the school setting has been limited to date. In this regard, it would be interesting and instructive to examine their language development in out-of-school contexts once they have left school in order to ascertain whether the non-native linguistic and communicative features of their performance evolve to more nativelike forms.

Comparisons between alternative forms of immersion have tended to find, with the occasional exception, that

1. early total IM students achieve higher levels of second language proficiency than early partial immersion students;
2. early IM students achieve second language proficency that is superior or equivalent to that of delayed IM students; and
3. early total IM students generally achieve higher levels of proficiency than one-year late IM students, and superior or equivalent proficiency when compared to two-year late IM students.

In general, then, early exposure and extended exposure are associated with relatively higher levels of second language proficiency. However, the findings from a number of specific studies indicate the following important qualifications are warranted. First, cumulative exposure alone may be less important than intensity of exposure so that less cumulative but more concentrated exposure can be as effective as more cumulative but extended exposure. Second, older students are more efficient second language learners than younger learners, other things being equal. This factor can be so influential as to offset any possible advantages associated with amount of exposure. Third, specific programmatic factors can be important determinants of the effectiveness of a particular program, irrespective of the age of the learners and the amount of second language exposure provided by the program. More will be said about programmatic factors in the next chapter when we consider a special activity-centered immersion program.

CHAPTER

5

Three Case Studies
in Immersion

The programs and evaluation results that have been reviewed to this point represent the most common prototypes of immersion and their associated pedagogical and linguistic outcomes. The preceding discussions are syntheses of research conducted in a number of major centers across Canada—Vancouver, Toronto, Ottawa, Montreal, and Fredericton, N. B. Such extensive replication of research lends confidence to the conclusions. In this chapter, we will examine three special immersion programs that have also been the object of systematic, albeit less extensive, investigation. These projects are of interest because, on the one hand, they reflect in interesting ways some of the principles of second language learning in immersion programs that have been identified already, and, on the other hand, they contribute to our knowledge of the immersion approach to second language learning because they represent extensions or pedagogically interesting modifications of immersion. More specifically, the first two projects to be reviewed—*double immersion* and *French-medium schooling*—extend the possibility of second language learning beyond conventional programs. In the case of the double immersion project, this is done by providing curricular instruction in *two* non-native languages instead of one. In the case of French-medium schooling, the possibility of second language learning is extended by postponing and limiting the use of English in the curriculum and thereby extending the use of French beyond the customary limits. The third project—*activity-centered immersion*—attempts to extend second language learning not by increasing exposure to the second language and not by increasing the number of second languages to be learned, but rather by providing a communicatively rich classroom environment to stimulate second language learning.

DOUBLE IMMERSION

By far the most common alternative forms of immersion, as already reviewed, involve the use of a single second language. Genesee, Lambert, and Tucker have investigated variations of immersion for English-speaking children in which two non-native languages (French and Hebrew) are used as major media of curricular instruction during the elementary grades (see Genesee & Lambert,

1983). French and Hebrew were selected as immersion languages for the programs in question because both have sociocultural significance for the participating children and their families. On the one hand, French has social and economic relevance on a day-to-day basis because it is one of the official languages of Canada and the only official language of Quebec, where the schools are located. In this regard, the Hebrew-French double immersion programs are the same as the St. Lambert program and other French immersion programs for majority language children in Canada. On the other hand, Hebrew is valued because of its religious and cultural significance and because of its increasing non-sectarian importance as a national language of Israel. In this respect, the Hebrew-French double immersion programs are like Ukrainian and Mohawk immersion programs which seek to promote heritage languages. The underlying principles of both components are the same. These programs are described in some detail here because they represent effective and feasible models of multilingual/multicultural education of possible interest to ethnolinguistic groups who are interested in revitalizing heritage languages and at the same time wish to acquire competence in an additional second language of some local or national relevance.

In two of the double immersion schools studied by Genesee and his colleagues, English-speaking children from Montreal received all of their curricular instruction during the primary grades in French and Hebrew only (see Table 6); there was no English language instruction during these grades. The French curriculum comprised language arts, mathematics, science, and social studies. The Hebrew curriculum comprised language arts, Jewish history, and religious and cultural studies. Native French- and Hebrew-speaking teachers were used to teach each curriculum. English was not introduced until grade 3 in the case of

Table 6   NUMBER OF HOURS OF INSTRUCTION PER WEEK IN ENGLISH, FRENCH, AND HEBREW IN DOUBLE IMMERSION SCHOOLS

	K	Grade 1	Grade 2	Grade 3	Grade 4	Grade 5
English						
DI1	0	0	0	5	5	7.5
DI2	0	0	0	0	5	6.5
DDI	12	12	12.5	11	9	9
French						
DI1	12.5	17	15	13.5	15	13
DI2	13.5	15	17	17	13.5	12.5
DDI	5	8	8	9	11	12
Hebrew						
DI1	10.5	13	15	13	12	12.5
DI2	10.5	15	12.5	13	12.5	12.5
DDI	15	12	12.5	13	12	12.5

DI1=double immersion school 1
DI2=double immersion school 2
DDI=delayed double immersion

one school (DI1—double immersion school 1) and grade 4 in the case of the other (DI2—double immersion school 2). We have referred to this form of the program as early double immersion. In contrast, in another double immersion school English along with French and Hebrew were used as media of instruction from kindergarten on. This program alternative has been referred to as delayed double immersion (DDI) because the amount of exposure to French increased systematically from five hours per week in grade 1 to twelve hours per week in grades 5 and 6. Instruction through English decreased somewhat from twelve hours per week in grade 1 to nine hours per week in grade 6 as a result. The Hebrew component also decreased somewhat.

These program alternatives raise some interesting psycholinguistic and educational questions that formed the basis of a longitudinal study. First, how effective is double immersion with respect to second language proficiency? As noted earlier, there is evidence that second language proficiency is less in single immersion programs in which both the first and second languages are used for instruction from kindergarten onward (i.e., partial immersion) when compared to early total immersion where use of the first language is delayed. Thus, the presence of the first language and/or the challenge of learning two second languages simultaneously might be expected to result in reduced second language proficiency in the case of the DI programs when compared to single immersion programs.

Second, as already noted, there is evidence that in the short term adolescents and adults achieve the same or higher levels of second language proficiency than children given the same or even less second language exposure; that is, older is better. Our discussion of the effectiveness of delayed immersion programs relative to early immersion programs in the preceding section indicated mixed results with respect to the older-is-better hypothesis—in Genesee's Montreal evaluations, early IM students generally outperformed delayed IM students, while in Lapkin's Ontario evaluations the delayed IM students performed as well as early IM students despite time differentials in favor of the latter. It was possible to examine this issue once again by comparing the performance of the early DI students and the delayed DI students.

Third, does simultaneous instruction in two second languages adversely affect first language development? While there is no evidence that single immersion adversely affects first language development, we do not know what effects double immersion will have. Also related to the question of first language development is the question of the effects of postponing and reducing English language instruction—in the DI2 program English instruction was delayed until grade 4 and at that time it was limited to five hours per week.

The performance of the DI groups was compared to one another and to that of 1) students in conventional single immersion programs (SI), and 2) students in non-immersion programs (i.e., EC). The SI students had accumulated more exposure in French (approximately 3,670 hours by grade 5) than the DI students (approximately 3,135 hours for DI1; 3,230 hours for DI2; and 2,185 hours for the delayed DI students). An extensive battery of English language, French language, Hebrew language, and mathematics tests was administered at the end of each school year from kindergarten onward. The students' general intellectual ability was assessed prior to their entering the program in order to determine the comparability of the various groups with respect to overall academic ability; *Raven's Progressive Matrices,* a widely used, standardized test of nonverbal reasoning, was used for this purpose. The SI and EC students had participated in Genesee's evaluation of the early total immersion program in Montreal, and they were selected for the present evaluation so as to be comparable to the double immersion groups on IQ, ethnicity, and socioeconomic status (see Genesee, 1978a). The results to be reported here are based on the performance of grade 5 students who had been in their respective programs for six years. These results, therefore, permit us to describe the long-term effects of the various double immersion options under investigation.

The results will be discussed in terms of each of the three questions identified earlier.

The Effect of Double Immersion versus Single Immersion on Second Language Achievement

This question was addressed by examining the French proficiency of students in the DI programs relative to that of students in the SI and EC programs and the Hebrew language proficiency of early DI students (i.e., DI1 and DI2) relative to that of delayed DI students. The first set of analyses allowed us to assess second language achievement (French) when there is simultaneous curricular instruction in two non-native languages (DI) as compared with programs in which curricular instruction is conducted through one second language only (SI) or through the native language (EC). The second set of analyses allowed us to assess second language achievement (Hebrew) in programs that provide equivalent amounts of instruction in the second language but have or have not given first language instruction from the beginning (i.e., delayed vs. early DI).

French.   The two *early* DI student groups scored as well as the SI students on all of the French language tests, except a vocabulary subtest. In contrast, the delayed DI students scored significantly lower than the SI students on all of the tests, except for one. All three DI groups scored significantly higher than the EC group on all of the French tests. Thus, on average, the performance of the groups could be ranked in approximately the following order from highest to lowest: DI1–DI2–SI, delayed DI, and EC.

Hebrew.   The delayed DI students scored significantly lower than the early DI students on a number of the Hebrew tests, including the grammar, vocabulary, and communication scales of the speaking test and a test of verb use; they scored at the same level as the early DI students on a test of reading comprehension. For the most part, there were no significant differences between the two early DI groups. Thus, there was a tendency for the delayed DI students who had received instruction through English simultaneous with instruction through French and Hebrew from the beginning to perform less well than the DI students who had not been instructed through English in the primary grades. This is so despite the fact that the Hebrew curricula in all three schools were quite comparable with respect to both content and amount of instruction.

The Effect of Double Immersion on First Language Development

This question was addressed by comparing the English language development of the DI groups with that of the SI and EC groups. There were no significant differences between the DI groups and either the SI or EC group on either a reading comprehension test or a spelling test; the DI2 students scored lower than the EC and the SI students on a vocabulary subtest, but there were no differences between the other groups on this test. Since the performance of the DI2 students had not been found in a follow-up evaluation conducted with students one grade behind the pilot group being discussed here, and because the performance of the DI2 group differed from that of the DI1 group, it is likely that their scores on the vocabulary test are idiosyncratic. Thus, the English language test results indicate overall parity between the DI students and both the EC students and the SI students.

The Effect of Postponing and Reducing English Language Instruction on English Language Development

Comparisons relevant to this question involve the DI1 group, who began English language instruction in grade 3, and the DI2 group, who began it in grade 4. Also pertinent here are comparisons between the SI program, which increased English language instruction quite quickly from grade 3 (five hours per week) to grade 5 (fifteen hours per week), and the two early DI programs, which provided only five to seven and a half hours per week in grades 3, 4, and 5. There were no statistically significant differences between the DI1 group and DI2 group on any of the English language tests, including reading, vocabulary, spelling, language arts, and writing. In terms of test norms, both groups scored at least one full year above their actual grade level, as would be expected from such a group of intellectually and socioeconomically advantaged students. As well, there were no statistically significant differences between the two early DI groups and the SI group.

Summary.   In support of previous findings, then, these results indicate quite clearly that English first language development was not adversely affected either by postponing English language instruction until grade 4 or by reducing its use. Nor was there an adverse effect on first language development as a result of simultaneous acquisition of two non-native languages. Once again, then, it appears that there is no long-term advantage to first language development as a result of early instruction in English. With respect to second language development, these results indicate that the early double immersion programs were almost as effective as single immersion programs in promoting French language proficiency, despite a time differential in favor of the single immersion program. This finding supports an earlier speculation that effective classroom participation and mastery of academic material may require a relatively circumscribed set of language skills that may be acquired quite quickly. It would appear that, notwithstanding time limitations, the early DI programs provided sufficient second language exposure for acquisition of the requisite skills.

It is also possible that the French language development of the early DI students profited from the concurrence of skills development in Hebrew. Ben-Zeev (1977) contends that early bilingualism requires the active deployment of attentional and linguistic strategies to avoid interlingual interference and that this in turn enhances general cognitive development. In a similar fashion, the more complex linguistic demands in double immersion relative to single immersion may promote general language learning strategies that are transferable from one second language to another. This may actually increase the efficiency of language acquisition in the DI programs.

In contrast to previous findings, reviewed in chapter four, these results do not support the older-is-better hypothesis. In fact, the delayed DI students tended to score less well than the early DI students; this was particularly evident from comparisons with SI students—the delayed DI students scored consistently lower than the SI students, whereas the early DI students scored at the same general level as the SI students. The differential effectiveness of the early and delayed DI programs with respect to French language development could be interpreted in terms of differences in amount of exposure. In particular, it could be argued that the delayed program offered less instructional time than the early immersion alternatives, both DI and SI; therefore, it resulted in less achievement. Time alone, however, does not provide an entirely satisfactory explanation of these results. First, it does not explain why the early DI and SI groups achieved comparable levels of French proficiency despite a time differential favoring the SI group. Second, it does not explain why the delayed DI group also performed less well than the early DI groups on the Hebrew language tests, even though the Hebrew components in all three DI schools were the same in terms of time and content. An advantage in Hebrew in favor of the early DI groups was even more evident in a follow-up evaluation carried out with grade 4 students (Genesee & Lambert, 1980).

An additional mitigating influence on the delayed DI students' second language achievement, both in French and Hebrew, may have been the presence of first language instruction during the initial years of the program. Evaluations of other French immersion programs that include English language instruction during the primary grades have also found lower levels of second language achievement than in programs without such instruction; comparisons between early total and early partial immersion alternatives are relevant here. The presence of English in these cases, however, has always been confounded by a corresponding reduction in exposure to the second language. This was not the case for Hebrew in the present programs, yet there was still a differential in favor of the programs that did not have early English language instruction. These results support the argument that simultaneous early instruction in the first language reduces second language achievement. The present findings do not allow us to specify a precise explanation of this effect. One possibility is that English may be so dominant as to interfere with the acquisition and use of the second language. It is interesting to note in this regard that Bruck (1978), working in French immersion programs with English-speaking children who have first language disabilities, recommends that first language instruction be postponed until after the primary grades, since earlier exposure seems to hamper these children's progress in French without yielding benefits to their English language development or academic achievement; these programs will be discussed in more detail in the next chapter.

These results illustrate the feasibility and effectiveness of educating English-speaking children in two second languages from kindergarten on. Consistent with findings from single immersion programs for children of similar backgrounds, it was found that DI students achieved significantly higher levels of second language proficiency than students in core FSL programs, and at the same time they experienced no long-term setbacks in first language development. It was also found that the DI programs that delayed the introduction of English language arts instruction until the middle elementary grades resulted in generally superior levels of second language proficiency. Since these experiments in trilingual education involved intellectually and socioeconomically advantaged children, it would be instructive to test their generalizability with less advantaged students. The suitability of immersion programs for all children will be discussed in chapter six.

ENGLISH-SPEAKING CHILDREN IN FRENCH-MEDIUM SCHOOLS

In this section, we will examine the results of an evaluation of all-French schooling on English-speaking children's language development (Genesee, Holobow, Lambert, Cleghorn, & Walling, 1985). Although the school programs under consideration here are not, strictly speaking, immersion programs, an evaluation of them contributes to our knowledge of the effectiveness of second language learning in immersion-type school contexts by indicating how far the immersion concept can be extended. The particular schools under investigation were typical of French-medium schools throughout the province of Quebec in a number of respects. First, the principal and all the educational and support staff, except for the ESL teachers, were native French-speakers and thus this school provided extended opportunities for the students to use French. At the same time, it is important to point out that informal observation of students in the hallways and in the schoolyard indicated that much of the social interaction between the English- and French-speaking students took place in English. This means that, although the schools provided an enriched second language learning environment by virtue of extended opportunities to use French with teachers, the principal, and support staff, they did not result in as much interaction in French with French-speaking peers as one might expect from the size of the French student group. Second, the curriculum of the schools was the same as that of other French schools, as prescribed by *Le ministere de l'education du Quebec*. Of most importance for the present discussion, English language arts were not taught until grade 4 and then they were limited to two and a half hours a week. The English language arts program was a native language program suitable for English-speaking students. These schools are of relevance here because of the language background of the participating students—the majority of whom (80 percent) were monolingual English-speaking. The restricted scheduling of English along with the almost exclusive use of French as a medium of instruction makes these schools a sort of "super immersion."

Evaluations of two cohorts of "experimental" students have been completed —a pilot group and a follow-up group. The evaluations have examined the performance of students in grades 4, 5, and 6. Grade 4 is the first grade when English language arts are taught, so we were able to assess the students' English language development immediately prior to and at the end of one year of English language arts instruction. In order to accomplish this, a battery of English language tests was administered in September of grade 4 and then parallel forms of the same tests were administered in June of grade 4. The tests assessed vocabulary, reading comprehension, spelling, and writing skills. The same kinds of tests along with tests of mathematics achievement were then administered at the end of grades 5 and 6. English-speaking students in a delayed immersion program were evaluated as a comparison group. These students were used as a comparison because they were from the same school district and therefore were socioeconomically similar to the experimental students. As well, previous research, as discussed in chapter three, had shown that students in partial immersion programs of this type demonstrate the same patterns of English language development as students in all-English schools, so that in effect these partial immersion students are equivalent to English control students as far as English language development is concerned.

The French language proficiency of the experimental students was also of some interest because of the enriched French language environment in which they were being schooled. Their French proficiency was compared to that of comparable English students attending an early total immersion program and to that of native French-speaking students attending a French school with a majority of French-speaking students. Tests of general language arts, reading, listening comprehension, speaking, writing, and mathematics in French were used. A test of nonverbal reasoning ability (i.e., *Raven's Progressive Matrices*) was administered at the beginning of grade 4 in order to assess the comparability of the various program groups.

English Language Achievement.   The results of the September testing in grade 4 indicated that there were statistically significant differences in favor of the English comparison students in the pilot group on two of the subscales of the writing evaluation: sentence variety and overall. There were no statistically significant differences between the experimental students and the English comparison students in either cohort (i.e., pilot or follow-up) on any of the other English language tests or test subscales. Since standardized tests were used to assess reading, vocabulary, and spelling skills, it was possible to assess the students' standing on these subtests relative to norming groups. When their raw scores were converted to stanine form, it was found that the pilot students, both experimental and control, generally scored at stanine 5 or 6 while the follow-up students scored at stanine 4 or 5. Both cohorts of experimental students generally scored at the 6 or 7 stanine level on the mathematics subtests. It is striking to see from this testing prior to the experimental students having English language arts that their performance was comparable for the most part to that of similar students who had followed a conventional English curriculum in the primary grades.

The June testing at the end of grades 4, 5, and 6 revealed that the experimental students from both cohorts scored as well as or better than the English comparison students on the English language and mathematics tests. The superior performance of the experimental students on some of these tests is surprising in view of the fact that there were *no* statistically significant differences between the groups on *Raven's Progressive Matrices.* That this occurred quite consistently on the mathematics subtests suggests that the math program in the French-medium schools was superior in some ways. This is confirmed by the French results insofar as the experimental students also scored significantly higher than the FC students on mathematics tests in French. That the experimental students also scored higher on some of the English language tests than the English comparison students suggests that their English language development was enriched by this second language experience.

French Language Achievement.   It is not possible to summarize the French language test results in detail owing to the large number of tests and comparison groups. A synopsis of the significant differences between the experimental and early immersion students and between the experimental and FC students is presented in Table 7 for the pilot groups; testing of the follow-up cohorts had not been completed at grade 6 at the time of this writing. In general, the results of the follow-up groups confirm the trends to be reported now for the pilot groups.

The entries in Table 7 indicate simply whether there was a statistically significant difference or not between the experimental group and each comparison

Table 7 TEST RESULTS OF ENGLISH STUDENTS IN FRENCH SCHOOLS

	Grade 4	Grade 5	Grade 6
	Experimental vs. Early Immersion Program		
Experimental=Immersion	reading test de rendement en francais test de rendement en mathematiques all scales of writing evaluation most scales of oral evaluation	reading test de rendement en francais test de rendement en mathematiques listening comprehension all scales of writing evaluation all scales of oral evaluation	most scales of oral evaluation
*Experimental > Immersion**	listening comprehension pronunciation scale of oral evaluation	none	reading test de rendement en francais test de rendement en mathematiques listening comprehension
	Experimental vs. All-French Program		
Experimental < All-French	reading test de rendement en francais some scales of writing evaluation all scales of oral evaluation	listening comprehension some scales of writing evaluation all scales of oral evaluation	most scales of oral evaluation
Experimental=All-French	listening comprehension test de rendement en mathematiques most scales of writing evaluation	reading test de rendement en francais test de rendement en mathematiques some scales of writing evaluation	reading listening comprehension test de rendement en francais test de rendement en mathematiques

*All reported differences are statistically significant at $p < .05$.

group on each test at each grade level. This is admittedly a crude method of synthesis, but it serves to summarize a great deal of data in a reasonably meaningful way. Notwithstanding performance on particular tests, there was an overall tendency for the early total immersions students to score as well as the experimental students in grades 4 and 5, but for the experimental students to outperform the immersion students by grade 6. One exception to this pattern was oral production—the early immersion students scored as well as the experimental students on all scales of the oral production evaluation (i.e., comprehension, pronunciation, grammar, vocabulary, and communicativeness) at all grade levels. This was largely true for the follow-up students as well.

Complementary to these findings, comparisons between the experimental and FC students by grade indicated that the experimental students performed relatively less well than the FC students in grade 4 but they improved relative to the FC students in grades 5 and 6. Once again, the oral production results were different—the experimental students were rated consistently less high than the FC students on oral production at all grade levels. There is no discernible pattern of improvement according to specific tests. Interpretation of these trends as developmental must be made with great caution since, in fact, not all the tests were developmental in nature; that is to say, the content of the tests did not reflect developmental changes in language proficiency.

Summary.   Both the English and French language tests results of this evaluation are interesting. There was no evidence either from the September grade 4 testings or from the June testings that the English-speaking students in either cohort had experienced any lags in their English language development as a result of attending these French-medium schools. This finding is particularly striking in the case of the grade 4 September testings, prior to formal English language arts instruction. Meetings with the parents of the pilot experimental student groups suggests that the parents may have been spending additional time with their students promoting English language skills—extra reading, and so forth. Notwithstanding this possibility, the present findings are noteworthy.

The French test results are interesting for a number of reasons as well. That the experimental students showed real improvement in proficiency over grade levels relative to French-speaking students would seem to indicate that the additional French they were exposed to in this program was paying off. This supports the suggestion made in chapter four that there are weaknesses in the later grades of some early total immersion program that arise from too drastic a cutback in French once English is introduced. Whether the experimental students in the French-medium schools under discussion here continued to show progress in French because they were simply getting more French, or because the communicative demands being made on them were increasing, is not clear from these evaluations. In either case, the present findings reinforce the suggestion that increased attention be given to the senior elementary grades of early immersion programs.

The French results are also interesting insofar as comparisons between the experimental and early total immersion students are concerned. On the one hand, the improvement in the experimental students' French proficiency that is discernible in these comparisons is encouraging. On the other hand, the similarity in performance of the two groups that does occur is somewhat surprising. In view of the considerably greater exposure to French provided by the French-medium schools, it might have been expected that the experimental students would have attained consistently and dramatically higher levels of proficiency than the students in the early total immersion program. That this was not found indicates that early immersion programs can result in relatively high levels of proficiency. At the same time, these results suggest that there is a limit to the level of second language proficiency that can be achieved in school settings that do not include a substantial opportunity for peer interaction in the target language or that do not otherwise use special pedagogical approaches to promote language development; more will be said about this in the final summary section.

ACTIVITY-CENTERED IMMERSION

In conjunction with the evaluation of a regular one-year late immersion program, Stevens (1976) evaluated the effectiveness of an innovative activity-centered late immersion program in the Montreal area. Both the regular immersion and activity-centered immersion programs she investigated were at the grade 7 level, and both were preceded by core French instruction from kindergarten. What distinguished the two programs was their pedagogical approaches. In the regular immersion program, teaching tended to be teacher-centered and group-oriented so that all students worked on the same topics, at the same time, and for the same length of time. Student participation generally involved reacting to teacher-led instructional activities and classroom routines; students seldom initiate the use of language in these types of classrooms. Such classrooms may be characterized as message-oriented or transactional as opposed to interactional, in that language is used to teach and display knowledge, linguistic or otherwise, rather than engage in open-ended social discourse (Ellis, 1984).

In contrast, in the activity-centered program, the students worked individually or in small groups on projects of their own choice, with general themes and guidelines prescribed by the teacher. This program was designed initially along Piagetian lines to capitalize on the individual learner's ability to learn for self-motivated reasons and according to his/her own learning style and rate. Piaget (1959) emphasized that children normally develop by interacting with and acting on their immediate environment and thereby build experience-based cognitive schema. The importance of an activity-based approach for language learning is described by Stevens (1983a):

> Another school event which occurs in Canada and in the colder parts of North America is the winter carnival. This event can give rise to both whole-class activities and individual activities. An example of a whole-class activity

is the making of an ice sculpture. During the decision-making process as to the subject and its size, everyone is involved in using language to express ideas, ask questions, or make comments. During the building process, different language is required, both for cooperation on the actual construction and for purposes of socialization. These are important opportunities for students to learn to experience real communication in which they can freely choose both the content and the form of what they want to say in conversational sequences. (p. 263)

Thus, an activity-based approach provides opportunities for students to experience a much wider range of speech events and to use a much wider range of speech acts than is possible in conventional medium-oriented classes in which the language is taught as a subject, or even in message-oriented classes in which regular content is taught through the second language.

Moreover, an activity-based approach incorporates individualization insofar as students choose the specific nature of the activities to be undertaken and are able to work at their own pace and according to their own personal learning styles in the achievement of their projects. While it is generally recognized that second language development both in naturalistic settings and in classroom settings proceeds according to some regular pattern, that may in fact be quite similar in both cases, there is nevertheless considerable individual variation and variability from learner to learner. The activity-based classes were student-centered and thus tolerated, and in fact capitalized on, such individual variation. Moreover, because the activities were not predetermined, the students were actively involved in defining the goals and means of attaining the goals of each project, and therefore they had a desire and a need to communicate. In most cases, the projects entailed much physical activity (e.g., designing blueprints, collecting materials for construction, and building itself) in addition to cognitive work. This means that there was contiguity between the students' immediate physical/perceptual world and their language learning. The importance of the "here-and-now" as a basis for language development has been emphasized by both first and second language researchers (Wells, 1981; Ellis, 1984).

An additional feature of the activity-based program was that it encouraged much student-to-student interaction in addition to or in lieu of the teacher-to-student interaction that tends to characterize regular immersion programs. Gumperz and Herasimchuk (1972, in Ellis, 1984) suggest that student-to-student interactions are "co-operative and characterised by syncopation, equal contributions and swift and direct exchanges" whereas teacher-to-student interaction is "hierarchical, involving monotony and teacher-dominated exchanges in which the teacher tries to guide the pupil through a series of pre-determined, pseudological steps" (p. 115). They suggest further that the former may be better suited to second language development insofar as it gives the learner opportunity to perform different interactive roles and engage in a wide range of speech acts. Student interlocutors may also provide extensive comprehensible input that is thought to be essential for second language acquisition (Krashen, 1981).

The activity-based and regular immersion programs evaluated by Stevens also differed in one other respect. Like most late immersion programs in Montreal, the regular late immersion program under investigation occupied approximately 80 percent of the school day. In contrast, the activity-centered program occupied only 40 percent of the school day, usually the afternoon; the rest of the day was spent in English. Thus, the time factor favored the regular immersion program. Despite this, the research results, gathered at the end of grade 7, showed that the students in the activity-centered immersion program had achieved the same level of proficiency as the regular immersion students in the interpersonal communication skills of speaking and listening comprehension, and almost the same levels of proficiency in reading and writing. Interestingly, it was also found that boys in the activity-centered program demonstrated generally higher levels of proficiency than girls; consistent sex differences have seldom been found or reported in other evaluations. Boys' higher level of activity in school, which can often be disruptive in regular teacher-centered programs, may be an advantage in a program that allows, and indeed encourages, active involvement in learning.

Stevens (1983a) suggests that the reasons for the evident success of the activity-centered approach to immersion can be found in the motivation provided by the use of language in situations of personal choice and in the opportunities provided for extended discourse among peers. It is interesting to note here that even discourse with other second language learners of the same level of proficiency appears to have been an adequate catalyst for second language development. Thus, peer interaction in this context may be beneficial, not so much because peers provide correct models of the target language, but because they elicit involvement in using the target language for meaningful and self-directed communication. Indeed, it is the infant's desire to communicate about matters of self interest that presumably motivate first language acquisition. In contrast, much of the communication that occurs in the more typical teacher-centered types of immersion programs is not only teacher-directed but syllabus-driven; that is to say, the content of communication is determined to a large extent by syllabus guidelines rather than students' or teachers' interests *per se*.

SUMMARY

The findings from these three special case studies corroborate findings from evaluations of more conventional immersion programs while extending our knowledge of second language learning in school in important ways. Thus, once again, we have seen that extended or postponed use of English has no apparent detrimental effects on the students' English language development. Conversely, there appears to be no pedagogical advantage to immersion programs that have an English language component during the primary grades. To the contrary, it has been suggested that an early English language component may detract from second language learning because it provokes a reliance on the first language. We have also seen once again that there is no simple relationship between time or exposure and second language achievement. This is not to say that time is unimportant, but that, beyond some critical limit, the exact relationship between time and achievement is not linear. The results of French-medium schooling for English-speaking children are interesting in this regard. On the one hand, they attest to the possibility of reducing English instruction even more than is customary in most immersion programs without engendering negative consequences. On the other hand, they call into question the utility of unlimited exposure to the second language if no special provisions are made to take advantage of the additional time being provided.

Class time must be used effectively. This is not a new observation. However, it may be especially relevant at this point in the development of communicatively based approaches to second language teaching. In question here is the identification of essential features of effective communicative approaches to second language teaching. In this regard, Ellis (1984) argues that "the process of language development, both first and second, is the same as the process of language use. The learner develops procedures for using whatever knowledge (linguistic or otherwise) he possesses to make sense. In so doing, he develops new rules to add to his existing knowledge" (p. 176). In other words, the learner acquires knowledge of language and how it works by taking part in discourse.

From a review of both first and second language acquisition research, Ellis identifies eight features of discourse that might be important for language learning and, therefore, language teaching:

1. quantity of intake
2. a need to communicate
3. independent control over the propositional content of discourse (i.e., the meanings to be expressed in discourse)
4. adherence to the "here-and-now" principle
5. the performance of a range of speech acts
6. an input rich in directives (e.g., imperatives: "Finish your work" and needs statements: "I want you to do exercise 3")
7. an input rich in "extending" utterances (e.g., expansions)
8. uninhibited practice

The relative effectiveness of the activity-based immersion program in comparison with regular immersion can be interpreted in terms of these features. They also provide a useful basis for both designing and evaluating other communicative approaches to second language teaching.

Also in question here is a theory or model of language *development,* or, according to Ellis's framework, "discourse development," that will serve to guide curriculum planners and teachers in their efforts to structure classroom activities so as to stimulate continuous language growth. As pointed out earlier, unless the communicative requirements in the second language classroom are consciously and systematically planned, language development may level off. Unfortunately, a model of discourse development that is sufficiently complete to inform curriculum designers is probably not possible at present given our current state of knowledge. In lieu of such a model, the academic curriculum itself may provide the basis for the development of discourse proficiency insofar as the curriculum is developmental in some cognitive and linguistic senses. That is to say, the content of the curriculum with its associated cognitive and linguistic demands may stimulate language development. The possibility of using academic tasks as a basis for organizing the curriculum to promote language development is discussed in chapter eleven. In fact, using the academic content of the curriculum to stimulate language development is the rationale behind immersion. However, maximum language learning in immersion will probably result only to the extent that the curriculum exploits opportunities for discourse in the service of academic achievement. It would appear that many immersion programs, and indeed many regular school programs, do not do this. More discourse-rich pedagogical approaches may be called for if immersion programs are to realize their full language teaching potential.

It also warrants repeating that there are real limits to the level of second language proficiency that can be achieved in school settings that do not include a substantial opportunity for peer interaction in the target language. Viewed differently, teachers and other adult educational professionals constitute language models that are limited. Even extended communication with such native speakers, as is provided in French-medium schools, may have restricted linguistic consequences. In schools where there are, in fact, native target language-speaking students, careful consideration needs to be given to how peer interaction or peer models might be better exploited.

6

The Suitability of Immersion for All Students

The research reviewed to this point has examined students from predominantly middle class backgrounds who speak English as a first language and who have average to above-average intelligence and no discernible language or learning disabilities. This focus reflects the composition of most immersion programs and thus has been a legitimate concern of researchers. With the well-documented success of the St. Lambert and Montreal immersion experiments in the mid 1960s, there was a dramatic increase in parental demand for the expansion of immersion. This brought about a broadening of the types of students enrolling in the program, including students with characteristics that might dispose them to do poorly in school; for example, students with below-average academic ability or with first language difficulties. While these types of children had never been systematically excluded from immersion, the concerns of educators and parents over their success in such an apparently challenging school program effectively limited their enrollment. It was feared that learning regular academic subjects through the medium of a second language might be an unmanageable burden to these students and thus contribute to their academic failure.

The suitability of immersion for all students is a question of more than academic interest. First of all, there is the danger that immersion programs could become elitist. That is to say, without substantive evidence to the contrary, it might be thought that such an extraordinary form of education is suitable for only the most capable academic students, thereby excluding less capable students. Indeed, this charge has been leveled against immersion. Such charges do not serve the educational community well because they threaten to sour the relationship between different sectors of the community—those involved in immersion and those not involved. Such charges may threaten the very existence of immersion because they call its continuation into question—if immersion is not good for all, it should not be offered to only a few; therefore, it becomes available to none. Second, in many parts of Canada bilingualism is not a privilege but a necessity for economic and social survival. To deny any or all children in these communities effective means for achieving bilingual competence through public education is ethically questionable. It is imperative that educational decisions concerning exclusion of subgroups of students from immersion be founded on systematic and objective investigation, and not on speculation or "common sense." The suitability of immersion for children with different characteristics is also, of course, of theoretical interest because the answers to this question will contribute to our understanding of the factors contributing to second language learning in school settings.

With these practical concerns and theoretical interests in mind, researchers have undertaken systematic investigations of 1) students of below-average intelligence; 2) students with specific language or learning disabilities; and 3) students from lower socioeconomic backgrounds. The results of these investigations will be reviewed in this chapter. We will also review evidence concerning the effectiveness of immersion for students in communities where there are few or no target language speakers, since the feasibility and effectiveness of such an intensive second language experience in settings devoid of target language speakers is sometimes called into question. The question of the suitability of immersion for children who do not speak the majority language will be considered in chapter nine.

ACADEMIC ABILITY

There has been considerable theoretical controversy over what intelligence is and how it should be measured (Gould, 1981; Kamin, 1974). For purposes of this review, intelligence will be defined in terms of student performance on standardized IQ tests. Although this definition is theoretically limited, it is nonetheless a useful definition for present purposes, given the influence that IQ scores often have on educational decisions. In addition, since most IQ tests are, in fact, standardized on the basis of academic performance, using IQ scores is a convenient index of academic ability, at least as it is traditionally defined.

In the past, studies in which intelligence and bilingualism have been investigated have viewed intelligence as the dependent variable and bilingualism or second language learning as the independent variable. In other words, the question was usually asked "What is the influence of second language learning or bilingualism on intelligence?" Without going into detail, early findings tended to show that bilingual students performed less well on intelligence and related tests than monolingual students (see Diaz, 1983, and Hakuta, 1986, for summaries of the early work). However, many of these early studies were methodologically flawed; for example, they failed to equate the monolingual and bilingual students on socioeconomic characteristics, or they ignored the bilingual students' proficiency in the language of the intelligence test. Studies since then have tried to correct these methodological shortcomings and, as well, have used more diverse and theoretically more interesting measures of intelligence. The results from these studies tend to show that bilinguals are not intellectually impaired and that, in some respects, they demonstrate cognitive advantages when compared with monolinguals (see Cummins, 1976, and Diaz, 1983, for reviews of this issue).

Cummins (1981) has proposed that there is a threshold of bilingual proficiency which if not attained will lead to negative cognitive consequences, as reported by early researchers. Cummins proposes further that there is a second, higher threshold of proficiency which if attained is associated with positive cognitive consequences. Bilingual proficiency falling between these two levels of proficiency is associated with neither positive nor negative consequences. Cummins reasons that language proficiency below the first threshold leads to cognitive deficits because the students' interaction with the learning environment is impaired. Proficiency above the second threshold enrichens cognitive ability because of the enhanced metalinguistic awareness that results from knowing two languages well. A recent study by Diaz (1983) suggests that cognitive enrichment is associated with early stages of second language acquisition and not later stages as contained in Cummins's threshold hypothesis. The important point for the present discussion is that under certain circumstances, as yet not completely understood, there may be a causal and significant effect of bilingualism or second language learning on intellectual ability.

For present purposes intelligence will be treated as an independent variable so that the question becomes "What is the influence of intelligence on performance in French immersion programs?" In light of the possibility that second language learning can have a significant impact on intellectual development, one should establish the IQ levels of the learners in question prior to their acquisition of the second language. Intelligence levels that are established after second language learning has begun can be influenced by the learning experience, or by pre-selection factors. As noted in chapter three, it is possible to partial out the effects of IQ using statistical procedures, but these procedures do not adequately control for differential experiences or educational treatments that might result from pre-existing differences in IQ. The studies to be reviewed in this section have been more or less successful in implementing these design considerations.

Evidence from Immersion

Genesee (1976b, 1978c) has systematically examined the importance of intelligence for performance in both early total immersion and one-year late immersion programs. Students in grades 4, 5, and 6 in early total immersion and in grades 7 to 11 in one-year late immersion programs in Montreal were classified as average (IQ score between 95 and 115), above average (IQ score above 115), or below average (IQ score below 95 but above 85). IQ scores were based on the *Canadian Lorge-Thorndike Test of Intelligence*. The IM students' performance on a battery of English language, French language, and mathematics tests was subsequently compared to that of students in the regular English program who had been similarly classified.

As expected, the below-average students in both the immersion and non-immersion programs scored significantly lower on the English language tests and on the mathematics tests than the corresponding average students, and likewise the average students scored lower than the above-average students. This is to be expected in view of the way that IQ tests are developed. Below-average students in immersion, early or late, did not score significantly lower than the below-average students in the English program on these same tests. This was also true of the average and above-average groups of students. Thus, the below-average students in immersion were not differentially handicapped in their first language development or academic achievement as a result of participation in immersion.

Comparisons of the French language test results revealed some interesting findings. Below-average IM students were found to score significantly lower than average and above-average IM students on tests that assessed literacy-based French language skills, such as reading and grammar. Again, this difference is to be expected in view of the way in which IQ tests are standardized. In contrast, however, the below-average IM students scored at the same level as the average and above-average IM subgroups on tests that assessed interpersonal communication skills in French-speaking and listening comprehension. More specifically, native French-speaking evaluators could not differentiate the below-average students from the above-average students on the basis of speech samples elicited in a face-to-face interview. The distinction between literacy-based language skills and interpersonal communication skills that emerged from these data resembles the distinction between context-reduced, cognitively demanding and context-embedded, cognitively undemanding language skills identified by Cummins (1981) as important dimensions of language proficiency; see chapter nine.

A differential relationship between IQ and type of French language proficiency was consistently characteristic of the performance of early total IM students in grades 4, 5, and 6. This pattern was also evident in the case of the one-year late IM students in secondary school, but it was somewhat less consistent. In particular, there was a statistically significant tendency for IQ to be positively associated with interpersonal communication skills in French among some of the grade 11 late IM students; that is to say, the above-average students spoke and comprehended French better than the average or below-average students (see Genesee & Chaplin, 1976; and Genesee & Stefanovic, 1976). Tucker, Hamayan, and Genesee (1976) reported similar findings in a study on individual differences in second language learning in early versus late immersion programs. They used regression techniques to investigate the relationship between a number of different predictor factors, including IQ, attitude, and personality factors, and second language achievement. Of particular relevance to the present discussion, they found that performance on an IQ test was more important in predicting speaking and listening comprehension skills among late IM students than among early IM students.

There is no ready explanation of why IQ seems to be a more important correlate of all types of second language proficiency among older students than among younger students. One possible explanation is that late immersion programs, and secondary school programs in general, are more academic and therefore call on the types of intellectual skills that are tapped by IQ tests. A second possibility is that the second language learning strategies used by older students are naturally different from those used by younger students. Krashen's notion of high monitor users who rely on the conscious manipulation of linguistic rules may be relevant here (Krashen, 1981). In other words, older learners may make greater use of conscious, intellectual strategies to learn language skills.

These results are consistent with the results of other researchers who have also found that intelligence is not necessarily the only or most important predictor of second language achievement. For example, in an early study, Malherbe (1946) compared the performance of Afrikaans- and English-speaking students attending unilingual- or bilingual-medium schools in South Africa. In the bilingual-medium schools, both Afrikaans and English were used as media of instruction. In the case of large bilingual schools, the Afrikaans-speaking and English-speaking students were taught separately in their respective native languages so that inter-language contact was limited to out-of-class contacts (parallel-medium schools). In the case of small bilingual schools, both English and Afrikaans were used to teach speakers of both languages (dual-medium schools). Unfortunately, Malherbe indiscriminately mixed both parallel- and dual-medium classes in his bilingual samples so that it is not possible to isolate the effects of each type of schooling; this fact must be kept in mind when interpreting his results.

Malherbe subdivided the students into above-average (IQ score above 100) and below-average (IQ score below 100) groups. Contrary to his expectations, he found that the below-average students in the bilingual-medium schools performed significantly better than the below-average students in the unilingual-medium schools on both language and academic achievement tests. In fact, he found that the below-average intelligence groups in the bilingual schools showed a gain over the below-average groups in the unilingual schools. The Afrikaans- and English-speaking students performed similarly. These results were the first to indicate that low intelligence and, by inference, low academic ability is not necessarily an impediment to successful performance in a bilingual school.

More recently, Robert Gardner of the University of Western Ontario and his colleagues have conducted a series of studies that have become classics in the field of second language learning (Gardner, 1986). In brief, Gardner's findings indicate that factors other than those related to intelligence or aptitude can have an important influence on second language learning and that these other factors are independent of intelligence. More specifically, they have argued and provided systematic evidence that positive attitudes and motivations can be related to second language achievement. The present results are also compatible with what we know about first language acquisition; namely, that all children, with a few pathological exceptions, acquire functional proficiency in their native language in natural contexts devoid of schoollike teaching.

It follows then that students other than the intellectually gifted can master a second language in school by virtue of positive attitudes and motivations. To the extent that French language learning in immersion is mediated through academic instruction, then students' attitudes toward schooling and their motivation to learn subject matter are especially important. This has important implications for curriculum development. More about the importance of attitudinal and motivational factors will be discussed in chapters ten and eleven. It also follows that second language programs designed to use naturalistic and incidental instructional procedures to develop the learners' interpersonal communication skills are likely to be more successful with a broad range of students than programs oriented toward formal, conscious instruction of literacy-based skills. The latter type of program is likely to produce the performance hierarchies that are characteristic of other types of school achievement.

Immersion Drop-Outs

Nothwithstanding the preceding findings, studies of students who have dropped out or transferred out of immersion have found that poor academic achievement is often a correlate of transfer (Bruck, 1978; Fletcher, 1976; Kamin, 1980; and Morrison, Pawley, & Bonyun, 1979). At the same time, it has been found that transfer out of immersion may also be associated with attitudinal, motivational, and/or behavioral concomitants. Bruck (1985a), for example, found that children who transferred out of an early French immersion program in Montreal expressed less positive attitudes toward learning French; they had parents who were less committed to their learning French; and they had teachers who were less supportive.

As Bruck (1985a) has pointed out, however, the results of these studies are difficult to interpret unequivocally. First of all, it is difficult to know whether the academic problems reported in these studies constitute a sufficient reason for the students transferring out of immersion, since appropriate control groups have not typically been included. It is known that on average students who transfer out of immersion programs have lower academic achievement than a randomly selected group of students who remain in the program. Thus, academic difficulties would appear to be characteristic of students who transfer. But not all students who experience difficulty transfer out of immersion, as evidenced by Genesee's (1976b) study of IM students with below-average levels of intelligence. Moreover, it is not known whether the academic difficulties faced by students who transfer out of immersion differ qualitatively or quantitatively from students who remain in the program despite difficulties. Thus, an appropriate control group to examine whether academic factors are a sufficient reason for students transferring out of immersion would include students with academic difficulties or poor academic achievement who remain in the program. Second, it is difficult to know whether the negative attitudes and low levels of motivation for second language learning reported for children who transfer out of immersion and for their parents are indeed precursors of transfer or whether, in fact, they are a consequence of transfer; that is to say, they may be rationalizations or justifications of transfer after it has occurred.

To address these issues directly, Bruck (1985a) conducted a prospective study of the predictors of transfer out of an early total immersion program. At the end of one school year, all French immersion teachers in ten schools were asked to identify students who were experiencing poor academic achievement and who the teachers thought would or should transfer to the English program. The teachers were also asked to identify students who were experiencing academic difficulties but who they thought would not or should not transfer out of immersion. All students so identified were tested at the end of the school year, prior to any of them actually transferring to the English program. They were examined with respect to cognitive ability, academic achievement, second language proficiency, and attitudes and motivations. Their status in the immersion program was determined in the fall of the next school year as either transfer or continuing. They were subsequently retested in the spring of that school year using the same types of tests that had been used previously. In addition, their teachers and parents were interviewed. The design of the study thus permitted the investigator to determine 1) whether the academic, cognitive, or linguistic profiles of the transfer students differed qualitatively or quantitatively from the non-transfer students prior to transfer; 2) whether there were any attitudinal, motivational, or behavioral differences between the transfer students and the non-transfer students prior to transfer; and 3) whether the latter differences were specific or general—that is, whether they characterized the students' predispositions in both the French immersion classes and the English classes and whether they were related to similar affective dispositions in the children's families.

Bruck found that although the transfer students had low levels of academic achievement and second language proficiency, they were no lower than the control students who remained in the program. Thus, the transfer students' academic difficulties were not different from those of the students who remained in the program despite difficulties. The major differences between the two groups of students were in the attitudinal, motivational, and behavioral domains. The transfer students' teachers rated them as having more behavioral problems—for example, they were rated more hyperactive and passive-inattentive than were the non-transfer students. The results indicated further that the transfer students' negative attitudes and motivations and their behavioral problems were not specific to the French classes—even their English teachers reported a higher incidence of behavioral problems for them than for the students who did not transfer. If the transfer students' difficulties were specific to learning through a second language, then one would have expected to find evidence of negative predispositions in the reports of the French teachers only.

The transfer students themselves indicated that they liked school, learning French, and using French *less* than the non-transfer students. Interestingly, there was no evidence that the transfer students' negative attitudes or low motivation were related to the attitudes or motivations of their parents. The parents of the transfer students did not differ from the parents of the non-transfer students with respect to their attitudes toward learning French and the French immersion program itself. Both groups of parents were committed to their children's bilingualism, and both were pleased with the immersion program. These findings run counter to Bruck's earlier findings, which indicated that the parents of children who switched out of immersion had less positive attitudes toward learning French. In light of the present findings, it seems likely that the attitudes reported by parents in Bruck's retrospective study reflect the consequences of transfer rather than being predisposing factors of transfer. These results underline the importance of assessing affective factors prior to a major change in the students' status in the program.

Taken together, these results indicate that 1) although academic difficulties may be necessary precursors for transferring out of an immersion program, they are not sufficient; 2) affective and behavioral problems appear to be the distinguishing factors that result in transfer out of immersion; 3) the affective and behavioral problems that result in transfer would appear to be enduring, general characteristics of the students who eventually transfer—such problems are not specific to the second language classroom; and 4) these predispositions cannot be traced to the students' parents or home. These findings corroborate Genesee's findings with respect to intelligence in indicating that low academic achievement is not an impediment to participation in and benefiting from immersion. At the same time, Bruck's results are significant in suggesting that academic difficulties may motivate transfer out of immersion once they become associated with negative attitudes or behavioral problems on the part of the student. Whether or not these latter problems are rectified once transfer to an English program occurs was addressed by Bruck in a follow-up to the study just reviewed; the results of this study will be discussed in the next section on language/learning disabled children in immersion.

LANGUAGE/LEARNING DISABLED CHILDREN IN IMMERSION

Two independent series of investigations of the suitability of early total immersion programs for students with language or learning disabilities have been carried out (see Bruck, 1978, 1982; and Trites, 1981). The research methods, findings, and implications of these two sets of studies are different and therefore warrant careful scrutiny. Similar research has not been undertaken in conjunction with delayed or late immersion programs.

Trites's Research

Trites (1981) contends that there is a subgroup of students who cannot make satisfactory progress in early immersion programs. According to Trites, these students experience difficulty in immersion because of a unique learning disability that is due to a developmental lag in the maturation of temporal lobe regions of the brain. He contends further that their disability can be diagnosed in pre-school and that they should not take part in early immersion programs until later in their development. His thesis is based on a series of three interrelated studies. There are a number of important reasons for questioning his interpretation of the results of each of these studies (see also Cummins, 1979; and Harley, 1976, pp. 208–215).

Trites's evidence for a unique disability profile underlying difficulty in immersion programs is based on the performance of IM students who were referred to the Neuropsychology Laboratory of the Royal Ottawa Hospital because they were experiencing problems in school. These students were examined using an extensive assessment battery that included the *Wechsler Intelligence Scale,* the *Peabody Picture Vocabulary Test, the Wisconsin Motor Steadiness Battery,* the *Frostig Visual Perceptual Battery,* the *Illinois Test of Psycholinguistic Ability,* and personality and neuropsychological tests. Their performance on these and other measures was compared to that of seven other groups: three normal control groups—English-speaking students in French schools, "ethnic" students (i.e., non-English, non-French speaking) in English schools, and French-speaking students in French schools; and four other "problem" groups—a reading disability group, a hyperactive group, a group with behavior and personality problems, and a group with minimal brain dysfunction. Inclusion of the last four groups made it possible to determine the specificity of the IM students' difficulty.

Analysis of the test results indicated that the performance profile of the IM group was different from that of the other control groups. That the IM students' profile was distinct from other groups of students who were also experiencing difficulty in school was interpreted by Trites as evidence that the IM students had a unique difficulty that could not be considered to originate from such problems as dyslexia or primary reading disability, hyperactivity, minimal brain dysfunction, or behavioral and personality adjustment. Trites's contention that the IM students' difficulty was due to a developmental lag in the maturation of temporal lobe regions of the brain was based on their relatively poor performance on the *Tactual Performance Test* (TPT). The TPT is

> a complex psychomotor problem-solving task in which the child, while blind-folded, is required to place six or eight blocks, depending on age, of varying shapes and sizes into a form board, first with the dominant hand, then with the non-dominant hand, and finally with both hands together. . . . Clinical interpretation of performance levels on this test can be complex, but under certain stringent conditions . . . performance on this test has specific implications with regard to the adequacy of the functioning of the temporal lobes. (Trites, 1981, pp. 33, 34)

The temporal lobes are areas of the brain that are associated with language, memory, and auditory-perceptual functions. Different parts of the temporal lobes are associated with different functions; furthermore, the left and right temporal lobes are associated with language and non-language functions respectively.

Despite Trites's efforts to equate his various control groups with the IM group on a variety of factors, the IM students were, on average, younger than most of the other groups by as much as 8 to 14 months. Thus, it is possible that the IM students' relatively poorer performance on the critical TPT reflects this fact. Trites, however, does not take this factor into account in his interpretation of the results. Trites also fails to point out whether the IM students' poor performance on the TPT occurred when performed with their left hand, their right hand, or both hands. This is an important detail because, as pointed out above, the left and right temporal lobes of the brain are not both associated with language functions to the same extent; it is the left hemisphere that is generally regarded as the "language hemisphere." One might expect the IM students' disability to be associated with left hemisphere function and not necessarily with right hemisphere function, since it might be assumed that their difficulties in school are language related. On the one hand, fine motor movements of the hands are under the control of the contralateral hemisphere; that is, fine movements of the right hand are controlled by the left hemisphere and vice versa for fine movements of the left hand. Thus, it might be expected that the IM students would have performed particularly poorly on the TPT with their right hands, thereby indicating a left hemisphere locus of difficulty. On the other hand, gross motor movements of the hands can be controlled by both hemispheres, in which case there is no way of knowing which hemisphere is more involved in performing the movements necessary to do the test. To the extent that the TPT was performed by gross hand movements, as appears to be the case from Trites's description, it is insensitive to left versus right hemispheric functioning and, therefore, insensitive to a language versus a non-language related disability. Even if one were to assume that the test requires fine motor movements, it is difficult to know how to interpret Trites's results without knowing which hand showed poorer performance.

Strictly speaking, it is not valid to conclude or imply, as Trites does, that the performance deficits that the IM students may have demonstrated on such an assessment battery are sufficient to cause the problems that necessitated their referral to the Neuropsychology Laboratory. First of all, referrals of the type that comprised Trites's samples constitute a clinical and therefore abnormal or non-random sample of IM students. Second, in order to establish whether the performance deficits constitute a necessary and sufficient cause of the students' putative difficulty, it is necessary to show that IM students who were not referred for clinical assessment do not demonstrate similar performance deficits. This would require much wider testing than was done in Trites's studies.

Trites's second study sought to address this latter issue. For this purpose, a group of students who had dropped out of immersion but who had not sought referral services were selected. These students were compared to a control group of students who remained in the immersion program. Both groups were assessed using a test battery similar to that used in the first study. Again, Trites reports that there were significant differences in performance on the TPT between IM students who were experiencing difficulty (i.e., the drop-out group) and those not experiencing difficulty. We do not know whether the drop-out group also performed more poorly on other tests in the battery, although the results from the third study strongly suggest that they in fact did. This is important, because it is critical in determining whether Trites's argument is true (that is, that the IM students experiencing difficulty have a unique disability due to temporal lobe immaturity) or whether the disability is due to generally low academic ability or some other factor.

Trites reports that the difference between the drop-out group and the control group was limited to the students who were below nine years of age; it was not evident among the students above nine years of age. He interprets this difference as evidence that the disability of the IM students is maturational and that it disappears with age. He goes on to conclude that "If the maturational-lag hypothesis is correct, it also seems clear that these particular children should be educated in their native language first and enter an immersion program only after nine or ten years of age" (1981, p. 38). This assumes that the putative disability of the drop-outs is a sufficient cause of the students' performance difficulties and that it is specific to second language learning environments. If this disability is specific to students experiencing difficulties in second language learning, then one would expect it to characterize children in other types of second language situations. Indeed, in his first study Trites found the same test profile to be characteristic of English children who were referred to him because they were having difficulty in French schools, but he did not find the same profile for minority language students (i.e., non-English, non-French speaking) who were having problems in English language schools. Are we to believe that this disability is specific to English-speaking children in French language schools? It is highly unlikely that the language centers of the brain, or for that matter the general cognitive abilities of children, are differentially attuned to different languages in this manner.

In his third set of studies, Trites sought to identify children likely to have problems in an early immersion program prior to their actual enrollment in the program. To this end, he administered an extensive battery of screening tests to a sample of 200 four-year-old children who were scheduled to enter a French immersion kindergarten class the following year. The performance of these children was subsequently monitored at the end of kindergarten and grade 1 as a function of whether they dropped out of immersion, stayed in immersion and were high achievers, or stayed in immersion and were low achievers. The results indicated that the students who dropped out of immersion had performed more poorly than students who stayed in the program on the TPT; but they had also performed more poorly on all 23 tests that comprised the *Early Identification Assessment Battery*. The battery included many tests that are commonly used for diagnostic purposes with school children. This suggests that the difficulty that the drop-out students were having could be described just as easily in terms of general learning or academic difficulties rather than in terms of a specific neuropsychological disability located in the temporal lobes.

Analyses were carried out to determine the validity of 35 tests, administered as part of the *Early Identification Assessment Battery,* as predictors of English and French language achievement. Trites notes that "Better prediction was accomplished for measures of English-language achievement than for measures of French-language achievement" (1981, p. 50). Given that the purpose of the battery is to predict which students will have difficulty in French immersion, these results would seem to call its predictive validity into question.

Finally, Trites's recommendation that students identified by the identification battery be excluded from or transferred to an all-English program assumes that such students do not benefit from participation in an immersion program. The evidence reviewed to date does not support this assumption. To the contrary, Genesee's study of students with low academic ability and Bruck's study of students with native language disabilities, to be discussed next, suggest that such students will progress at the rate and to the limits posed by their particular problems. At the same time, they acquire higher levels of second language proficiency than they would in a regular program, thereby attesting to the benefits of participation in the program.

In sum, because of shortcomings in Trites's interpretation of his data, it is not possible to conclude from this research whether the difficulties experienced by the drop-outs he examined are uniquely characteristic of children who are experiencing difficulty in second language learning or who are just drop-outs; whether or not these students might not have the same difficulties were they in an all-English program; whether the putative source of their difficulties (i.e., developmental lag in temporal lobe maturation) is a necessary and/or sufficient cause of their difficulties; or even whether their difficulties are specific to this neuropsychological disability and not to more general learning disabilities or some other factors.

Bruck's Research

In a similar vein, Bruck (1982) has examined the progress of children with impairments in native language development:

> The term language impairment refers to a heterogeneous group of children who, despite physical well being, normal intelligence and a healthy personality acquire first language with painful slowness. Such children may display a number of different symptoms. For example, many children are relatively late in using words, in combining them, and in developing clear articulation and syntactic sophistication. These children may have problems in comprehending as well as producing speech. At school age, they often lack facility in oral language and miss the point of instructions, explanations, and informal conversations. Language impairment is usually sufficient cause for school difficulty. (p. 47)

Bruck screened kindergarten children attending early total immersion and regular English-medium schools in one school district near Montreal in October of each year for six consecutive years. The children were screened for language impairments using a number of procedures: 1) all French immersion and English kindergarten teachers in the district were asked to identify any children in their classes who they felt had problems with language; 2) the children thus identified were then interviewed by Bruck; and 3) they were administered a short, diagnostic battery of tests specially developed for the research project to diagnose children with and without language difficulties.

Four groups of children were subsequently constituted: two groups with language difficulties—those in French immersion and those in the English program; and two control groups without language difficulties—those in immersion and those in a regular English program. The control students were matched with the IM students on the basis of sex, age, classroom teacher, and father's occupation. The progress of the groups of students so identified was monitored each year until the end of grade 3. Their progress was assessed using a battery of English language, French language, and mathematics achievement tests. Since, in fact, the number of children qualifying for inclusion in the language disabled groups was quite small for any given year, it was necessary to aggregate children for these groups by repeating this procedure for a number of consecutive years. In the final analysis then, the children who comprised each grade level sample (e.g., grade 3) were drawn from successive cohorts of school children; in other words, they were not all tested during the same school year.

Comparisons between the disabled groups, both those in immersion and those in the English program, and non-disabled groups permit an assessment of the disabled students relative to non-disabled students regardless of school program. Comparisons between disabled students in the immersion program and disabled students in the English program permit an assessment of the impact of immersion schooling on children with language disabilities relative to the impact of regular English schooling on similarly disabled children. The results at the end of grade 3, the last year of the evaluation, indicated that it was in fact taking the disabled children in both programs, immersion and English, longer to attain basic literacy skills in English and academic skills than their non-disabled peers, as would be expected from their disability. Nevertheless, the disabled students in the immersion program had developed "linguistic, cognitive, and academic skills at a rate similar to that at which they would develop were they placed in an all English classroom" (Bruck, 1978, p. 65). At the same time, the disabled students in the immersion program showed good progress in French language learning to the point that they could cope with classroom instruction in French within the limits posed by their disability. Bruck concluded that "children with language disabilities can benefit from and learn in French immersion programs" and they "should not be excluded from such programs merely because it is felt that their first language development is poor" (p. 70). Were Trites's screening procedure used, many children who might benefit from immersion could be unjustifiably excluded. It is important when applying the findings of this research to understand that it is based on the performance of *groups* of students and that therefore individual cases must be considered special.

As Bruck points out, many language disabled children cannot cope with traditional core second language courses, possibly because such courses, which emphasize conscious and rote learning of formal linguistic rules and structures, inadvertently exploit the language weaknesses of these children. Immersion programs, in contrast, may be relatively more suitable and effective with language disabled children because they put less emphasis on such teaching strategies and relatively more emphasis on incidental, student-based learning. Bruck's results corroborate Genesee's results with students of below-average intelligence. Both sets of findings indicate that students in immersion programs who are disadvantaged with respect to school learning achieve to the same level and at the same rate as similarly disadvantaged students in all-English programs, albeit at lower levels than children who are not disadvantaged. In other words, they do not experience additional disadvantages as a result of the immersion experience, and, to the contrary, they benefit from it in terms of improved second language proficiency.

One major criticism of Bruck's findings might be that they are based on the performance of language disabled students who choose to stay in the immersion program despite their difficulty; therefore, they do not reflect the performance of a non-select group of language disabled students. Indeed, this criticism could be leveled at any findings pertaining to subgroups of disadvantaged students who remain in immersion, including Genesee's below-average subgroups. As noted in chapter three, such self-selection is inevitable in any school program that is voluntary, and therefore the results of assessments based on such self-selecting populations are valid for, albeit not generalizable to, any and all students. In a later section of this chapter we will examine the academic, linguistic, and affective consequences of switching to an English program.

Switching as a Solution

Before leaving this topic, it is worthwhile to examine the effects of switching students who are experiencing difficulty in immersion to an English-medium program. Switching to an all-English class is often suggested as a solution for such students by parents, teachers, and school administrators alike, for no other reason than it makes a lot of common sense. It merits careful examination because of the possibly negative rather than positive consequences it might have. Thus, for example, transferring students from immersion deprives them of the benefits of intensive French language learning, which, as has been pointed out earlier, may be an essential skill in bilingual areas of Canada. Transferring students out of immersion may also have immediate negative effects on the transferred students' self-perceptions, since it may stigmatize the student or result in the student feeling that he or she has failed. The recommendation that students experiencing difficulty in immersion be transferred to an English program implies that participation in an immersion program contributes to or causes the difficulty that has led to the students' academic problems. At the very least, such a recommendation assumes that transfer to an English program would eliminate or reduce significantly the difficulties that such students might otherwise have in immersion programs. To the extent that this does not actually happen, then disappointment and disillusionment might be the result. Existing evidence does not support this implication. In fact, the results of a study by Bruck (1985b) indicate that transferring students out of immersion programs does not necessarily result in significant changes in their academic performance.

Bruck (1985b) examined the consequences of transfer out of an early immersion program as a follow-up to her earlier study on predictors of transfer out of immersion. As reported earlier, Bruck found in her first study that while academic difficulties were necessary for students to transfer out of immersion, they were not sufficient to explain transfer. Rather, attitudinal, motivational, and behavioral problems were found to distinguish students who transferred out of immersion from students who stayed in immersion despite academic problems. Bruck examined the academic, behavioral, attitudinal, and linguistic performance of these same transfer students one year after they transferred. The same types of assessment instruments were used in the follow-up study as had been used in the prediction study. The progress of the transfer students was compared to that of the students who remained in immersion, in order to determine whether transfer had resulted in better academic performance, more positive attitudes, and/or improved behavior.

Academically, all students—transfer and non-transfer alike—demonstrated better academic performance in the follow-up testing than in the initial testing; this is to be expected because of normal age-related development. Improvement in academic performance was evidenced from the teachers' ratings of student performance as well as from the students' actual performance on a number of standardized tests. Particularly noteworthy was the finding that the transfer students did not demonstrate greater improvement than the students who remained in immersion. The parents of the transfer students perceived more improvement from the pre-transfer period to the post-transfer period than did the parents of the students who did not transfer, even though such differential improvement was not actually manifest in the students' measured performance.

Since it had been the behavioral and affective factors that differentiated the students who eventually transferred from the students who remained in the program, it was particularly interesting to monitor their affective status after transfer for possible positive changes. The teachers' ratings of the students' behaviors in school showed some improvement among the transfer students with regard to passive/inattentive behaviors, but no improvement with respect to hyperactivity or general conduct—the transfer students received poorer ratings on these last two scales than the non-transfer students. It will be recalled that the transfer students had been rated more poorly on these dimensions during the pre-transfer testing. The transfer students continued to report that they did not like going to school, and they also felt that their friends made fun of them. There were no differences on 16 other attitudinal scales given to the students. The transfer students also continued to express less positive attitudes toward learning French than did the non-transfer students on 11 of 17 related items. Thus, the negative predispositions that characterized the transfer students before they transferred persisted for the most part once they had switched to the English stream, confirming, as initially suggested by Bruck, that the problems that underlay the transfer students' difficulties were not program-specific, but rather reflected enduring personality characteristics.

Interestingly, when the parents were questioned about their children's adjustment to the English stream, the parents of the transfer students made more positive comments about their children's attitudes to school after transfer (83 percent) than prior to transfer (37 percent); the comments of the parents of non-transfer students changed little from pre- to post-testing—73 percent of the non-transfer parents made favorable comments during the initial testing and 77 percent made favorable comments during the follow-up testing. The transfer parents were also less supportive of second language learning in general after their children's transfer; and they felt that the importance of second language learning had been overemphasized to the detriment of their children's development. These sentiments had not characterized their reactions prior to the transfer, indicating that they were a consequence of the transfer rather than a reason for it. These findings underline the importance of *prospective* research designs in the study of factors affecting educational decision making.

Thus, contrary to common-sense expectation, Bruck's results indicate that transfer of students experiencing difficulty in a second language program to a native language program will not necessarily result in academic, linguistic, or affective improvements. These results are important in indicating that second language education does not necessarily contribute to poor levels of academic achievement; rather, achievement is "associated primarily with individual differences in psychological functioning" (Bruck, 1985b, p. 22). Trites's suggestion, and the common-sense notion that problems in immersion programs can be rectified by switching the students in question out of the program, need careful reexamination. On the one hand, more serious consideration needs to be given to identifying and treating these students' difficulties in immersion, without automatically transferring them to an English program. On the other hand, if transfer does take place, it seems advisable to continue to monitor these students' progress in the English program and to provide them with the special attention and treatment they need if real improvements are to occur. The apparent improvements that seem to result from transfer can probably be attributed in most cases to normal development rather than to a switch in the language of instruction *per se*. In other words, it may not be sufficient to simply switch students experiencing difficulty to an English stream in order to treat the root problem of their difficulties.

SOCIOECONOMIC BACKGROUND

The majority of immersion programs in Canada are populated by children from middle to upper-middle class families, and consequently most of the research findings are based on similarly constituted student samples. The suitability of immersion for children from lower socioeconomic backgrounds has been explored systematically in three studies in Canada, all in Montreal (Bruck, Tucker, & Jakimik, 1975; Cziko, 1975; Tucker, Lambert, & d'Anglejan, 1972). In these studies, the performance of IM students from "working class" families was compared to that of comparable working class children in the English program using a battery of English language and mathematics tests. Their performance was also compared to that of working class FC children attending French-medium schools using a battery of French language tests. The socioeconomic status of the students was assessed using the Blishen scale (1958), which considers the father's occupation, father's years of schooling, and family income. Generally speaking, the average scale values of the student groups was around 4, with 7 being the maximum value.

It was found that in most cases the IM students scored as well as the EC students on the English language tests. There were some instances when the IM group scored lower, but these only occurred in grades prior to the introduction of English language instruction. There was no indication that the IM students were having difficulty in mathematics relative to the EC students. With respect to French achievement, it was found, as in other evaluations, that the IM students scored as well as the FC students on some of the tests, such as listening comprehension. In the Cziko study, it was also found that the working class IM students scored as well as a control group comprised of middle class IM students on the French language tests. The working class and middle class students examined by Cziko, however, were enrolled in the same classes, suggesting that his results might not generalize to the performance of working class students in separate classes.

One final study deserves mention here since it also included a group of students from working class families. These students were part of a larger evaluation of alternative immersion programs being carried out by Holobow, Chartrand, and Lambert (1985). The original design of the study did not call for students from working class families. However, *a posteriori* examination of the students' socioeconomic status revealed one subgroup in which a majority of their mothers and fathers had technical occupations and earned low incomes. These students had been in a two-year late immersion program. When their scores on a French reading comprehension test, a French cloze test, and a listening comprehension test were compared to those of early total IM students from predominantly middle class families, no statistically significant differences were found. A significant difference was found between these groups, in favor of the early total IM students, on a test of French language arts (i.e., grammar, spelling, vocabulary, etc.).

Taken together then, there is nothing in the results of these four studies to suggest that students from lower socioeconomic groups will experience difficulties in English language development in immersion programs or that they cannot benefit from immersion in terms of second language achievement. It must be acknowledged that there are limitations to all of these studies that limit their implications. None of them has examined student progress over a long term. As well, none of the student groups examined can be said to be representative of working class children from inner-city settings where low socioeconomic status is extreme or endogenous. This gap in our knowledge will be filled to some extent by a study in progress that is examining the outcomes of an early partial immersion program for children from lower social class backgrounds in Cincinnati (Holobow, Genesee, Lambert, Met, & Gastright, 1987). This project will be described in greater detail in chapter eight.

That none of the groups examined in the Canadian research comes from truly low socioeconomic communities is due to the fact that members of these communities have not sought immersion programs in their schools for some as yet unknown reason. Investigation of the reasons why working class parents are not likely to seek immersion programs is an important empirical question with significant social implications. As long as these parents do not request immersion education in their communities, their children will be effectively precluded from what is generally regarded as the most effective school-related means for achieving bilingual proficiency. As noted earlier, this may be an important skill for residents of bilingual communities where both languages are in fact used on a daily basis. Bilingual proficiency may be particularly important for children of working class backgrounds to the extent that many of them pursue service-related careers and therefore require proficiency in both languages to provide the necessary services. Children who pursue professional careers may be less dependent on their language proficiency for employment to the extent that their professional skills are more important than their language skills *per se*.

GEOGRAPHICAL SETTING

As pointed out in chapter two, since their inception in 1965 in Quebec, French immersion programs have been instituted outside Quebec and are now available in communities where there is no large local population of French speakers, such as in Vancouver or Toronto. Furthermore, in contrast to immersion in French which is recognized as an official language by the Canadian federal government, immersion is also now available in non-official languages; for example, there is a partial early immersion program in Ukrainian in Edmonton, Alberta (Lamont, Penner, Blowers, Mosychuk & Jones, 1976), and, as already noted, there are Hebrew and Mohawk immersion programs in Montreal. Immersion programs in non-official languages have been motivated in Canada by a desire to revitalize and maintain heritage languages. Thus, the majority of students in the Edmonton Ukrainian immersion program are second- or third-generation Ukrainian children who speak English as a first language. The children in the Hebrew immersion program in Montreal are Jewish and are also native English speakers, while the children in the Mohawk immersion program are Mohawk by descent and speak English. In all three cases, the parents of the participating children wish to revitalize or maintain their culture and language and view the school as an important means of achieving this.

The availability of systematic and methodologically similar evaluations of immersion programs in a number of Canadian cities makes it possible to examine the effectiveness of immersion in different types of settings. In general, the pattern of results found in the bilingual city of Montreal by Lambert, Genesee, and their colleagues has been found in other Canadian cities regardless of the relative presence or absence of target language speakers. In particular, there has been no evidence of long-term deficits in English language development or academic achievement, and at the same time the participating students achieve noteworthy functional proficiency in the second language. Moreover, the results from evaluations of heritage language immersion programs, including the Hebrew immersion program discussed earlier (see also Adiv, 1983, for similar Hebrew programs in Toronto), reveal similar patterns of results.

These results tell us nothing about the relative success or effectiveness of programs in different community settings. It might be expected that a lack of target language speakers would diminish the actual level of effectiveness of immersion programs in such areas; that is to say, it might be expected that the lack of target language speakers or even the lack of official status of the target language might reduce second language achievement. Unfortunately, no planned, direct comparisons of second language achievement in immersion programs in different geographical settings have been carried out. However, Swain (1981) has made a number of *post hoc* comparisons of the French proficiency of students enrolled in French immersion programs located in Canadian cities that differ with respect to number of French-speaking residents. Her analyses were based on existing test results collected by independent researchers, so her comparisons were necessarily limited to standardized language proficiency tests that had been used in common by these researchers—they included listening comprehension and reading tests. She found that, overall, IM students living in bilingual communities, such as Montreal or Ottawa, did not score higher than students living in relatively monolingual communities, such as Toronto or Vancouver. Swain concluded: "Generally speaking, there seems to be little relationship between the use of the second language in the broader environmental context and the acquisition of second language skills" (1981, p. 118).

This interpretation must be accepted with caution, however (Genesee, 1981d). It is possible that the listening and reading tests that were available to Swain for her comparisons were not sensitive to the types of language styles that IM students in bilingual communities might be exposed to extracurricularly. First of all, it is probably in the domain of interpersonal communication skills (i.e., speaking and listening) and not reading that one would most expect the impact, if any, of the broader linguistic environment to be evident. In fact, it is difficult to imagine many out-of-school activities in the second language that would involve elementary school-aged children in reading to the extent that would be necessary to influence their general reading proficiency. On the other hand, one could well imagine numerous types of activities for school children that might involve extensive oral/aural language skills, e.g., sports teams, Scouts, or Girl Guides. Indeed, Swain found that there was a tendency for IM students in Montreal to outperform IM students in less bilingual settings on listening comprehension tests. As well, it is likely that the language variety assessed by the standardized second language tests at Swain's disposal was formal; in contrast, it might be expected that the linguistic advantage that accrues from living in a bilingual community is most likely to be found in informal or colloquial language usage.

It is also possible that Swain failed to find differences in second language proficiency as a function of setting because the students attending immersion in different cities are not entirely comparable. The greater availability of immersion programs in bilingual regions of the country, and particularly in Quebec, along with the greater felt urgency to learn French in these regions, has probably resulted in greater participation by students with a broad range of ability levels than in relatively monolingual regions. If this is in fact true, and it seems a reasonable speculation, then any possible positive effects of the environment on second language proficiency might be offset or obscured by the countervailing depressing effects of lower levels of intellectual ability. This would be particularly evident in the types of tests that Swain had at her disposal; namely, tests of formal language proficiency.

Regardless of the overall composition of the IM students in different settings, it is also possible that the student samples used in the evaluations examined by Swain were not comparable. In Genesee's evaluations of the early immersion programs in Montreal, for example, he was careful to select samples of students with above-average, average, and below-average levels of academic ability. While this selection procedure may have resulted in a nonrepresentative sample of IM students, since it may have over-included below-average students, it was a useful means of exploring the suitability of immersion for below-average students. However, such a sample selection procedure poses problems for comparisons involving samples that were not similarly selected or in programs whose student populations were not similarly constituted.

Until planned, direct comparisons of the French language proficiency of students in immersion programs located in different settings are carried out, we cannot tell whether the presence of target language speakers in the community influences the students' second language achievement. The available data do indicate, however, that neither large numbers of target language speakers nor official status for the target language is necessary for the overall success of a second language immersion program. It would appear that the parental and student motivation that underlie such programs are sufficient to ensure some fairly high minimal level of success.

SUMMARY

Evaluations of IM students with characteristics that are typically disadvantageous have revealed that such students demonstrate the same levels of first language development and academic achievement as similarly disadvantaged students in all-English schools. Three learner characteristics have been examined extensively: academic ability, first language ability/disability, and socioeconomic background. At the same time, the disadvantaged students were found to achieve significantly higher levels of second language proficiency than control students receiving core FSL instruction. To their advantage, students with below-average levels of academic ability achieved the same levels of proficiency in speaking and listening comprehension in French as average and above-average IM students.

Innovative research by Bruck of McGill University's Learning Centre has shown that, while academic difficulty may predispose students to switch out of immersion, such difficulty by itself is not sufficient to result in transfer, and therefore the presence of academic problems is probably not the underlying causal factor. Rather, it appears that behavioral and/or attitudinal problems associated with academic difficulty distinguish students who switch out of immersion from those who remain in, notwithstanding academic difficulties. Additional evidence reported by Bruck suggests further that the root cause of some students' inability to cope in immersion reflects enduring personal/affective problems which are not tied specifically to immersion in a second language program. Thus, transferring students who are experiencing difficulty in immersion out of the program should not be expected to result in quick remediation of the students' problems. To the contrary, as the available evidence suggests, unless special measures are taken to address these students' enduring problems they may continue to experience difficulty even in an all-English classroom.

There is an evident need in many immersion programs for more specialized remedial services for students who are experiencing difficulty but do not intend or want to switch to an English program. The provision of such services is no simple task. It is difficult even when working with English-speaking children in English classes to know precisely what their problems might be. The task of identifying and treating difficulties is compounded in second language classes by not knowing what is a developmental lag associated with the second language and what is an underlying problem. Nevertheless, the availability of immersion classes also presupposes the provision of a normal range of remedial and special services for the participating students.

A corollary issue concerns the provision of programs for gifted immersion students. A survey carried out by Canadian Parents for French (1985) in immersion schools across Canada revealed that relatively few school districts provide programs for gifted education and that both parents and educators feel that not enough is being done in this area to serve the needs of such students.

Systematic, longitudinal evaluations of immersion programs in communities across Canada have revealed that immersion is a relatively effective approach to second language education even in areas where there are few target language speakers. This conclusion will be confirmed when we examine the effectiveness of United States immersion programs in chapter eight.

Overall, immersion has shown itself to be an effective form of second language education for students with diverse learner characteristics and from different kinds of communities.

CHAPTER 7

Social-Psychological Studies of Immersion

The goals of French immersion programs, at least in bilingual regions of Canada such as Montreal and Ottawa, are not only linguistic and academic. As noted in the opening chapter, it was fundamental sociocultural changes in Quebec society that gave rise to immersion in the first place. Although centered in the province of Quebec, these changes had far-reaching economic and political implications throughout the country. The impact of these changes is evident in the nationwide proliferation of immersion programs that we have already noted (Stern, 1984). The original founders of immersion hoped that, in addition to second language proficiency, the immersion experience would engender among English Canadian students more positive attitudes toward the French language and French Canadians than those previously held (Lambert, Hodgson, Gardner, & Fillenbaum, 1960). It was also hoped that the immersion experience would predispose young English Canadians to use French in day-to-day situations wherever possible, thereby leading to some form of cross-cultural contact and communication. It is not uncommon to find some of these hopes expressed formally in the statements of program goals of some school districts. These social issues have given rise to a number of empirical investigations concerning the social-psychological consequences of immersion, mostly in the region of Montreal where these issues are of immediate practical significance.

The immersion programs are of some social-psychological interest for theoretical reasons as well. Bilingualism has been examined systematically as an important independent variable in numerous subareas of social psychology including, for example, studies of stereotyping and ethnic attitudes (Lambert et al., 1960), research on social interaction and person perception (Ryan & Giles, 1982), and studies of intergroup conflict (Tajfel & Turner, 1979). There are a number of specific reasons for hypothesizing that learning a second language or being bilingual might have significant social-psychological consequences. Acquisition of a second language may have social-psychological effects on the individual through a process of cognitive restructuring. It has been proposed that stereotyped attitudes toward unfamiliar social groups may develop and be maintained, at least in part, because perceptions of the other group are undifferentiated (Katz, Johnson, & Parker, 1970). Accordingly, perceptual training in differentiating members of a stereotyped group might be expected to lead to attitude change;

and, in fact, there is some evidence to support this expectation (Katz, 1973; Hohn, 1973). Zajonc (1968) has hypothesized that increased familiarization with unfamiliar groups through mere exposure will lead to more positive attitudes toward the group. Others contend that intergroup contact is necessary and, moreover, that the nature of the contact will have important consequences for the nature and extent of the attitudinal change (Amir, 1976). By providing students with opportunities to interact with French Canadians, such as their teachers or other students, or to become more familiar with French Canadians vicariously through their program of studies, immersion programs might be expected to have some of the cognitive restructuring effects discussed by these researchers.

Second language acquisition might also be expected to have significant social-psychological implications for the individual, since language can be an important symbol of ethnic identity. Indeed, research in Canada has shown this to be the case for English and French Canadians (Taylor, Bassili, & Aboud, 1973). Thus, to learn another group's language may influence one's perception of oneself or of other groups insofar as one is acquiring a salient and distinctive characteristic of another group.

To mention one last example, Gardner (1986) has proposed a social-psychological model of second language acquisition in which second language proficiency and other aspects of second language learning are related to a complex of attitudinal and motivational factors; Gardner's model will be described in more detail later in this chapter. Much of Gardner's early research has been carried out with adolescent learners in largely monolingual Canadian settings or in schools with conventional second language courses. The immersion programs provide an interesting opportunity to examine this model in truly bilingual settings with young second language learners.

In short, social-psychological research undertaken in conjunction with evaluative studies of Canadian immersion programs has been motivated on the one hand by practical social issues within the community and on the other hand by theoretical issues of general social-psychological interest. The extant research findings can be summarized in terms of two broad issues: 1) bilingualism, ethnic identity, and intergroup perceptions; and 2) attitudinal and motivational factors and second language use in a bilingual setting. Before reviewing this work, let us first of all review research that has examined immersion students' attitudes toward the immersion program itself, since this is an important aspect of any pedagogical innovation of such broad scope.

STUDENT ATTITUDES TOWARD IMMERSION

Genesee (1978b) asked grade 6 students from an early total immersion program and grade 11 students from a one-year late immersion program their opinions of their respective programs. Grade 6 and grade 11 students taking core French were similarly surveyed. Despite the fact that 29 percent of the early IM students and 35 percent of the late IM students sampled said that they thought the program entailed more work than the English program, both groups indicated they were very happy to have taken it—on a scale from 1 (very happy) to 7 (very unhappy), the average rating of the early IM students was 1.55 and of the late IM students 1.72. Furthermore, 82 percent of the early IM sample and 77 percent of the late IM sample said they would recommend it to younger brothers and sisters. Lambert and Tucker (1972) similarly found that grade 5 students in the St. Lambert early immersion program were happy with school and the way French was being taught, whereas students in the English program with core French instruction were much less so. For example, 52 percent of the IM students but only 16 percent of the core French students agreed with the statement, "I enjoy studying French the way it is taught in school." In fact, 19 percent of the core students reported that they would prefer not to study French anymore, whereas virtually none of the IM students responded in this way.

Swain and Lapkin (1982) have reported similarly positive reactions from students attending French immersion programs in Ontario, despite the fact that in some cases the students were attending schools in regions of the province where there were very few French Canadians and, therefore, virtually no public evidence of their existence. Edwards, Colletta, Fu, and McCarrey (1979), also working in Ontario schools, questioned the teachers of early IM and EC students concerning the students' classroom behaviors and general adjustment to school. The teachers' reports gave no indication that the IM students were having trouble adjusting to the immersion program.

Cziko, Lambert, Sidoti, and Tucker (1980) carried out a retrospective study of students who had graduated from the early immersion program in St. Lambert. The students were contacted one year after they had completed grade 11 and were asked to give their impressions of the immersion program now that they had left school. Their reactions were elicited during an interview and in a questionnaire. The IM graduates and their parents expressed very clearly an appreciation for the early immersion experience, and the majority of those interviewed said they would choose the immersion option again if they had to do it over. In contrast, graduates of the English program with FSL expressed general disappointment with their language program and leveled harsh criticism against the school system for having failed them and their children. The early IM graduates expressed feelings of well-being, self-assurance, and satisfaction with their level of proficiency in French. In fact, a number of them indicated that they felt quite capable of working in French and studying further in French at the college or university level. They also said they were eager to study other languages. A larger proportion of IM students than EC students indicated a desire to stay in Quebec, even though a majority of both groups thought that they would probably leave within ten years.

On balance, the contrasts between the EI (i.e., IM) and EC groups that . . . emerged portray the early-immersion experience as a means of developing high degrees of skill in the French language, a feeling of confidence among graduates that they could work, study, and live in a French environment as well as in an English one; a belief that they could, given simple opportunities to use French, become fully bilingual; and a willingness and desire to meet and integrate with French-speaking Canadians. (Cziko et al., 1980, p. 155)

BILINGUALISM, ETHNIC IDENTITY, AND INTERGROUP PERCEPTIONS

In a review of early work relating bilingualism to personality formation, Diebold (1968) concluded that "the popular consensus about the effects of early bilingualism on personality integration and emotional adjustment is that this experience is detrimental" (p. 236). Diebold indicated that thinking among early researchers in the field tended to view bilingualism as giving rise to two distinct personality structures which in turn implicated psychodynamic conflict, anomie, and schizophrenia in the extreme case (see Christophersen, 1948). It has been argued that in learning two languages the bilingual internalizes two systems of "shared meanings or world views" (Lamy, 1979), one from each ethnolinguistic group, and that identity problems may arise, either because these meaning systems are inherently irreconcilable or because they are reconcilable but yield a hybrid reality system that is not compatible with either of the systems which gave rise to it. It is interesting to note the parallel between Diebold's negative conclusion and that of early researchers investigating the relationship between bilingualism and intellectual development (see Cummins, 1976, and Hakuta, 1986, for reviews of this research).

Since that time, we have come to appreciate that such categorical conclusions are a gross oversimplification. Even in social settings where language may be an important aspect of ethnic identity, as in Canada, this may not be true of all members of the community. Adiv (1977), for example, found that native French-speaking Jewish Canadian children saw themselves as more similar to other Canadians who were Jewish but English-speaking than to French-speaking Canadians. Apparently, Jewishness offered a more salient basis for intergroup distinctiveness than did language and, therefore, figured more prominently in the children's ethnic identity.

The complexity of social-psychological outcomes that can be associated with bilingualism is illustrated in studies by Gardner and Lambert (1972) on the ethnic identity of Franco-Americans in New England and Louisiana. They found that different subgroups of respondents had different patterns of reactions to their dual ethnolinguistic backgrounds. There were subgroups who seemed not to think of themselves in ethnolinguistic terms at all; there were subgroups of individuals within the larger samples who appeared to orient themselves exclusively toward one of their ethnolinguistic reference groups while ignoring the other; and there were subgroups who identified positively with both reference groups. The fact of such subgroup differences is an important empirical finding, indicating that the relationship between bilingualism and its associated dual culturalism is much more diverse than Diebold's conclusions would indicate. Such diversity should not be unexpected since the circumstances, individual and sociocultural, in which people learn a second language can be quite different. Why these different reactions occur is an important theoretical and practical question.

In this regard, Lambert (1980a) has suggested that the social-psychological consequences of bilingualism and its associated dual culturalism will depend upon the sociocultural dominance of the two language/cultural groups in question. He contends that acquisition of a second language and contact with the second language group by members of a dominant or majority ethnolinguisitic group are likely to lead to an *additive* form of bilingualism. By this he means that acquisition of a second language and contact with another culture are not likely to displace or replace the individual's first language or home culture. Thus, this type of bilingual will have two mutually viable language systems within his/her repertoire and will have access, at least in principle, to two cultures. Consequently, such bilinguals are not likely to reject their first language or culture or to otherwise express generalized negative feelings toward the second language and culture. In contrast, Lambert contends that acquisition of a second language and contact with another culture, where these are socially dominant, by members of minority ethnolinguistic groups may lead to *subtractive* bilingualism, in that the majority language and culture may replace or undermine the individual's first language and culture. The latter type of bilingualism may be expected to be associated with negative feelings toward the first language and culture since they constitute a marker of minority group status.

Research on the ethnic identity of English Canadian students in immersion programs supports Lambert's notion of additive bilingualism. Genesee (1977b) and Cziko, Lambert, and Gutter (1980) examined the ethnic identity of early immersion students in two separate studies using multidimensional scaling techniques. Each student was simply asked to indicate how similar or dissimilar he/she thought a number of personal and ethnic concepts were to one another. For example, the student might be given the pair French Canadian—English Canadian and asked to indicate on a rating scale how similar they are. In order to determine the students' perceptions of themselves relative to the other concepts, they were asked to indicate how similar they themselves were to each of the other concepts. In total, 14 concepts were presented to the respondents to be compared; they included the concepts *MYSELF*—an *English Canadian,* a *French Canadian,* a *Canadian,* a *Quebecer,* an *American,* and others. The advantages of this technique are that it does not require that the respondents evaluate any of the concepts positively or negatively, and it leaves each respondent free to use whatever criteria of similarity he/she wants. The statistical analysis of the ratings yields a type of psychological "map" depicting the students' perceptions of their social environment as it is tapped by the concepts included for comparison. Essentially, the technique represents the students' subjective perceptions of similarity in terms of spatial distances and configurations—concepts that are perceived to be more similar to one another are located closer together in space.

The results from the two studies revealed that the social perceptions of IM and EC students were similar in two important respects. First, two major clusters of concepts could be identified in the responses of each group: one associated with the English language and English Canadians and one associated with the French language and French Canadians. Second, both the IM students and the EC students perceived themselves to be associated with the English clusters, indicating that both groups tended to identify primarily with English Canadians. At the same time, the IM students differed from the EC students with respect to their perceptions of French Canadians. The IM students tended to perceive the English and French clusters as more similar. They also tended to view themselves as more similar to French Canadians. Genesee has noted these effects as early as grade 1 (Genesee, Tucker, & Lambert, 1978).

Thus, participation in immersion has been found to be associated with perceptions of a reduction in social distance between English and French Canadians. The social distance reported by monolingual English Canadian students may have been reduced in the case of IM students, because the acquisition of a second language results in perceptions of oneself as bilingual and therefore similar to others who speak the target language. It may also be that the IM students' familiarization with French Canadians through interaction with French-speaking teachers or through exposure to curricular material in French has made them realize fundamental similarities between the two ethnolinguistic groups that might otherwise be masked by superficial language differences. The development of such perceptions could be an important precursor for establishing social contact and relationships with members of the other group, leading ultimately perhaps to more positive intergroup attitudes.

Studies of IM students' ethnic attitudes have yielded more complex results. In their longitudinal evaluation of the St. Lambert early immersion program, Lambert and Tucker (1972) assessed the attitudes of IM and EC students toward themselves, English Canadians, and French Canadians. Attitude profiles were generated repeatedly at successive grade levels, thereby allowing the investigators to map out changes in attitude over grades. Attitudes were measured mainly by having students indicate their responses using 7-point rating scales describing a variety of personal and social traits (e.g., likeable, smart). The results indicated that in the primary elementary grades the IM students saw themselves and English Canadians in general in a more favorable light than did the EC students. Similarly, their attitudes toward French Canadians were more positive than were those of the EC respondents. When the attitude profiles of the same students were examined in the senior elementary grades, relatively few significant differences were found between the IM and EC students' perceptions of French Canadians. Similar patterns of attitudes and attitude change have been found in the case of students participating in late immersion programs (Genesee, Morin, & Allister, 1974); namely, grade 7 late IM students exhibited more positive attitudes toward French Canadians than did EC comparison students, whereas there were no such differences between similar student groups by grade 11, the final grade of the program. At no time were the attitudes of IM students less positive than those of the EC students.

IM students' attitudes toward French Canadians, while initially more positive, may come to be the same as those of students in an English program, because there is an absence of real social contact with French Canadians and therefore a lack of behavioral or social evidence on which to sustain positive attitudes over an extended period of time. The potential importance of such contact for inter-group attitudes is demonstrated in a study in which the attitudes of grade 7 students attending late immersion programs in otherwise English schools were compared to those of students attending a similar late immersion program but located in an otherwise all-French school. The latter program allowed for day-to-day contact between the two ethnic groups (Genesee, Morin, & Allister, 1974). The results indicated that, while the attitudes of the late IM students in the English schools tended to be positive relative to those of EC students, they were not as positive as those of the IM students in the program located in an otherwise all-French school. Thus, there may be limits to the extent of attitude change that can be achieved and sustained in second language programs that do not provide real meaningful contact between the learner and members of the target language group. Students may need opportunities to form friendships or to interact with members of the other language group before they can develop stable positive attitudes toward them.

Another possible explanation of the IM students' attitudinal shift can be found in the general sociopolitical climate of Quebec where these studies were conducted. The period from 1965 to 1977, when these studies were carried out, was marked by rapid and radical changes in Quebec politics, culminating in 1976 with the election of a provincial government that advocated an independent, monolingual French state for Quebec. Tensions between French and English Quebecers reached an all time high during this period. It seems quite likely that some of the tensions, fears, and hostility experienced by the English community at large at this time filtered down to students in immersion schools and colored their perceptions of French Canadians. Schools are part of large, complex social systems and therefore are likely to reflect and perpetuate the sentiments charac-teristic of ethnolinguistic groups toward one another in the community at large. More will be said of the importance of intergroup factors for second language learning in the next section.

ATTITUDES, MOTIVATION, AND SECOND LANGUAGE USE

A number of surveys have been conducted by Genesee (1978b, 1981a) to examine the language habits and attitudes of IM students outside the school setting. After all, it was the growing importance of French in normal day-to-day events that led to the development of immersion in the first place. Genesee used a diary method to study the extracurricular language habits of groups of grade 6 IM and EC students in Montreal. Students were asked to indicate in specially prepared diaries, as best they could, what they had done during the preceding day from the time they got up in the morning until the time they went to bed. In addition to indicating what they did and when they did it, the students were asked to indicate what language was used. Either a researcher or the students' teachers helped the students fill out their diaries at the beginning of each school day. This was done for several consecutive days and for weekdays as well as weekends.

The same type of information was solicited from the students' parents. However, since a diary was impractical in this case, the parents were asked to describe their language habits in a questionnaire by estimating which languages they used, when, and in what circumstances. The parents' estimates were limited, in most cases, to the three days preceding their receiving the questionnaire; this was done in order to increase the reliability and validity of their responses by reducing demands on their memory. The response rate from the parents was quite high—65 percent—and the responses they provided appeared honest and realistic. The students and parents also answered a number of additional questions regarding their feelings about learning and using French.

In response to these latter questions, the IM students reported that they felt more comfortable and confident when speaking French with francophones than did the EC students. They also indicated that they were more likely to respond in French when spoken to in French and that they were less likely to avoid situations where French would be spoken. In fact, their diary entries revealed that they actually used French significantly more often than the EC students in interpersonal situations—e.g., with friends, with salespersonnel, and in public settings. At the same time, there was little indication from their diaries that the IM students were more likely to use French in other contexts—they were no more likely than EC students to watch French television, listen to French radio, or read French books for pleasure. Furthermore, the actual frequency and duration of usage of French in these contexts was negligible when compared to their use of English in the same contexts. The same patterns of language use were reported by the students' parents. It is interesting to speculate that the parents may have provided influential role models for the students.

One feature that distinguishes the use of French in interpersonal contexts, in contrast to its use in conjunction with the media, is the degree to which personal control and choice are exercised by the individual in initiating use of language. Use of the media is entirely under individual control and depends upon personal choice. Thus, use of language in conjunction with the media may be characterized as *active.* In contrast, use of language in interpersonal situations is often contingent on other individuals and/or social circumstances—an individual's use of his/her second language might be required in an interpersonal encounter, either because this is the only language the interlocutor understands or because the social situation requires its use. Language use under these circumstances might then be characterized as *reactive.* If this is in fact an accurate basis for distinguishing the IM students' second language use in these two contexts, then it would appear that their second language habits are largely *reactive.* This characterization of the IM students' language habits is compatible with their reported motivations for learning French, which tend to be more instrumental than integrative (Genesee, 1978b). Gardner, Gliksman, and Smythe (p. 182, 1978) define an integrative motive as a "high drive on the part of the individual to acquire the language of a valued second language group in order to facilitate communication with that group." An instrumental motive has been defined as the feeling that "learning a second language is important for pragmatic or utilitarian reasons" (Gardner, p. 209, 1979). One might expect an instrumental motivation to be sufficient to promote reactive language use, whereas it may not be sufficient to result in active language use.

Studies by Genesee and Bourhis (1982) provide additional evidence that IM students' willingness to use French may be somewhat limited. This research examined evaluative reactions toward the use of French and English in public situations in Montreal. Sixteen-year-old late IM and EC students were asked to listen to and give their impressions of two people depicted in simulated dialogues involving a salesman and a customer. In one study, the salesman was played by a French Canadian actor and the customer by an English Canadian actor. In certain conditions the French Canadian salesman persisted in using French with the English-speaking customer. By doing so, he violated a social norm that the customer be served in his first language. When this occurred, the salesman was rated negatively on a number of personal traits by both the IM and EC students. In fact, the IM respondents tended to evaluate the salesman even more negatively than did the relatively monolingual EC students. Having made personal efforts to learn French through extended intensive French language programs, the IM students may have expected reciprocal effort and therefore accommodation on the part of French Canadians. Alternatively, being able to communicate in either language, French IM students may be especially sensitive to basic social norms regarding appropriate language use in public situations. The salesman–customer encounter is an especially rigorous test of the students' tolerance toward the use of French because the social norm in this situation does not support the use of French—in fact, even French Canadian students presented with the same scenario also tended to downgrade the French Canadian salesman when he maintained French with an English-speaking customer. In any case, these findings illustrate further that bilingualism through schooling alone may not be sufficient to effect unlimited social-psychological changes.

It should probably not be too surprising that the social-psychological consequences of participation in an immersion program may be somewhat limited. After all, language is simply one variable in a complex network of social, economic, and political factors that can influence intergroup relations which in turn will influence second language learning and use. The importance of social factors for second language learning was drawn to the attention of second language researchers and educators by Gardner and Lambert in their 1972 book, *Attitudes and Motivation in Second Language Learning.* In this and subsequent publications Gardner has articulated a social-psychological model of second language learning. Very simply, Gardner's model holds that second language learners must have positive attitudes toward the target language and the target language group if they are to sustain the motivation necessary to undertake the extended and at times arduous efforts required to master a second language. The model goes on to say that second language learning is mediated directly by the learner's own motivations. Thus, variations in second language behaviors are associated directly with variations in individual motivation, among other factors. Gardner (1986) has provided empirical support for this model.

Some of the research findings just cited, however, suggest that in bilingual, cross-cultural contexts it may be necessary to consider *intergroup* factors in addition to the strictly individualistic factors outlined by Gardner. In this regard, Genesee, Rogers, and Holobow (1983) have argued that second language learning will be influenced by perceptions of motivational support; that is, the learners' belief that their motives for learning a second language are supported by the target language group. The notion of motivational support can be illustrated using Gardner's notion of an integrative motivation—individuals with a strong motivation to learn a second language in order to become part of the target language community may be discouraged from doing so by their perceptions that the target language community does not want them to integrate or will not let them integrate.

In order to test this possibility, Genesee et al. (1983) asked groups of second language learners in core French programs and in French immersion programs in Montreal to indicate how much they agreed with a number of motivational statements (e.g., "I want to learn French so that I can get to know French Canadians better.") They were also asked to indicate how much they thought French Canadians would agree with the same kinds of statements (e.g., "French Canadians want English Canadians to learn French so that we will get to know them better.") The students' responses to these questions indicated that they perceived a noticeable lack of motivational support from French Canadians relative to their own motivations; this was particularly true with respect to motives that appeared to be pragmatic or instrumental in nature. For example, the IM students did not think that French Canadians wanted them to learn French so that they (i.e., English Canadians) could get better jobs, become politically influential, and so on. The IM students themselves, on the other hand, reported that these were important motives for their learning French.

The relationship between the learners' own motives, their perceptions of motivational support, and their second language achievement was examined using step-wise multiple regression techniques. The results of these analyses indicated that, as predicted, not only did the students' own motivations for learning French have a significant positive correlation with their second language achievement, but so did their perceptions of motivational support. In other words, the more the English Canadian students believed that French Canadians wanted them to learn French the greater was their proficiency in French. Moreover, there was a positive correlation between the students' perceptions of motivational support and their reported *use* of the second language, so that those students who perceived more motivational support from French Canadians reported using

French in a variety of social situations. In some cases, the students' perceptions of motivational support were more important than were their own motivations. The analyses indicated that the importance of motivational support as a correlate of second language learning was independent of the students' own self-reported motivations. These results underline the importance of intergroup factors by indicating that second language learning does not take place in a sociocultural vacuum and that intergroup factors outside the school setting can influence school achievement in significant ways.

It is important to point out that all of the social-psychological research reviewed here, and in fact most of the social-psychological research conducted in conjunction with immersion programs, has been carried out in the metropolitan Montreal area (see Swain & Lapkin, 1982, for a review of other studies). This is not surprising in view of the fact that immersion is relatively more prevalent in Quebec than elsewhere—including approximately 13 percent of the anglophone student population, in contrast to New Brunswick with 9 percent and Ontario with 3 percent (Stern, 1984). Nor is it surprising in view of the sociopolitical climate and the very real social implications of bilingualism and language-related issues in Quebec. Nevertheless, the fact that different results and therefore different conclusions might be found elsewhere in Canada or in the United States where intergroup dynamics are different must be borne in mind.

Even within the province of Quebec itself, the nature of intergroup relations and particularly French–English relations vary from region to region. In a study of the social-psychological significance of bilingual code switching in Quebec City, Genesee (1984a) found that situational norms that prescribe appropriate language choices by a salesman and a customer were much less in evidence than had been found in an earlier study conducted in Montreal (Genesee & Bourhis, 1982). In other words, the English- and French-speaking interactants in Quebec City were much more likely to be evaluated in terms of interpersonal factors than situational ones. Genesee suggested that situational norms were salient for judging language behaviors in Montreal because they provide a relatively neutral basis for carrying out and interpreting cross-cultural dyadic interactions in a city where language is a source of conflict. Quebec City, in contrast, is much more French dominant and has experienced far less language-related conflict than Montreal. Thus, the need for a basis of social interaction that is neutral with respect to its intergroup implications is less in Quebec City. Gardner (1986) has also found that the relationships outlined in his social-psychological model of second language learning are sensitive to sociocultural context. In particular, he found that an integrative motivation is more strongly associated with second language learning in monolingual settings where the second language is not present than in bilingual settings, such as Montreal. By way of explanation, he has suggested that, where opportunities to experience the second language are not readily available, motivated individuals will nonetheless seek them out, and their added exposure will promote achievement.

Cleghorn and Genesee (1984) have proposed that the influence of intergroup factors can be found within bilingual schools themselves (see also Paulston, 1977). They argued that, since bilingual schools are part of the fabric of society at large, they reflect major social patterns and processes that characterize that society. It follows, therefore, that since the staffs of French immersion schools are made up of French and English Canadian teachers who are members of ethnolinguistic groups in conflict, one might expect immersion teachers to experience conflict in school. The nature of this conflict has been described briefly in chapter one. Thus, Cleghorn and Genesee argued that one might expect English and French Canadian teachers working in immersion schools to bring to their professional roles as teachers the same conflicts and antagonisms that characterize English–French relations in the community at large.

Using ethnographic research techniques, they sought to investigate 1) whether the interactions between the English and French Canadian teachers in an early total immersion school would in fact reflect societally based conflict; 2) in what specific ways this conflict would be expressed; and 3) how they, along with the principal of the school, would manage such conflict so that it did not interfere with the normal functioning of the school.

Cleghorn spent most of one school year systematically observing the social interaction patterns within the target immersion school; her observational results were supported by interview and questionnaire data. The school in question was typical of many immersion schools in Montreal in terms of its size, suburban location, and predominantly middle class student group. All-English classes were available along with immersion from grades 4 to 6; there was no English stream in the primary grades since there was an insufficient number of students interested in this program to warrant it. A majority of the teachers were French speaking and taught in the immersion classes. The principal was native English speaking with some proficiency in French. The overall climate of the school was congenial and open, and evaluations carried out in the past indicated that the results of this school were as good as most other immersion schools and better than some.

In support of their argument, Cleghorn and Genesee found that there were in fact divisions between the French and English teachers that could be traced to intergroup conflict in the community at large. There was evidence of intergroup division within the formal organization of the school itself—the members of each teaching stream (i.e., English and French) associated predominantly with members of their own group. Even when the formal organization of the school would under other circumstances bring about intergroup interaction and cooperation (in grades 3 to 6 where English and French teachers taught the same students), there was virtually no evidence of interaction between the English and French teachers. Similarly, staff meetings, which included all the teachers and which provided a forum for the discussion of pedagogical issues pertinent to the whole school, were characterized by a *de facto* split between English and French. The topics of discussion showed an almost exclusive preoccupation with pedagogical issues of relevance only to the English stream teachers. Furthermore, English was used almost exclusively in these meetings, despite the fact that the majority of the teachers were francophone and all of the English teachers could speak and understand French.

There was also ample evidence of an ethnolinguistic split in the teachers' informal social interactions. In the staff room, for example, the English and French teachers were seated separately, and there was little communication between members of the two groups. Observations of encounters between teachers in the hallways and elsewhere in the school also indicated a lack of interaction, verbal or otherwise. Private interviews with individual teachers revealed that both teacher groups, and especially the English teachers, felt there was tension between the French and English teachers. Their comments revealed further that these tensions stemmed from reactions to changes in the school that reflected the growing size and importance of the French immersion component of the school and an accompanying diminution of the English component. These changes threatened their job security and power. These changes in turn were linked to changes in the community at large—more specifically, a resurgence of the French language and culture and a waning of the English language and culture in Quebec.

It was evident from the teachers' private comments as well as from the observational data that the avoidance or lack of interaction noted above was both an expression of intergroup conflict and a strategy for minimizing conflict and maintaining harmony among the staff. Social or linguistic avoidance by the teachers could be interpreted to serve two goals. It allowed the English teachers to establish a "myth" that they did not know French, so that when French and English teachers were gathered together as a group the use of English was necessary. It also allowed the French teachers to uphold a rule that is sacrosanct in most immersion schools; namely, that only French be spoken with IM students by immersion teachers in and out of the classroom. Thus, silence between the English and French teachers during encounters in the school corridors allowed the French teachers to comply with an important norm of their profession, and it protected the English teachers from deviating from their preferred pattern of using English in mixed-language groups.

These interaction patterns were not necessarily conscious or malevolent. Rather, they comprised an implicit part of the school's "culture"—a tacit agreement among the school participants that maintained harmonious relationships. Viewed from the teachers' and administration's point of view, these patterns of interaction were rational and comprehensible within the general norms of the teaching profession and within the specific norms of immersion education. The coexistence of English and French teachers in the same school and their implied support for French language learning are consistent with a new social order in Quebec and Canada which aims to improve relations between English and French Canadians. Viewed from the students' point of view, however, the picture may be quite different. It is possible that the language models posed by the English and French teachers in this school and in similar schools are seen by the students as perpetuating the two solitudes that have traditionally characterized French–English relations.

Instances when intergroup interaction or cross-language communication did occur tended to favor English, the traditionally dominant language. A particularly striking example of this occurred one day when the principal of the school entered a French immersion class to speak to the students about the English compositions they had handed in to their English teacher. The principal conscientiously reviewed student work and was generally highly informed of each student's progress. Disappointed by their generally poor submissions, he decided to "take them to task." The principal entered the French class, unannounced and uninvited, ignored the French teacher who was in the midst of a lesson, and, using English, proceeded to admonish the students for their poor performance; once finished, he hastily retreated, again largely ignoring the class teacher. Viewed from the principal's perspective and from the norms of immersion, the principal's language behavior can be explained easily and rationally. This particular principal felt that he was a poor language model for his students because his French language skills were poor; consequently, he was prone not to use French, except for short, perfunctory purposes. Thus, it is quite likely that he ignored the French teacher and used English in order not to exhibit his poor French in front of the students and risk loss of face. At the same time, he could not address the teacher in English because this would have broken the all-French rule that characterizes immersion classes. Viewed from the students' perspective, however, this episode could easily have been seen as a reaffirmation of the dominance of English over French.

That the French teachers were never seen to contest the differential preference enjoyed by English can be interpreted as their tacit acceptance of this norm, possibly as a means of maintaining harmonious relationships in this otherwise English school. The important point here is that both the English and French teachers participated in formulating the sociolinguistic norms of the school; neither should be viewed as victim or perpetrator.

The strategies used by the teachers to create a harmonious school atmosphere can be traced to sociolinguistic norms that prevailed some years ago, when social and economic power rested with English Canadians. In contrast to traditional norms, the sociolinguistic norms that were emerging in Quebec at the time of this study favored the use of French over English; indeed, the use of French was required under certain conditions by law. These emerging societal norms were evidently not yet sufficiently entrenched to break down the ethnolinguistic barriers that were observed to characterize the teachers' interactions. Indeed, it is striking that, despite the fact that the teachers were working in a setting in which the two solitudes were under pressure to dissolve, such rigid barriers persisted. It has been argued that ethnic boundaries play an important role in personal identity (Barth, 1969). Thus, the maintenance of ethnic barriers in an immersion school may serve to protect the identities of the teacher groups involved. The maintenance of traditional interaction patterns that favor English over French in immersion schools may in turn serve to preserve the school's traditional identity within the English community. Attempts to break down ethnic boundaries are likely to be threatening and lead to resistance.

If the social goals of a bilingual school are to provide students with models of bilingual, cross-cultural interaction, then it would appear that changes in teachers' interactions with one another are needed. Teachers may have to be trained to renegotiate their identities in a changing bilingual/bicultural society, and systematic efforts may need to be undertaken to address thorny issues concerning language usage in school. To this end, it would seem important for teachers as well as principals to receive special in-service training to heighten their awareness of the sociocultural context within which they work, so that they are better able to consciously and systematically cope with that reality in an educationally constructive way.

It would be important in subsequent research to examine more fully students' perceptions and interpretations of the sociolinguistic norms of the school. Such research could establish whether or not the social interaction patterns revealed in the Cleghorn and Genesee investigation have any discernible and noteworthy consequences for second language learning or attitude development in bilingual schools. Notwithstanding the lack of direct data on students' reactions to language use in immersion schools, the present results are certainly compatible with and serve to explain in part some of the limitations in language use and attitudes noted earlier in this chapter.

SUMMARY

Research findings concerning the social psychological implications of second language learning in immersion programs suggest two major conclusions. First, it appears that second language learning in such settings has social-psychologically relevant consequences for the participating students. Second, the social-psychological effects of immersion that are discernible are likely to be specific and tied fairly closely to the particular experiences that comprise immersion education. More specifically, it has been found that English Canadian students in immersion programs are not likely to experience a loss of ethnic identity with respect to their home language group, as some earlier theories might have predicted and as some parents might have feared. At the same time, IM students report a greater sense of similarity to French Canadians, possibly as a result of linguistic similarities. IM students have been found to express more positive attitudes toward French Canadians during the initial stages of the immersion program. However, over time their feelings come to resemble those of students in English schools. This shift may occur as a result of the absence of real sustained social contact with French Canadians.

It may be unrealistic to expect English Canadian students to like French Canadians simply because they have learned French. Nevertheless, it is evident that IM students have more positive attitudes toward the use of French in most situations; and, in fact, they report using it more often than do EC students in interpersonal encounters. Use of French in other contexts, especially when individual initiative and personal choice are involved, is less likely. It was suggested that parents and teachers may provide language models that shape students' use of French and their attitudes toward it in important ways. The relationship between second language learning in immersion and other bilingual schools and extracurricular factors, including the role of parents and of societal norms and processes at large, remains a largely unexplored but potentially critical issue in our understanding of bilingual forms of education. We will return to some of these issues in chapter ten.

CHAPTER
8

Immersion in the United States

It was not long after the introduction of the St. Lambert early total immersion program that American educators began to explore its use in the U.S. context. American immersion programs have not attained the popularity of their Canadian counterparts, but they have been applied in interesting ways that are distinctive from their use in the Canadian context and are worthy of attention. For the most part, immersion programs in Canada can be said to have been developed in response to official policies of bilingualism and to the practical realities of bilingualism in the country. A number of immersion programs have also been adopted in the pursuit of heritage language maintenance and/or revival —the Ukrainian program in Edmonton and the Mohawk program in Montreal are two examples. Immersion programs in the United States can be classified according to one or more of three different purposes: 1) as linguistic, cultural, and general educational enrichment; 2) as magnet schools to bring about a balanced ratio of ethnolinguistic groups; or 3) as a means of achieving some degree of two-way bilingualism in communities with large populations of non-English speaking residents. This classification is somewhat arbitrary, but it serves to highlight some important program variations. Examples of each type of program have been carefully documented and evaluated. In this chapter, we will review and examine the available research findings pertaining to each.

IMMERSION AS EDUCATIONAL ENRICHMENT

Throughout history, bilingualism and a bilingual education have been seen as the hallmark of a "well-educated person." This is no less true today. Indeed, it is not uncommon to find private schools offering special foreign or second language courses as part of their curriculum. There are numerous international schools located throughout the world that have established their reputations, in part at least, on the opportunities they provide their students to become bilingual; for example, the J. F. Kennedy School in Berlin (Mackey, 1972). The attractiveness of these schools is based not only on their language programs but also on the opportunities and rewards they offer students who wish to study in a foreign country. Attendance in these schools provides an enriched cultural and language experience seldom found in public schools in the home country. Second language immersion programs also offer students the possibility of an enriched educational experience without having to travel abroad and without considerable expense for either the school system or the parents. To the extent that immersion programs exceed the demands of regular public schooling, they also provide a challenging educational experience that some parents feel is missing in regular school programs. This aspect of the programs is often cited by Canadian parents who send their children to immersion. The first experiment in second language immersion in the United States reflects this tradition.

1st in US

The Culver City Immersion Program

The first replication of the Canadian immersion experiment in an American setting took place in Culver City, California, in 1971. The comments of some of the parents who took part in this experiment indicate their motives for wanting their children to be in an immersion program (from Rhodes, 1982, in Campbell, 1984):

"I felt it would give her an added dimension to her education and provide insight into another culture."

"I wanted my child to learn a foreign language. [I] also felt that she was ready for more challenge than the regular kindergarten provided."

"My husband and I had a deep desire for our daughter to learn of another cultural background and have some fluency in that language." (p. 119)

A survey of parents in Holliston, Massachusetts, who also opted to send their children to an immersion program, revealed similar motives (Irujo, 1984).

The program in Culver City is an early total immersion program in Spanish. The selection of Spanish as the language of immersion reflects the prevalence of Spanish in southern California and parental interest in the practical benefits their children might derive from knowing Spanish. Immersion programs have been offered elsewhere in the United States using languages that have no immediate practical relevance to the participating children. For example, French immersion programs are available in Montgomery County, Maryland, and Holliston, Massachusetts, even though there are no French-speaking residents in these areas.

Following the St. Lambert model, the Culver City program provides all curricular instruction in kindergarten and grade 1 in Spanish. English is introduced into the curriculum for the first time in grade 2 when English language arts are taught. As in other immersion programs, instruction through English is expanded progressively until there is an approximately equal split between English and Spanish instruction by the end of elementary school. The teachers are either native Spanish speakers or they have nativelike proficiency in Spanish. The kindergarten and grade 1 teachers present themselves as monolingual Spanish speakers in order to encourage the students to use Spanish as much as possible.

However, in contrast to most Canadian programs where different teachers are used to teach the French and the English curricula throughout the elementary grades, in Culver City the same bilingual teachers teach both the Spanish and the English curricula from grade 2 on. The two languages are never mixed during the same instructional period, however.

Participation in the program is voluntary, and the participating children come from backgrounds that represent a wide range of socioeconomic levels, with the majority of them coming from middle class families. Campbell (1984) characterizes the Culver City immersion program as additive; "that is, in addition to the full and complete development of English, the home language of the children, they are provided with opportunities to acquire a foreign language" (p. 123).

The development of the Culver City program has been accompanied from the beginning by a close working relationship with the departments of English as a Second Language and Applied Linguistics at UCLA. The researchers from UCLA have undertaken extensive, longitudinal assessments of the program and particularly student outcomes, including English language development, academic achievement, second language proficiency, and attitudes toward the program and other ethnolinguistic groups. The results of the Culver City evaluations correspond in most major respects to the results of evaluations of early total immersion programs in Canada. Culver City IM students have been found to lag behind non-immersion students in their English language development during kindergarten and grade 1 when no English language arts are taught. Within one year of receiving English language arts instruction, however, they perform as well on standardized tests that assess their English language development and academic achievement as do carefully selected comparison groups of students attending regular English language programs (Cohen, 1974).

Assessment of their Spanish language skills has indicated that the IM students attain high levels of functional language proficiency. This has been evidenced in their use of Spanish for scholastic purposes and for social purposes outside school and in their performance on standardized tests of Spanish (e.g., *Comprehensive Test of Basic Skills: Español*). At the same time, it has been found that they "do not sound like native speakers of Spanish, nor can they perform as well as native speakers in reading, writing or aural comprehension" (Campbell, 1984, p. 131). A similar differential between functional proficiency and native-like competence has been found for French IM students in Canada, as noted in chapter four.

It has been customary in evaluations of Canadian programs to evaluate the second language achievement of immersion students with that of students participating in conventional second language programs. Equivalent comparisons have not been undertaken in evaluations of most American immersion programs because of the absence of second language instruction at the elementary school level in school districts offering immersion. In a national study of the relative effectiveness of alternative second/foreign language teaching programs, including immersion and FLES (foreign languages in the elementary school), Gray, Campbell, Rhodes, and Snow (1984) found, as might be expected, that students in American immersion programs achieved higher levels of second language proficiency than students in FLES programs. These findings substantiate Canadian findings based on similar program alternatives.

The Montgomery County Immersion Project

Similar outcomes have been reported from assessments carried out in Four Corners Elementary School, Montgomery County, Maryland (see Montgomery County Public Schools, 1976). In the Four Corners program, all curricular instruction in kindergarten to grade 2 was given in French, with the exception of physical education and music which were taught by English-speaking specialists. English language arts instruction was introduced into the curriculum in grade 3, one year later than in Culver City. Class groupings included multiple grade level combinations so that students from different grades shared the same classrooms. The evaluation results from Four Corners School are particularly interesting because the second language tests that were used allow for comparisons with students attending early French immersion programs in Canada and also with native French-speaking students attending public schools in Montreal.

Comparisons between the Four Corners IM students and native French-speaking students from Montreal indicate that most of the Four Corners students scored in the above-average stanine range on tests of French language arts and mathematics. It should be pointed out that as a group the Four Corners students were above average with respect to academic ability—on a test of cognitive abilities they scored at the 83rd percentile on the verbal subtest and at the 77th percentile on the quantitative subtest. Undoubtedly, this contributed to their high level of performance on the French reading, language arts, and mathematics tests which are probably sensitive to overall ability, as noted in chapter six. Nevertheless, these results are positive in indicating that the Four Corners students demonstrated a high level of proficiency on tests of French language proficiency, as would be expected of a group of such capable students.

When the achievement of the Four Corners students was examined, using tests of French reading and listening comprehension that were standardized using Canadian IM students, it was found that they scored at an impressively high level. It is not possible to be more precise than this, since neither test norms nor comparison group results were presented in the evaluation report.

Their performance on a number of English language and academic achievement tests was compared to that of other students in the same school who were equally capable—no differences were found except for spelling and punctuation, with the IM students scoring lower than the control students. As noted previously, such lags are not uncommon among early IM students; they are self-correcting usually within one or two years of receiving English language arts instruction.

Summary

Taken together, the results from the Culver City and Four Corners projects attest to the effectiveness of second language immersion programs in communities that lack either a local presence of the target language (i.e., the Four Corners program) or national political recognition of the target language. The participating students achieved noteworthy levels of target language proficiency at no expense to their native English language development or academic achievement. As Campbell points out, immersion programs present an alternative to FLES programs that are cost- and pedagogically effective and therefore may serve to dispel some of the misgivings Americans have traditionally expressed about the time and expense of foreign language education.

IMMERSION AS "MAGNET SCHOOLS"

Immersion programs have been instituted in a number of American school districts in an effort to achieve a balanced ratio of students from different ethnic, linguistic, and socioeconomic groups. Immersion programs in these districts then offer alternative forms of education that might be sufficiently attractive to students from diverse family backgrounds to result in racially, linguistically, and socioeconomically mixed schools without having to resort to compulsory busing or other enforcement procedures. Alternatives besides immersion are also offered in these districts as an enticement to integration. The attraction of "magnet schools," including immersion, is based in part at least on their education enrichment value, and to this extent this form of immersion is similar to the preceding one. Immersion schools have been used as magnets in Cincinnati, Milwaukee, and San Diego. Spanish has been used as the language of immersion in San Diego, and French and German in addition to Spanish have been used in Milwaukee.

The Cincinnati Immersion Project

The first use of immersion programs for this purpose was in the Cincinnati Public Schools in 1974. At present, the Cincinnati immersion programs are the nation's most extensive, with over 2,000 students in attendance and employing approximately 80 immersion teachers (see Campbell, 1984). Programs are available in French and in Spanish and are of the partial immersion variety—with approximately 50 percent of the curriculum taught in English and 50 percent taught in the second language. This program is pedagogically similar in most important respects to other immersion programs in Canada and the United States.

Holobow, Genesee, Lambert, Met, and Gastright (1987) have undertaken a systematic evaluation of the French immersion program in the Cincinnati Public

Schools. Like other immersion evaluations, the design of their research is longitudinal in nature and will involve evaluating both pilot groups and follow-up groups in order to assess the generalizability of the findings. Because the Cincinnati immersion programs function as magnet schools, they have attracted both black students and white students as well as students from working class and middle class backgrounds. Thus, it is possible to assess the program's effectiveness for students from these different subgroups. The design of their research is shown in Figure 4.

The participation of black students is particularly interesting since many of them speak a nonstandard dialect, namely, black vernacular English, as well as being from a minority ethnic group. A systematic evaluation of the suitability of immersion for such students has not been undertaken before, although it is clear from other magnet school projects that use immersion that such students are in attendance. Nonstandard dialect speakers of English arc not available in sufficiently large numbers in Canadian immersion programs to permit a systematic assessment of their progress in that setting.

The Cincinnati research is ongoing. The baseline performance of each subgroup of students will be assessed at the beginning of kindergarten using *Raven's Progressive Matrices* and the *Peabody Picture Vocabulary Test,* widely used tests of nonverbal reasoning ability and verbal ability, respectively. Pre-testing is an important feature of the research design because it allows the evaluators to pre-select groups of students who are comparable from the beginning with respect to these two important school-related abilities. Any subsequently measured differences in achievement between these groups can then be reasonably attributed to other factors. The *Metropolitan Readiness Tests* are also being administered at the beginning of the kindergarten year in order to assess the students' readiness for school learning. The kindergarten level of this test assesses skills related to auditory memory, rhyming, letter recognition, visual matching, listening comprehension, quantitative language skills, and copying.

The progress of each subgroup will be monitored each spring until grade 3.

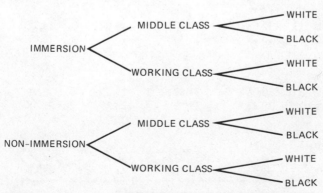

Figure 4   Diagram of Research Design for Cincinnati Evaluation

A battery of English language, French language, and mathematics tests, where appropriate, will be used for this purpose. Only English language achievement is being assessed at the end of kindergarten. The French language achievement of each immersion subgroup will be compared to that of the other immersion subgroups, and their English language and academic achievement, where assessed, will be compared to that of non-immersion students attending the same schools. To date, pilot groups have been evaluated as of the end of kindergarten and grade 1, and follow-up groups have been tested in kindergarten.

The results of the pilot kindergarten groups will be presented in detail here since they have been fully analyzed. Their grade 1 results will be summarized briefly. The kindergarten year is a full-day program with half the day being spent in French and half in English. This must be borne in mind when interpreting the English language test results. The following discussion will focus on each ethnic and socioeconomic subgroup separately (see Table 8).

All pre-test scores and the spring English language results were submitted to three-way analyses of variance, with program (immersion, non-immersion), socioeconomic status (middle class, working class) and ethnicity (black, white) the independent variables. As expected on the basis of the pre-selection procedures, the IM and EC students did not differ significantly on the pre-test measures, including the Metropolitan Readiness Tests (Table 8). Furthermore, the IM and EC students did not differ signficantly from one another when examined according to socioeconomic and ethnic subgroupings. Thus, one can be reasonably confident that the respective IM and EC subgroups were comparable from the outset with respect to nonverbal and verbal ability.

There were no significant between-group differences on the English language tests administered in the spring (see Table 8), nor were there significant interac-

Table 8   CINCINNATI PARTIAL IMMERSION PROGRAM: PRE-TEST RESULTS

	Middle Class		Working Class	
	IM	Non-IM	IM	Non-IM
Raven's Progressive				
Matrices (36)*				
Group $F=.43$ (1,134)				
White	15.08	15.93	14.69	14.77
Black	15.89	15.33	12.53	13.05
Peabody Picture				
Vocabulary Test (45)				
Group $F=.38$ (1,137)				
White	32.08	31.32	29.65	30.93
Black	29.22	29.89	26.35	27.68
Metropolitan Readiness				
Test (76)				
Group $F=1.61$ (1,136)				
White	60.52	58.43	58.76	54.77
Black	61.56	56.33	48.50	48.95

Note: Maximum test scores are presented in parentheses after test names.

tion effects between program type and either social class or ethnicity. This means that, taken as a whole, the IM group did not differ significantly from the EC group in English at the end of kindergarten. That there were no program by social class interaction effects means that the working class students from the immersion group scored just as well as the working class students from the regular English program and, similarly, the middle class IM students scored just as well as the middle class EC students. When the raw scores from the Metropolitan tests were converted to stanine equivalents, it was found that all four subgroups scored in the average stanine range (i.e., 4–5–6) and thus were performing on par with average kindergarten students throughout the United States.

That there were no statistically significant program by ethnicity interaction effects means that the black students from the immersion group scored just as well as the black students from the regular English program; similarly, the white students from the immersion program scored just as well as the white students from the English program. Thus, apparently students from both the majority white group and the minority black group experienced no setbacks in their native English language development as a result of participation in this partial immersion program. This is particularly interesting in the case of the black students who, for the most part, come to school speaking a nonstandard dialect of English and who, therefore, can be said to be functioning in both a second language during half the school day (French) and a second dialect during the other half (Standard English). The present results are encouraging because they indicate that these nonstandard dialect speakers appear to have no difficulty mastering literacy skills in the standard dialect. The same pattern of results was found one year later when the students were in grade 1. Follow-up testing of kindergarten students who were one year behind the pilot students also revealed no significant differences in English performance for those in immersion when compared to non-immersion students.

Turning now to French language development (Table 9)—the IM students were administered two French language tests, the *French Comprehension Test* (Barik, 1976) and the *Test linguistique maternelle* (Stevens, 1983b). The *French Comprehension Test* was designed to assess the listening comprehension skills of Canadian IM students. It assesses comprehension of words, sentences, and stories. Percentile scores, based on the performance of IM students attending half-day programs, are provided, making it possible to compare the achievement of the Cincinnati IM students to that of Canadian IM students. The *Test Linguistique Maternelle* has two components, one assessing listening comprehension and the other oral production skills in French. The comprehension component tests comprehension of vocabulary, short phrases, and short stories using a variety of toys, realia, and pictures. The test is administered to small groups of students. For the oral production component, the students are asked to name objects (vocabulary), to use complements and prepositions by describing the relationships of objects to one another, to produce short phrases in response to questions from the examiner, and to express themselves freely by telling a short story based on

Table 9   CINCINNATI PARTIAL IMMERSION PROGRAM: SUMMARY OF SPRING KINDERGARTEN TEST RESULTS

English Language Results

		Middle Class		Working Class	
		IM	Non-IM	IM	Non-IM
Metropolitan Readiness Test (73)*					
Group $F = 1.47$ (1,133)					
	White	58.61	61.04	56.12	55.46
	Black	57.13	57.33	45.19	51.11

French Language Results

	Middle Class		Working Class			
	White	Black	White	Black	F Ratio	df
French Comprehension Test						
raw score (45)	33.50	35.11	32.25	29.42	3.45	(1,68)
percentile	67	74	62	53		
Test linguistique maternelle						
listening (20)	13.12	15.33	13.31	12.37	.63	(1,68)
speaking (17)	5.31	5.00	5.50	4.17	.26	(1,67)
total (37)	18.42	20.33	18.81	16.44	.55	(1,67)

Note: Maximum test scores are presented in parentheses.

a sequence of cartoonlike pictures. The test is administered to each student individually and is scored using both objective and subjective criteria.

The French language test results were analyzed, using analysis of variance procedures, with social class, ethnicity, and sex of student as the independent variables. There were no significant differences between middle class and working class students or between black and white students on either test. In particular, the working class students scored just as well as the middle class students and the black students scored just as well as the white students. When the comprehension test results were converted to percentile form, it was found that all of the Cincinnati groups scored at the 50th percentile or better; that is, they scored better than 50 percent of the Canadian norming group. It can also be seen from Table 9 that the students' comprehension skills were generally better than their production skills. This is characteristic of both first and second language acquisition and has been noted frequently in evaluations of Canadian immersion programs. Their oral production skills, in fact, were very rudimentary and did not permit a detailed analysis; this is also common among Canadian kindergarten IM students.

Testing of the pilot students one year later, in grade 1, revealed that the Cincinnati students compared favorably with a norming group from Canada that consisted of grade 1 students who had been in a half-day French immersion program in kindergarten followed by an enriched French program of 90 minutes per day in grade 1. It was also found that there were no significant differences between the working class students and the middle class students on either French test or between the black students and the white students on Stevens's *Test Linguistique Maternelle.* In contrast to the kindergarten results, however, the black students scored significantly lower than the white students on the *French Comprehension Test* in grade 1. It is not clear whether these results represent an emerging ethnic group effect of a general nature or whether they also reflect differences in the nature of the skills evaluated by these two tests. Insofar as the *French Comprehension Test* is standardized and more cognitively loaded than Stevens's test, then it may call on the kinds of academic skills that black students have often been found to do poorly on. It is certainly the case that Stevens's test is more authentic with regard to naturalistic speaking and listening skills. It is these latter kinds of skills that have been found to be less susceptible to subgroup differences (see, for example, Genesee's, 1976a, and Bruck's, 1982, results for low achievers and language disabled students). We will be examining the performance of these subgroups carefully in subsequent evaluations in order to try and clarify these results.

Summary

Although these results are preliminary, they are highly consistent with evaluation results from Canada. Indeed, the results of the middle class students replicate the Canadian findings. In addition, the present results are encouraging insofar as they indicate that children from lower socioeconomic and/or from ethnic minority backgrounds can benefit from second language immersion programs. In some cases, in fact, these students attained the same levels of second language proficiency as did students from more advantaged families. These findings are consistent with Genesee's and Bruck's earlier findings concerning academic and native language ability and second language achievement in demonstrating that the acquisition of interpersonal communication skills in a second language is relatively insensitive to individual differences of a cognitive, linguistic, and, we can now add, albeit tentatively, social nature. It is important to emphasize here that these results pertain only to ethnic minority group children who speak a nonstandard dialect of English and therefore cannot necessarily be generalized to ethnic minority group children who do not speak English or who have limited proficiency in English. This issue will be discussed in the next three chapters.

IMMERSION AND TWO-WAY BILINGUALISM

The final application of immersion programs in the United States to be discussed here is similar to the preceding cases but at the same time distinctive in certain respects. Immersion programs have been used in a number of American school districts in conjunction with Title VII bilingual education programs for non-English proficient (NEP) or limited English proficient (LEP) students; New York State has a number of two-way programs in operation, and a number of two-way programs are being developed in California (see San Diego City Schools, 1982, and Cohen, 1975, for documented examples). In these cases English-speaking American children receive instruction through a second language during a substantial part of their elementary school program; English is gradually and slowly introduced until the curriculum is divided approximately equally between English and the second language. What distinguishes these programs from the enrichment programs described in the first section of this chapter is the inclusion of NEP or LEP students who are native speakers of the second language. In fact, these programs are usually designed initially to provide bilingual instruction to NEP/LEP students in compliance with guidelines from the Office of Civil Rights. What distinguishes these programs from conventional bilingual education programs is the inclusion of majority language, English-speaking students during both the non-English and English portions of the program. These programs, therefore, aim for two-way bilingualism in that they promote bilingual proficiency in English and the non-English language among both native English-speaking students and NEP/LEP students. Thus, these programs represent an innovation on both the Canadian immersion programs and the United States bilingual programs.

The San Diego Immersion Project

The first program of this sort was instituted in San Diego in 1975. It was designed to meet

> the instructional needs of Spanish-speaking students with limited proficiency in English. . . . In addition, since the program also includes native English-speaking students, it allows minority language students to enjoy full integration while it provides exemplary second-language instruction for native speakers of English. (San Diego City Schools, 1982, p. iii)

Approximately 60 percent of the students in the program are Spanish-speaking and the remaining 40 percent English speaking. They are grouped together in multi-level grades. Participation in the program is voluntary for both the Spanish- and English-speaking students. Project schools are located in areas of the district where there is a sizeable population of Spanish-speaking students. As of 1982, there were six project schools. Although no information concerning the students' socioeconomic characteristics is contained in the project report, it seems likely that the Spanish-speaking students are from predominantly working class homes.

Spanish is the main medium of instruction during a pre-school year and in kindergarten to grade 3. English is taught for approximately 20 minutes per day in pre-school, 30 minutes per day in kindergarten, and 60 minutes per day in grades 2 and 3. There is a strong emphasis on oral language training and readiness training in these grades. Instruction is divided approximately equally between English and Spanish during the remainder of the program, i.e., grades 4, 5, and 6. Spanish language instruction during pre-school to grade 3 is provided by a bilingual teacher with the assistance of a bilingual aide. English language instruction during these grades is provided by a different English-speaking teacher. This strategy of language separation has been adopted from the Montreal immersion model in order to promote the use and acquisition of Spanish to the maximum. It is felt that mixed use of the two languages by the same teachers even during different instructional periods might lead the students to use English as much as possible, since it often tends to be the preferred language even among young non-English-speaking children.

In grades 4 to 6, the teacher uses both Spanish and English to teach the curriculum but never during the same instructional period. This is a marked departure from the "concurrent method" of instruction commonly used in many early bilingual education programs. According to this strategy, both English and the non-English language were used interchangeably and in some cases non-English translations of English utterances were even provided. It is now generally felt that this approach engenders confusion or disregard for the language in which the students are not proficient and is, therefore, counterproductive. The San Diego project has sought to create a Spanish-only setting during the early elementary grades. This is very important since it means that both the Spanish- and English-speaking students are given every opportunity to develop high levels of proficiency in Spanish for academic purposes. As Cummins (1981) has pointed out, high levels of proficiency in the bilingual's two languages may be necessary to incur positive cognitive effects. As well, a high level of proficiency in Spanish is necessary if both the Spanish- and English-speaking students are to benefit from positive interdependence between their two languages.

In order to maximize the language learning benefits to be derived from having native speakers from both language groups in the same class, students from both language groups are always mixed for instructional purposes. However, since the curriculum developers felt that simply mixing both language groups would not ensure interaction and communication, they have incorporated a good deal of structured classroom activities that encourage interaction. A detailed and coherent syllabus based on current thinking regarding language and learning has been designed to integrate and reconcile the different instructional and linguistic needs of these students. An example from the Kindergarten and Grade 1 instructional guidelines will illustrate this point:

Two instructional techniques compensate for the differences in the Spanish vocabulary and language patterns at the command of the K–1 class's two native language groups at this early grade level. First, when the K–1 class's students are receiving Spanish oral language instruction as a total class, visual aids—in the form of pictures, chalkboard drawings, gestures, and pantomines

—are used to insure that the native speakers of English comprehend what is being discussed. Second, when the class is divided for individualized oral language instruction, the instructional emphasis for native-English-speaking students is on reinforcing beginning Spanish vocabulary and language patterns. (These same techniques apply to native-Spanish-speaking students during the English language period.) (San Diego City Schools, 1982, p. 41)

The San Diego *Bilingual Demonstration Project,* as it is officially called, has been evaluated on an annual basis by an independent evaluator. Both Spanish- and English-speaking project students have been assessed for 1) English and Spanish oral language proficiency, 2) English and Spanish reading achievement, and 3) math tested in Spanish and in English. Student performance in each domain has been interpreted with respect to norms provided by test developers. In general, this is a less satisfactory basis for interpretation than the performance of local comparison groups of the type used in the Canadian evaluations or in Culver City. The results of the Spanish- and English-speaking students in the project were combined and treated as a single group "since instructional goals are the same for students of both native language groups." (1982, p. 185) Thus, it is not possible to examine the results of each group separately. It is possible that the English language results are inflated by the results of the Spanish-speaking students and vice versa for the English language results of the Spanish-speaking students. Additional analyses were planned to examine the results for each language subgroup (Lear, 1985, pers. comm.). In the meantime, the results of the combined analyses will be reviewed.

The results of these analyses revealed that, as a group, the students entered the program below grade level in English but had either attained grade level proficiency by the end of the program (i.e., grade 6) or had made good progress toward grade level proficiency. More specifically, kindergarten-entry students progressed from an average rating of "limited" proficiency in *oral* English to an average rating of "proficient" in three years; they progressed from one year below grade level in English *reading* in grade 2 to eight months behind grade level in grade 5; and they progressed from six months behind grade level in *math* tested in English in grade 2 to one month below grade level in grade 5. A second cohort of students who entered the program in grade 1 fared better in the long run than those who entered in kindergarten—by grade 6 the grade 1-entry students had achieved a "proficient" rating in oral English and they scored one year above grade level in English reading and in math tested in English. The differences between the kindergarten-entry and the grade 1-entry student results may be due to the fact that the latter were gathered in grade 6 and the former in grade 5. Or, they may be due to initial differences in ability or in socioeconomic characteristics. The use of carefully selected comparison groups from the same communities as the project students' would help to unravel these possibilities.

The Spanish language results are quite variable. The students received an oral rating of "proficient" within two years of entering the program; kindergarten-entry students scored five months behind grade level on the Spanish reading subtest in grade 5, while the grade 1-entry students scored *two years above* grade level by grade 6, having scored five months below grade level in grades 3, 4, and 5. The evaluator offers no explanation for this rapid improvement, nor for the discrepancy between the two cohorts. Both cohorts scored between two and three months above grade level by the end of grades 5 and 6 on the Spanish math subtest. Variability in the test results may be due in part to the use of grade equivalent scores which are generally regarded as problematic and difficult to interpret (Cronbach, 1984).

A final assessment of the San Diego project awaits the results of analyses of each language group considered separately. Notwithstanding the inconclusive nature of these results, they illustrate the importance of longitudinal evaluations of school programs of this sort. This point has been illustrated repeatedly in the Canadian evaluations where it has generally been found that there is a lag in the development of English language literacy skills during those grades of the program when English language arts are not taught. As noted in chapter three, follow-up testing of these students has found that they achieve the same level of proficiency as English control students within one year of receiving English language arts instruction. Had the programs not been viewed as longitudinal from the beginning, then the results from early evaluations might well have led to their abandonment because of putative English language deficits. It was only through longitudinal testing that these "deficits" were seen to be short term.

This issue warrants particular emphasis in the case of bilingual education programs for LEP/NEP students where there is often an urgency, sometimes required by law, to "exit" students from the program as quickly as possible, thereby increasing the risk that normal grade level proficiency in language skills and/or academic achievement will not be attained. In fact, as we shall see in the next chapter, legal guidelines in some districts permit mainstreaming of LEP/NEP students as soon as they score at the 25th percentile on a standardized test of English language achievement. Such low-level performance would hardly ensure successful integration into an all-English class.

SUMMARY

The evaluation results reviewed in this chapter suggest a number of general conclusions concerning the effectiveness of second language immersion programs for educating American students. The conclusions to follow are somewhat tentative pending the outcomes of ongoing research, including, for example, follow-up testing in the Cincinnati project and the results of subgroup analyses in San Diego.

With respect to English language development, the Culver City, Cincinnati, and Montgomery County evaluations indicate that English-speaking American students experience no deficits in their English language development as a result of participation in an immersion program of either the total or partial type. The results from these three projects are especially important because appropriate comparison groups were included in the evaluations. The Culver City and Montgomery County results are highly consistent with Canadian results, as one would expect in view of the fact that these two projects are highly similar to many of the Canadian projects.

Of particular interest are the Cincinnati results which go beyond the Canadian findings in indicating that children from a minority ethnic group, many of whom probably speak a nonstandard dialect of English and/or come from lower socioeconomic backgrounds, also show normal levels of first language development in immersion programs. These findings extend Genesee's and Bruck's findings concerning the suitability of immersion programs for students with characteristics that might otherwise put them at a disadvantage in school. We can now add that second language immersion programs can be used effectively with not only students with below-average intellectual and first language ability but also students from minority ethnic backgrounds and/or possibly from minority dialect backgrounds as well. Studies of this sort are important because they provide an empirical basis for formulating policy regarding eligibility for immersion. In fact, these results provide no justification for local educational policy that seeks to exclude such children from participating in immersion programs.

With respect to academic achievement, and mathematics in particular, the Culver City and Montgomery County results indicate that the students had no difficulty assimilating new academic knowledge and skills, even though they were taught through a second language. The English language and mathematics results from the San Diego evaluation corroborate the above findings but are less conclusive, owing to the use of a combined-groups analysis in that study.

The second language results are more complex and varied. With regard to speaking and listening comprehension, it can be said that the American IM students under evaluation attained functional proficiency in the target language. This was evidenced by their performance on speaking and listening tests standardized on native speakers or on Canadian students participating in early immersion programs. Observations of the students' second language use both in school and outside school, as reported by the Culver City evaluators, also attest to high levels of functional proficiency. The Cincinnati results are important in suggesting that IM students from lower socioeconomic backgrounds and/or from minority ethnic groups may be as effective in developing speaking and listening skills in the second language as students from middle socioeconomic backgrounds and/or from the majority ethnic group. At the same time, it has also been reported in the Culver City evaluations that the IM students had not attained truly nativelike mastery of the target language even after six years of immersion in Spanish. This has been found by Canadian evaluators as well and is probably not unexpected given the language-learning limitations of most school environments. What is noteworthy is that their linguistic deficiencies do not seem to impair their communicative proficiency. In view of these findings, extracurricular second language experiences, such as summer camps or exchange visits, seem advisable in order to bring the students up to native levels.

Assessments of IM students' second language reading skills have varied from approximately one year below grade level (Culver City) to above average (Montgomery County) or above grade level (San Diego). Variations in grade level, student ability, socioeconomic status, and other factors may account for these differences. Notwithstanding this variation, even the lowest reading assessment results attest to relatively high levels of achievement.

It is interesting to note that all of the U.S. immersion projects have been of the "early" type; there are no "late" immersion programs. This option may be of potential interest to American educators and parents who wish to concentrate on first language development prior to extensive exposure to a second language.

The conclusions reported here corroborate the Canadian findings in most important respects. In summary, they indicate that immersion programs constitute a feasible and effective way for English-speaking American students to attain high levels of second language proficiency without risk to their native language development or academic achievement. At the same time, the American projects afford researchers and educators an opportunity to extend their knowledge of the immersion approach by providing a number of program variations which, although not as popular as their Canadian counterparts, are truly innovative. Thus, the magnet immersion school projects have been instructive in demonstrating the suitability of the immersion approach for students from diverse socioeconomic and ethnolinguistic backgrounds, in contrast to the majority of Canadian programs and the American enrichment programs which involve predominantly middle class, white, Standard English-speaking students. The two-way bilingual/immersion projects are instructive as examples of truly integrated bilingual programs involving participants from both language/cultural groups. By providing peer contact in the target language, this approach offers a solution to some of the shortcomings inherent in immersion programs in which only the teacher has native proficiency in the target language.

At a time when a growing number of educational authorities—including, for example, the President's Commission on Foreign Language and International Studies—have expressed concern over Americans' general incompetence in foreign languages and their ignorance of foreign cultures, the immersion approach offers an educational response that is showing itself to be both feasible and effective within the American public school system.

CHAPTER 9

Educating Minority Language Children: The Case for Bilingual Education

At about the same time that Canadian educators were developing innovative second language immersion programs for English-speaking children, American educators were beginning to address equally important and related issues concerning the education of non-English or limited English proficient children in the United States. As in Canada, there are sociopolitical and psychoeducational aspects to the American story; both will be touched on briefly in this chapter (see also California State Department of Education, 1981, and Kloss, 1977).

HISTORICAL ANTECEDENTS OF BILINGUAL EDUCATION

In contrast to the documented success of English-speaking students in second language immersion programs, children from minority language groups who either lack or have limited proficiency in English often experience disproportionately high rates of failure in schools where the majority language is used as the sole medium of curricular instruction—so called "submersion" programs (Aguirre & Cepeda, 1981, in Parker, 1985a; Ogbu, 1978). This has been the case for minority groups in other developed areas of the world as well as North America (see Skutnabb-Kangas, 1980, for a discussion of the European case; and deVos, 1973, for the Japanese case). Non-English speaking children have always constituted a large percentage of the North American school population and, contrary to commonly held beliefs, their cultural adaptation and economic success are not largely the result of education (Greer, 1972; Steinberg, 1981). As Parker (1985a, p.2) points out, the belief that schools have been the great vehicles of adjustment, assimilation, and upward economic mobility for the millions of immigrants who came to America in the first half of this century is unsubstantiated by the evidence. On the one hand, high percentages of children who were eligible for public education did not, in fact, attend school. For example, as late as 1914, there were only five high schools in Manhattan and the Bronx, a remarkably small number for an urban area that even at that time was one of the most densely populated in the United States (Steinberg, 1981). On the other hand, even those students who attended school dropped out in high numbers before completing high school. Greer (1972) has documented that retention rates among Russians, Germans, and the Irish, for example, were very low: Russian—16 percent; German—15 percent; and Irish—.1 percent. Even when the compulsory age of attendance was raised from 12 to 16 years of age between 1917 and 1925, attendance in high school remained low—4.7 percent to 6.6 percent of eligible students in New York were registered in high school. Thus, school failure and drop-outs are not a recent phenomenon in public education.

The 1960s marked the beginning of a period of serious discussion and debate concerning the lack of academic success of minority group students, including the economically underprivileged and ethnically different as well as language minority students. Indeed, the sixties were a period of significant social reevaluation and change on a number of different fronts. Castellanos (1983) has identified a number of sociopolitical factors and events of particular significance for the development of bilingual education in the United States, including immigration patterns following the Second World War, events following the Cuban Revolution in 1958, and the Civil Rights Movement of the 1960s. Whereas previous immigrants to the United States had come mainly from Western European countries (e.g., Britain, Germany, or Scandinavia), immigration following World War II was increasingly from Eastern Europe and the Caribbean (i.e., Puerto Rico and Cuba). Like other immigrant groups, the new waves of European and Puerto Rican immigrants were poor and often uneducated, but unlike previous immigrants, they were culturally and even physically quite different from other Americans. Puerto Ricans presented a particularly interesting case. Technically speaking, they were not immigrants since Puerto Rico had been a U.S. territory since the turn of the century. They, therefore, often arrived in the United States expecting to be treated like citizens, and many of them expected to travel freely between the mainland and Puerto Rico. The existing school system was not prepared for these new kinds of immigrants—immigrants who could not or did not want to assimilate readily. Furthermore, since public education was more available and attendance more strictly enforced than previously, these students were not so likely to drop out of school as previous generations of students had. As a result, they posed a persistent "problem" for educators.

Of particular importance for the future education of minority language groups was the influx of Cuban refugees in 1959 following Castro's coup d'etat. Unlike previous immigrants and indigenous Spanish-speaking Americans, the Cuban refugees were middle and upper-middle class and were professionally trained. Moreover, they were victims of a Communist takeover and therefore were welcomed heartily by the citizens and government of democratic America. Moreover, they were thought to be transient and thus were provided with educational services befitting a group that was likely to return once Castro was overthrown. The Dade County school system, in fact, established a Spanish language school for the children of Cuban refugees. This program paved the way in 1963 for the first bilingual (Spanish–English) education program in the United States after World War II—Coral Way Elementary School in Miami. Approximately half of the students in this program were Cuban and half were Anglo-American. Districts in other parts of the United States with heavy concentrations of Spanish-speaking, largely Mexican-American children soon followed suit with similar bilingual schools.

About the same time, sweeping civil rights legislation also prepared the way for nationwide programs of bilingual education. The Civil Rights Act of 1964 declared that no person on the basis of race or national origin be excluded from or discriminated against in any program receiving federal financial assistance. In 1964 President Johnson declared the "War on Poverty," and in 1965 restrictive immigration quotas were lifted and the Voting Rights Act was passed ensuring the suffrage of minority citizens. All of these events marked the beginning of the end of an era of laissez-faire attitude toward economically disadvantaged and ethnolinguistically different citizens of the United States. The first federal initiative in support of bilingual education for minority language children followed these events shortly.

In 1967, Senator Ralph Yarborough of Texas proposed to amend the Elementary and Secondary Education Act (ESEA) of 1965 in order to assist local educational authorities to establish bilingual education programs for Spanish-speaking children. The original proposal underwent numerous revisions until it was finally passed by Congress in 1968 as Title VII of ESEA—the Bilingual Education Act. The legislation that was finally enacted applied to all non- or limited English proficient students, and while it supported "new and innovative elementary and secondary school programs to meet the special needs" of these children, it did not in fact specify the exact form of these programs—Yarborough's original proposal for bilingual education was no longer part of the legislation. The amendment left local educational agencies to decide what specific programs they would provide. The conditions of the Act determined that these special educational programs would be compensatory or remedial in nature, however. The compensatory nature of the program derived from two aspects of the Act. First, it stipulated that these special services or programs would be offered only temporarily until such time as the student could function effectively in an English classroom. Second, the Act gave priority to low-income families and, thereby, branded non-English speaking children with socioeconomic stigma; this provision has since been changed. These two provisions of the Act then effectively defined the situation as one of linguistic deficiency and social inferiority. Bilingual education has never recovered from these assignations.

Additional support for bilingual education, as yet still not specified, came from two other events. In 1970, the U.S. Office for Civil Rights issued an official memorandum to all school districts with 5 percent or more national origin minority students. The memorandum was motivated by concerns that these children were not being treated within the spirit of the 1964 Civil Rights Act which forbade discrimination and segregation on the basis of race and national origin. In particular, contravention of the equal treatment clause might be pleaded insofar as national-origin students were precluded from effective participation in school because they could not speak or understand English. Therefore, local school agencies were directed to take affirmative action to rectify such situations.

Around the same time, a class action suit was filed in 1969 on behalf of the Chinese community in San Francisco against the San Francisco school system—*Lau* v. *Nichols*. The plaintiffs claimed that their children were denied "equal educational opportunity" since they were compelled to attend schools in which instruction was provided in a language they did not understand—just as the Office for Civil Rights had feared. The case eventually reached the Supreme Court of the United States, and in 1974 it was decided in favor of the plaintiffs. As Circuit Judge Hufstedler argued:

> There is no equality of treatment merely by providing students with the same facilities, textbooks, teachers and curriculum; for students who do not understand English are effectively foreclosed from any meaningful education. (in Castellanos, 1983, p. 117)

The Court did not specify what educational action would be satisfactory, but it did issue a number of specifications which could be best fulfilled by bilingual education.

Also in 1974, the U.S. Congress passed the Education Amendments Act which superseded the 1968 Title VII ESEA and for the first time provided a definition of what constituted bilingual education:

> It is instruction given in, and study of, English and (to the extent necessary to allow a child to progress effectively through the education system) the native language of the children of limited English-speaking ability; and such instruction is given with appreciation for the cultural heritage of such children, and (with respect to elementary school instruction) such instruction shall (to the extent necessary) be in all courses or subjects of study which will allow a child to progress effectively through the educational system.

Thus, federally funded programs were to include native language instruction and cultural enrichment; ESL alone was not sufficient. In effect, the legislation recognized the importance of instruction through the native language as a means of promoting academic achievement during that time when the students lacked the English language skills necessary to attain and maintain grade-appropriate levels of achievement. At the same time, the students were to be receiving English language instruction so that they could make the transition to an all-English instructional curriculum.

In 1975, the Office of Education of the Department of Health, Education and Welfare convened a panel of bilingual experts to establish guidelines that could be used by local educational agencies in serving minority language students and that could also be used by the Office for Civil Rights in monitoring compliance with the Court's ruling on the Lau versus Nichols case. The "Lau Remedies," as the commission's guidelines came to be known, supported and reinforced the definition of bilingual education contained in the Education Amendments Act of 1974. Guidelines concerning eligibility for bilingual education were initially established by the Lau Remedies and tended to restrict participation to students with limited or no proficiency in English. These have since been dropped and at present eligibility criteria are much broader than previously so that students with some proficiency in English and even native English-speaking students are eligible. "Exit" guidelines have been established through a combination of federal and local policies. In general, exit criteria encourage "mainstreaming" the students into all-English classes as quickly as possible; for example, in some districts, students can be moved out of a bilingual class if they score at only the 25th percentile on a standardized English language test.

Thus, in brief, bilingual education for minority language students in the United States has come to be defined in the following terms: initial academic instruction through the medium of the students' home language accompanied by English-as-a-Second-Language instruction. Use of the home language during this time serves the dual functions of 1) allowing academic instruction to be given in a language that the students know and therefore can learn through; and 2) making more time available for English language learning—both in school, through ESL instruction unencumbered by the necessity to use the language for academic purposes, and out of school, through normal contact with native speakers. This is continued until it is deemed that the student can receive all curricular instruction through English, at which time instruction through the home language is usually discontinued. The programs are also expected to teach and support the students' home culture. The primary goal of the majority of programs is clearly to teach the students enough English language skills so that they can be integrated into all-English classes; very few of the programs espouse continuing support for the home language. Thus, in contrast to the Canadian immersion programs, these programs clearly aim for transitional bilingualism.

This characterization of U.S. bilingual education is necessarily general and oversimplified. There is, in fact, considerable variation among programs. The present characterization is nevertheless the basis for a model of bilingual education that has been the topic of discussion, analysis, and controversy. It is this model of bilingual education that has been scrutinized by researchers and debated by politicians, educators, and the public alike. Therefore, this model will be the focus of discussion in the remainder of this chapter. Unlike the preceding chapters on immersion, this one will not attempt to be comprehensive in its coverage, especially of the research. The sheer volume of research, much of it below acceptable scientific standards, as well as the tremendous unsystematic programmatic variation, would make such an approach intractable and of dubious merit. Rather, a number of issues pertaining to the psychoeducational (this chapter) and the sociocultural (chapter ten) bases of bilingual education will be examined. Chapter eleven will then examine what immersion education has to say about teaching English as a Second Language to minority language students.

PSYCHOEDUCATIONAL FOUNDATIONS OF BILINGUAL EDUCATION

In addition to sociopolitical hurdles, bilingual education has had a number of conceptual hurdles to jump in order to convince both educators and the lay public of its educational validity. On the one hand, it seems to make patently good sense that children be educated through their home language if schooling is to be effective. In fact, in an historic document, UNESCO (1953) declared that every child has the right to receive primary education through the medium of the vernacular. On the other hand, it has seemed counterintuitive to many Americans that primary education through the medium of a non-English language is the most effective means for teaching non-English speaking children English. In particular, it is not immediately obvious to most how reducing English instruction, as is the case for bilingual education in comparison with all-English education, can be a better way to promote English language learning than teaching the students only in English. Cummins (1981) has labeled this the "less is better" hypothesis in contrast to the common-sense notion that "more is better."

Acceptance of bilingual education in the United States has also been made somewhat difficult by the success of the Canadian immersion programs. If, it has been argued, English-speaking Canadian students can be educated successfully through the medium of a second language in immersion programs, then why should a similar approach not work for minority language children in the United States? To the extent that this means placing minority language children in ordinary classrooms where English is spoken without making special linguistic or cultural adjustments (so-called submersion), then this approach is tantamount to advocating educational practices that were prevalent prior to the 1968 Bilingual Education Act. However, as we noted earlier, it was precisely the documented failure of this approach that led to bilingual education in the first place. Since this approach has become unacceptable, arguments have also been made for a modified or structured immersion approach for the education of minority language students (Baker & de Kanter, 1983; Epstein, 1977). Baker and de Kanter defined structured immersion as instruction in English, the students' second language, by teachers who understand the students' home language. The teachers permit the students to respond in their first language even though the teachers themselves always respond in English. Furthermore, the curriculum is structured so that prior knowledge of English is not assumed and content is taught in ways that can be understood by the students. An evaluation of the relative effectiveness of bilingual education versus structured immersion is currently underway by Ramirez et al. (1986) and will be discussed later. Let us now examine the prevailing psychoeducational rationale underlying bilingual education.

Cummins's Theoretical Framework

Cummins (1981) has argued that an understanding of bilingual education requires an understanding of both the development of bilingual proficiency and the relationship between language proficiency and academic achievement. The theoretical framework that Cummins has developed to describe these relationships also proposes to reconcile second language immersion programs for English-speaking, majority group students and use of the home language in bilingual education for non-English speaking, minority group students. There are basically three components to the model: 1) the nature of language proficiency and its relationship to academic achievement; 2) the relationship between first and second language development; and 3) sociocultural factors and language proficiency development. Each will be described and their interrelationships examined.

The Nature of Language Proficiency

Cummins (1981) has proposed that language proficiency, first and second, can be conceptualized in terms of two distinct continua (see Figure 5). One of these continua is related to the degree of contextual support available for expressing or comprehending meaning through language. This continuum is characterized at one extreme as context-embedded and at the other extreme as context-reduced. In the case of context-embedded language use, meaning conveyed by language is supported by a wide range of non-linguistic or para-linguistic cues.

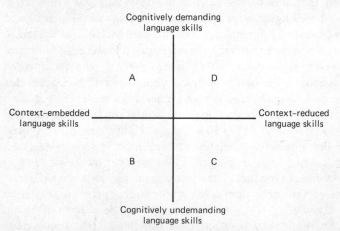

Figure 5 Cummins's Model of Language Proficiency Development (1981)

An example of such language use would be a conversation between two individuals who know one another and who are talking about a familiar topic. In such communication, there is no need for the interlocutors to use linguistically elaborated or precise messages to convey the intended meaning; much of what they want to convey can be left unsaid or implicit. Context-embedded communication of this type is characteristic of much day-to-day language use. Furthermore, children's experience with language prior to formal schooling is usually of this sort. In fact, one could say that this is the type of language proficiency that all children acquire when learning their first language.

In contrast, context-reduced communication lacks such contextual support so that the message must be conveyed in a linguistically explicit and detailed fashion if it is to be effective. An example of context-reduced communication would be listening to a lecture on an unfamiliar topic. In this case, meaning must be conveyed in a linguistically explicit and elaborated way. Much of what goes on in school during academic instruction is of this sort—the teacher is trying to convey information or to teach skills to the learner that are not already known and that cannot be explicated easily by reference to their day-to-day experiences. Certainly the essence of reading and writing for academic purposes is explicit and precise use of language to convey meaning.

The second continuum which is independent of the first one is defined in terms of the degree of active intellectual or cognitive involvement required by the communication task that the interlocutors are engaged in. Cognitive involvement can be conceptualized in terms of the amount of information the individual must process simultaneously or in close succession in order to carry out or complete communication. Another way of conceptualizing this continuum is in terms of the degree of automaticity or mastery of the linguistic skills needed to achieve communication. The kind of language used to do one's shopping, buy lunch in a cafeteria, or talk about last night's television programs would be examples of cognitively undemanding communication tasks. Cummins (1981) suggests that examples of cognitively demanding communication would be writing an essay on an abstract topic or persuading others that your point of view rather than theirs is correct:

> In these situations, it is necessary to stretch one's linguistic resources (i.e., grammatical, sociolinguistic, discourse, and strategic competencies) to the limit in order to achieve one's communicative goals. (p. 13)

The cognitive continuum of Cummins's model is intended to address developmental issues of language proficiency. Tasks may often be cognitively demanding the first time they are performed, but become less demanding with practice. Thus, language tasks and skills move from the cognitively demanding to the cognitively undemanding end of the continuum as the individual achieves mastery of the requisite linguistic skills.

Cummins's model of language proficiency is defined largely in terms of *linguistic* skills and factors. There are good reasons for extending the model to incorporate processing information and performing tasks that are essentially sociocultural in nature. This extension seems justified in view of the fact that the knowledge contained in or presupposed by much verbal communication is often culturally based and culturally transmitted. Inclusion of sociocultural factors is also justified on the grounds that most communication takes place in a social situation and effective communication requires analysis, comprehension, and reaction to social parameters of the situation. In fact, frequently the social parameters that describe the context of language use require explicit marking in the verbal messages or at least require modifications of the message. For example, in French, the social status of the listener dictates which form of the second person pronoun (*tu* or *vous*) will be used. Or, communication in an informal situation calls for the use of certain lexical items and not others. The social parameters may not always be physically present and yet may still be important. For example, there are social conventions pertaining to writing business letters versus personal letters. Effective letter writing may be impeded if one does not know these conventions, even though one may actually have the linguistic competence to respond to the relevant parameters in linguistic form.

Other things being equal, social situations that require processing complex social information or sociocultural information that is unfamiliar to the individual will be cognitively demanding, whereas social situations that do not require such information processing will be cognitively undemanding. It follows that a given situation can make different cognitive demands on different individuals. For instance, situations that are cognitively undemanding for native speakers familiar with the sociocultural parameters of the situation can be cognitively demanding for second or foreign language speakers who are not familiar with them. For example, buying groceries, which is a simple routine in one's home country, can be a demanding task in a foreign country where one does not know what the social norms are. An inability to processing the social cues that define the interactional context can effectively block or impede verbal communication to the extent that one does not perceive and/or understand the pertinent social parameters of the situation.

Research, cited earlier, on the relationship between IQ and second language achievement among French immersion students in Montreal supports Cummins's distinction (Genesee, 1976b). It will be recalled that this research found that there was a positive association between proficiency in French as a second language for literacy purposes (i.e., reading and writing) and overall level of intellectual ability among elementary school students in early French immersion programs, but no such relationship was found for the same students in the case of interpersonal communication skills, i.e., speaking and listening comprehension. That overall intellectual ability has a differential relationship with academic language skills and interpersonal communication skills of a non-academic nature implies that there are two distinct types of language proficiency. Other researchers have proposed distinctions that are similar to Cummins's (see, for example, Olson, 1977; and Snow, 1985).

It is important to emphasize that the distinctions being made here are not simply between literacy skills and oral language skills. Oral use of language for interpersonal communication can also be characterized as context reduced and cognitively demanding; for example, a lecture on astrophysics. Conversely, written language can be context embedded and cognitively undemanding; for example, a note to one's spouse to "pick up the bread on the way home." Literacy skills will be used as an example of context-reduced, cognitively demanding language skills for convenience and because literacy skills as practiced in most school situations are of this type.

Cummins argues that a major reason why minority language students often fail in all-English programs is because the language proficiency required of them in such programs (namely, context reduced) is not the same as the kind of language proficiency they bring to school with them (namely, context embedded). Moreover, he argues, because of their non-English background the English curriculum is more context reduced and cognitively demanding than for native English-speaking students. Cummins points out that educational personnel are often "fooled" by minority students' glib use of English for primary social interaction to think that they are prepared to handle academic instruction through English. We would also add that all-English schooling could impede the academic development of minority language students, insofar as the cultures of the classroom and school are different from that of the student's home and therefore are so cognitively demanding that they effectively preclude the student from full participation in the curriculum.

It follows, therefore, that effective pedagogy that seeks to promote language skills for context-reduced, cognitively demanding situations will initially provide instruction that is context embedded from the learner's point of view. Effectively, the task of the educator is to move students from quadrant A types of language proficiency to quadrant C (see Figure 4). This probably applies to some majority language children as well. Minority language students have the added task of having to learn basic language skills in English before they can proceed to learn the kinds of language skills needed for academic work.

Bilingual Proficiency Development

The second component of Cummins's framework concerns the developmental relationship between first language proficiency and second language proficiency. As Cummins (1981) notes:

> The argument that if minority children are deficient in English, then they
> need instruction in English, not in their L1, implies: a) that proficiency in L1
> is separate from proficiency in English, and b) that there is a direct relation-
> ship between exposure to a language (in home or school) and achievement in
> that language. (p. 22)

Cummins has referred to this conceptualization of bilingual proficiency as the Separate Underlying Proficiency (or SUP) model. In fact, there is no evidence in support of this notion. Rather, the available evidence supports a model of bilingual proficiency that is developmentally interdependent; that is to say, development of proficiency in one language can contribute to development in another language (see also Snow, 1985). Cummins has referred to this as the Common Underlying Proficiency (or CUP) model. He postulates further that interdependence between first and second language proficiency development is most characteristic of context-reduced, cognitively demanding language proficiency (e.g., literacy skills for academic purposes). It is less likely to characterize the development of interpersonal communication skills of the context-embedded, cognitively undemanding nature. Indeed, there is much evidence that second language literacy proceeds quite quickly if literacy skills have already been learned in the first language (Cummins, Swain, Nakajima, Handscombe, & Green, 1981; Skutnabb-Kangas & Toukomaa, 1976).

It follows, therefore, that educating minority language students through the home language, especially insofar as they acquire context-reduced, cognitively demanding kinds of language skills, can facilitate English language development through linguistic interdependence. Viewed from another perspective, one does not have to begin teaching minority language students English reading and writing skills from the beginning if they have already acquired literacy skills in their home language and if they have acquired some oral/aural proficiency in English. This phenomenon is also referred to as "positive transfer." It is likely that transfer will occur only if the students have achieved some high level of proficiency in the skills in question; conversely, it seems unlikely that skills that are poorly mastered in one language will transfer to another language. This point is very important because it means that bilingual education programs should seek to develop a high level of proficiency in the students' academic language skills in the home language before exiting them to all-English classrooms if they are to take advantage of this interdependence effect. Indeed, this is the primary linguistic justification for bilingual education. Unfortunately, this is all too infrequently the case, as we have already seen.

Neither the language proficiency model nor the developmental interdependence hypothesis proposed by Cummins is adequate to account for the high levels of school failure experienced by minority language students relative to majority language students, since they beg the question of why the former come to school lacking the requisite language experiences more than majority group children. It is the third component of Cummins's framework that addresses this issue.

Sociocultural Factors and Bilingual Proficiency

Any conceptual framework that attempts either 1) to explain the disproportionate failure of minority language students in all-English schools or 2) to reconcile the effectiveness of immersion programs for majority language children with the advisability of bilingual education programs for minority language children must ultimately be based on sociocultural or group-related factors. This follows logically from the fact that the phenomenon in question pertains to groups of students. Whatever the ultimate explanation of this complex phenomenon, it cannot be in terms of a simple language mismatch effect, whereby the school failure of minority language students is explained by a mismatch between the language spoken at home and the language spoken at school; otherwise, one could not explain the success of immersion programs. It cannot be a simple socioeconomic effect or cultural mismatch effect, whereby the failure of minority language students in school is explained by their disadvantaged socioeconomic status or by the cultural mismatch between their homes and the school; otherwise, one could not explain the noteworthy success of students from some minority language groups. Ogbu (1986), for example, notes that a longitudinal study carried out in Stockton, California, found that over a twenty-year period Asian students achieved disproportionately high levels of attendance at the junior college level but that Mexican-American students continued to be underrepresented. Others have reported similar "success stories" for some minority language students (see Coleman, 1966, and Gibson, 1983, for other examples).

Cummins (1981) has proposed that an explanation may be found in the feelings of some minority language groups toward themselves and toward the majority group (see Cummins, 1985, for a discussion of sociocultural factors in bilingual education). In particular, he notes that minority language student groups that do poorly in school often have ambivalent or negative feelings toward their own culture and language and toward the majority culture and language. He suggests that these feelings can influence patterns of child–parent interaction that, in turn, can influence the development of communicative proficiency. Specifically, he has suggested that parents from groups that are ambivalent about their own culture and language may be prone to discourage development of the home language and concomitantly encourage development of the majority language. Such parents may attempt to use English with their children in the home. Because of the parents' limited proficiency in English, this in turn may lead to language use in the home that is relatively restricted and therefore does not prepare the children for the kinds of language skills that are required in a school setting. In effect, these parents may be limiting the range of language experiences that they offer their children because their own proficiency in English is not sufficient to provide a wide range of language experiences.

In contrast, minority language parents who are proud of their cultural heritage are more likely to promote development of the home language and to provide language experiences that prepare their children for the kinds of context-reduced, cognitively demanding language skills they will need in school. In fact, research by Dolson (1985a) has indicated that Hispanic students in Los Angeles who used Spanish at home performed as well as or significantly better on a number of academic tests than similar students who used English at home.

If Cummins's explanation is to account for the success of immersion programs for majority language children, then it must follow that English-speaking parents are proud of the English language and culture and consequently promote the development of a wide range of English language skills, some of which are useful in school. The students' English language proficiency as developed in the home can in turn contribute to their second language development in school, at least insofar as academic language skills are concerned. However, Cummins does not explicate this part of his model.

Heath (1986) concurs with Cummins that language experiences in the home can be important for children's later success in school. According to Heath, different sociocultural groups and institutions in society use only a sub-set of the total possible set of language patterns that make up language. Children who are experienced in using language in the home in ways that are similar to its use in school are likely to be more academically successful. In the case of non-English speaking children, Heath emphasizes, it is not so much which language is used at home that is important, but rather the way in which language is used (see also Snow, 1983). She urges much language experience in the home with written material and positive reinforcement as preparation for learning the language patterns characteristic of schooling.

In summary, according to Cummins, native language instruction for minority language students is advisable and beneficial because it serves to strengthen and broaden the language skills that they have upon starting school. Their first language skills, at least insofar as these have been developed to be adequate for academic purposes, will then support and facilitate English language development as a result of linguistic interdependence. In addition, use of the home language and positive support for the home culture will serve to create positive attitudes toward the students' ethnolinguistic group, which in turn will dispel ambivalence that they might hold toward the majority language and culture. Since majority language English-speaking groups value their home language and culture, they are more likely to provide the kinds of language experiences in the home that make transition to school painless and successful. Therefore, majority language children can be immersed in second language immersion programs easily and successfully. We will return to the issue of sociocultural factors in bilingual education in chapter ten.

AN ASSESSMENT OF BILINGUAL EDUCATION

There have been many evaluations of bilingual education programs. They can be classified as primary or secondary in nature. Primary evaluations include both studies of single programs in particular school districts and studies of programs nationwide. The evaluation studies of Canadian and U.S. immersion programs are examples of primary single program evaluations. This is by far the most common type of evaluation of bilingual education. They number in the hundreds since school districts are required by the terms of their contracts with the federal government to conduct evaluations of bilingual programs funded under Title VII monies. Two nationwide primary evaluations of bilingual education with a focus on student outcomes have been undertaken—one by Danoff et al. (1977a, 1977b, 1978), also known as the AIR study; and one in progress by Ramirez et al. (1986). Secondary evaluations of bilingual education consist of reviews of primary studies; they can be of two types—narrative reviews or meta-analyses. Narrative reviews consist of systematic but non-statistical analyses of selected primary evaluations (Baker & de Kanter, 1983; Cummins, 1981; Dulay & Burt, 1978b; Troike, 1978; and Zappert & Cruz, 1977). Meta-analysis is a procedure that compares the results of primary studies using statistical procedures. Only one meta-analysis of bilingual education has been carried out to date (Willig, 1985).

In comparison with immersion programs, bilingual education programs for minority language children are inherently more difficult to evaluate (McLaughlin, 1985). Willig (1985) has identified three aspects of bilingual education that have been problematic for program evaluators: 1) issues concerning language dominance or proficiency, 2) the composition of bilingual and non-bilingual school groups, and 3) other program variables. These factors create problems in evaluating bilingual education, either because they tend to result in experimental and comparison groups that are not comparable or because they invalidly minimize putative differences in program types and therefore mask or counteract any real effects of the educational programs under evaluation.

Unlike majority language English-speaking students in immersion programs, minority language students in bilingual programs differ greatly with respect to both English language proficiency and non-English language proficiency. Therefore, when constituting experimental and comparison groups for evaluation purposes, it is necessary to assess the students' proficiency in both languages in order to establish equivalency of both groups. Assessment of proficiency in language for academic purposes is problematic, owing to the general lack of testing instruments with demonstrated reliability and/or construct validity; this problem is particularly acute for tests of proficiency in non-English languages. These problems are compounded in evaluations of bilingual education by having to assess proficiency in two languages.

Willig points out that regression effects associated with language proficiency can also pose problems for program evaluators. Students in bilingual education programs tend to be from populations whose distribution of language scores, at least in English, is relatively low. Students who are not in bilingual education programs for some reason or other tend to be from populations whose distribution of language scores is relatively high. Notwithstanding differences in the distributions of scores of the populations from which they are drawn, experimental bilingual and non-bilingual comparison groups can be constituted to have comparable pre-test scores by using matching procedures—the students in the bilingual programs will be drawn from the relatively high end of their population distribution, while the students in the comparison group will be drawn from the relatively low end of their distribution. Despite such matching procedures, however, the experimental and comparison students' scores on evaluation tests will tend to regress toward their respective population means; that is, the bilingual program participants' scores will regress downward while the non-bilingual program participants' scores will regress upward. These regression effects will occur independently of any educational treatment effect, and they will tend to mask any possible treatment effects. Random assignment of students selected from a homogeneous group of students, all of whom are otherwise eligible for bilingual programs, will ensure true equivalence of experimental and comparison groups. Other, non-random procedures for constituting experimental and comparison groups will tend to result in non-equivalent groups.

There are other factors associated with the composition of bilingual and non-bilingual classes that can also result in non-equivalent experimental and comparison groups if precautions are not taken to avoid their influence. For example, it is common practice in bilingual programs to exit students from the program once they have achieved some minimum level of proficiency in English. This means that students in non-bilingual programs may in fact have been in a bilingual program at one time. As well, new students with limited English proficiency are continually enrolled in bilingual education programs. This means that the composition of the experimental group can change during the course of evaluation. Both of these practices will counteract any beneficial effects of bilingual education by lowering, or maintaining at a low level, the test scores of the experimental group and raising the scores of the comparison group.

The true consequences of bilingual education can also be masked by other program variables. In this case, the effect is to minimize rather than maximize group differences. To the extent that non-bilingual comparison school programs contain features of bilingual school programs, such as the use of bilingual aides or classroom teachers with bilingual training, then comparisons between bilingual and non-bilingual programs will be misleading in suggesting that there is no difference between program types. In question here is the valid selection of educational treatments to be compared. In a related vein, there is a question of the overall quality of the programs under evaluation. To the extent that bilingual programs are disadvantaged relative to non-bilingual programs, owing to lack of qualified teachers, insufficient instructional materials, inadequate facilities, or overall program instability, then any comparison with a non-bilingual program is unfair and invalid. In her meta-analysis of bilingual program evaluations, Willig (1985) found that, indeed, program instability had a measurable impact on students' academic performance. In fact, Willig found that many of the factors mentioned here had measurable and significant effects that counteracted the positive effects of bilingual education.

Problems in program evaluation inherent in bilingual programs themselves have been exacerbated by the poor research designs, statistical analyses, and psychometric procedures of many of the primary evaluation studies (see Baker

& de Kanter, 1983, and Willig, 1985, for discussions of research methodology in bilingual education). In fact, the results of many primary evaluation studies are uninterpretable because they fail to meet basic standards of sound research methodology. Secondary reviews of primary evaluation studies have found it necessary to reject the majority of primary studies in order to arrive at valid conclusions. For example, Troike (1978) rejected all but 12 of 150 studies in his review and Baker and de Kanter found only 39 of some 300 primary studies that met their criteria of methodological adequacy. Methodological problems include

1. failure to address the main issues concerning the effectiveness of bilingual education;
2. non-random assignment of students to experimental and comparison groups with no other controls for establishing equivalency between groups;
3. inadequate or nonexistent pre-test assessments, including failure to adequately assess students' language proficiency;
4. lack of appropriate statistical analyses;
5. inappropriate use of gain scores, grade-equivalent scores, or other norm-referenced scores; and
6. failure to establish or document the nature of the differences in educational treatment, if any.

An additional problem faced by evaluators is that there is no single model or limited set of well-defined models of bilingual education in operation. As a result, it is not possible to determine conclusively whether bilingual education *in general* works. However, insofar as individual programs of bilingual education can be shown to facilitate English language development and academic achievement, then it is possible to conclude that it *can* work. Of course, such a conclusion depends upon sound evaluation studies carried out on programs with educational practices that in fact differ from non-bilingual programs in ways that conform to some acceptable definition of bilingual education. A minimum definition would require that the program provide some academic instruction through the students' home language prior to or along with instruction through English. It is not possible to ascertain from many evaluation reports precisely what use was made of the students' first language because details concerning specific aspects of the program under evaluation are often lacking.

The narrative reviews of Dulay and Burt (1978b), Cummins (1981), Troike (1978), and Zappert and Cruz (1977) examined fairly limited sets of carefully selected primary studies. Cummins's review, for example, was limited to five studies of U.S. programs that provided a test of his interdependence hypothesis, and Troike deliberately selected 12 studies of programs with positive effects in order to document that bilingual education can work. All secondary reviewers have found that at least some of the studies they reviewed facilitated English language development and/or academic achievement in comparison with English-only programs.

By far the most comprehensive narrative review has been carried out by Baker and de Kanter (1983). They examined several hundred primary studies and identified 39 that met their standards for sound research methods. They then examined the results of these studies to ascertain whether bilingual education accelerated, slowed down, or had no significant effects on the participating students' English language development and academic achievement in comparison with that of students in non-bilingual programs. They reported that 11 of the studies found that minority language students participating in transitional bilingual programs performed better on English language tests than students in non-bilingual programs; 26 found no statistically significant differences between bilingual program participants and comparison students; and 9 found bilingual education to be less effective than non-bilingual programs. More than 39 sets of findings are cited here since some of the studies reported the results of more than one evaluation. Baker and de Kanter (1983) concluded that "the case for the effectiveness of transitional bilingual education is called into question by studies that found no difference in second-language performance between treatment and comparison groups" (p. 43). That some bilingual programs did not result in significantly better performance than some comparison programs may be due to any number of factors, with the obvious possibility being the quality or nature of the programs in question. In fact, Baker and de Kanter did not examine program variables so that the negative or null results they found could reflect poor quality bilingual programs and/or inappropriate comparisons. Contrary to their conclusion, the results of the 11 evaluations reporting better academic achievement by bilingual program participants can be interpreted to mean that bilingual education *can* work.

Meta-analysis is a statistical procedure that can assess the effect of variations in programs and in program evaluations. It, therefore, provides a more systematic and detailed means of analyzing and interpreting the kind of variation that characterizes primary evaluations. Willig (1985) has reexamined the primary studies reviewed by Baker and de Kanter using this procedure. She excluded a number of studies included in the Baker and de Kanter review because they were conducted on programs outside the United States (e.g., the Canadian immersion programs) and therefore do not pertain to the main issue in question. Willig's analysis revealed overall significant effects in favor of bilingual education in reading, language, mathematics, and total achievement whether assessed using English tests or non-English tests. In other words, students in bilingual programs scored significantly higher than students in non-bilingual programs in each of these areas.

Willig also found that the quality of the evaluations and characteristics of the programs themselves contributed significantly to program outcomes so that the overall positive effects she noted were evident in some studies and not in others. The pattern of results revealed by her analysis was interesting and instructive. Positive effects in favor of bilingual education were evident when 1) random assignment was used to constitute the experimental and comparison groups, 2) both the experimental and comparison students were Spanish dominant, 3) the comparison groups did not include students who had previously been in a bilingual program, and 4) the experimental groups did not change during the evaluation by admitting new students in need of bilingual education. Positive effects in favor of bilingual education were also found when 5) the bilingual program appeared to be stable, and 6) the comparison program did not have features of the bilingual program. In other words, when the students and programs under evaluation were equivalent in appropriate psychometric respects but different in relevant educational respects, positive effects emerged.

Positive effects in favor of bilingual education have also been reported by Ramirez et al. (1985) in a nationwide comparison of bilingual education and structured immersion programs. In their first year's evaluation, Ramirez and his colleagues compared the performance of kindergarten, grade 1, and grade 3 students in early-exit and late-exit bilingual programs to that of students in structured immersion programs. Early-exit bilingual students are mainstreamed into English-only classes as soon as they demonstrate proficiency in English. Late-exit students are not mainstreamed into English-only classes until the 5th or 6th grade. Tests of English language, Spanish language, and academic achievement were used. The research is being carried out in four states: California, Texas, New York, and Florida. The results of the first year's evaluation indicated that bilingual students in all three grades outperformed or made larger gains from fall to spring than students in structured immersion programs in which all instruction was given in English. The researchers stress that these results are preliminary and await follow-up testing. They are nevertheless important because this is the first systematic comparative evaluation of structured immersion programs versus bilingual education.

SUMMARY

Since its beginning in 1968, bilingual education in the United States has faced a number of political, legal, and pedagogical hurdles. It is likely that the political and legal hurdles will continue to pose formidable challenges to advocates of bilingual education. Indeed, in a news conference in September, 1985, the federal Secretary of Education, William Bennett, questioned the effectiveness of bilingual education and called its continuance into question. As well, a recently established group called *U.S. English* is seeking to make English the only official language in the United States and thereby reduce federal support for the use of non-English languages in U.S. schools. Such events do not augur well for bilingual education on the political front.

Evaluations of bilingual education provide empirical evidence of its effectiveness. The most compelling evidence in favor of bilingual education comes from Willig's meta-analysis of 28 methodologically sound primary evaluations. If the results of Ramirez's first-year evaluation of bilingual education versus structured immersion hold up in follow-up testing, then they too will be of major importance. It is also clear from primary evaluations of individual programs that bilingual education can work. Earlier declarations that bilingual education does not work are based on the faulty logic that, because particular examples of bilingual education have not resulted in English language and academic achievement that is superior to that in all-English programs, then bilingual education in general is ineffective. Such declarations testify to a naive acceptance of the results of blatantly flawed research designs.

Cummins's theoretical framework provides a coherent and useful conceptual rationale for bilingual education. It is unlikely, however, that the question or "problem" of minority language students' disproportionately poor performance in school can be understood completely in the largely individualistic and cognitive terms that have been emphasized in this chapter. Broad-based sociocultural factors are probably implicated as well (Hernandez-Chavez, 1984; Ogbu & Matute-Bianchi, 1986; Paulston, 1980). Even the sociocultural basis of language proficiency development contained in Cummins's original framework, as described here, may be too individualistic or narrowly conceived to encompass all relevant causal factors (see Cummins, 1985, for a more detailed consideration of sociocultural factors). In other words, different kinds of underlying causal variables may be needed to explain the performance of minority language students in school in addition to the largely linguistic and cognitive ones. If this is true, then providing primary language and academic instruction through students' home language, and delaying transition from a bilingual program to a mainstream English program, may enhance minority language students' academic success relative to the consequences of submersion or other all-English schooling alternatives; but this approach may not maximize their performance, or it may lead to mixed results if other factors are in fact operating.

For example, if students from minority language groups are unlikely to do well in school for motivational reasons (e.g., they feel that they are doomed to fail in school because of discrimination) rather than for specific linguistic or cognitive reasons, then the approach currently practiced would not address all of the factors acting to depress their academic achievement. An understanding of all underlying causes of minority language students' difficulties in school is more than a theoretical issue. It is essential if educators are to develop rational educational interventions that will optimize minority language student performance and maximize their scholastic achievements. In the next chapter, we will examine some sociocultural perspectives on bilingual education.

CHAPTER 10

Sociocultural Perspectives on Bilingual Education

It is widely recognized that education does not take place in a social vacuum. Indeed, the origins of the immersion programs can be traced to sociocultural changes in Canadian society. Sociocultural factors can influence the form of specific educational innovations; as well, they continue to influence educational processes and outcomes in important ways once innovation has been instituted. As will be seen shortly, in the case of bilingual education, the source of these influences can often be linked to factors associated with ethnolinguistic diversity and, specifically, to status and power relationships associated with such diversity. In this chapter we will examine ways in which sociocultural factors associated with 1) society at large, 2) minority–majority group relations, and 3) schools can influence the social organization of schools and the academic performance of minority language students. The theoretical issues presented in the following sections should be regarded as working hypotheses that can broaden our perspective on bilingual education and its consequences; they all await empirical verification.

SOCIETAL FACTORS

Paulston (1980) argues that a true understanding of bilingual education and its consequences requires an understanding of the larger social context of which schools are a part. She suggests more specifically that bilingual education can be examined from two broad sociological perspectives; one she refers to as the equilibrium paradigm and the other the conflict paradigm. According to Paulston, North American bilingual education, including the Canadian immersion programs, have been developed, implemented, and evaluated within the perspective of the equilibrium paradigm. This is probably the predominant ideological and political perspective of most North Americans.

Equilibrium Paradigm. A specific example of the equilibrium paradigm which has been particularly influential among North American social scientists is structural-functional theory of social change. According to this theory, society is a complex system of functional components that interact harmoniously. The components include, for example, institutions such as schools, subsystems such as the economic system, and social processes such as social mobility. Social change is said to occur as a result of gradual, accumulative changes in the various components, and social forces within society work to ensure that any transformations of the system are smooth. Conflict and disharmony between or among the component parts are to be avoided because they are associated with instability and breakdown of the system. Radical and conflictual change are viewed negatively and are avoided or minimized. Dysfunction within the system is seen to be a problem in the functioning of one or more of the components in need of modification; the system itself, however, is to remain relatively unchanged. Failure is regarded as a problem or weakness of the components, subgroups, or individuals involved, and is to be rectified by changing the individuals or subgroups that are failing. In essence, society is regarded as a homeostatic system working to maintain the integrity and effectiveness of the whole while allowing for changes to its parts or members.

Paulston (1980) has argued that the very structure and philosophy of bilingual education in the United States as well as its consequences can be understood within this paradigm. Accordingly, it is assumed that the lack of social and economic success of minority language groups is due to unequal opportunity stemming from differences in their linguistic, cultural, and learning styles in comparison with those of the majority group. The lack of scholastic success of minority language students, in particular, is assumed to be related directly to their poor English proficiency, which is linked to their ethnicity. Hence, the academic achievement of minority language students can be improved by the provision of better English language instruction and ultimately improved English language proficiency. Social and economic opportunity will follow in turn as a result of the improved scholastic achievements that minority language students bring to the job market. In other words, providing minority language students with age-appropriate English language proficiency and academic skills will allow them to compete on an equal footing for jobs, status, and privilege in the world of work.

According to this perspective, the immediate objective of bilingual education should be to equalize the educational opportunity of minority language students by compensatory training in English. Bilingual education so defined is regarded as a balancing mechanism that compensates for the children's linguistic disadvantage and that thereby maintains societal equilibrium. It is not surprising then that *transitional* bilingual education has been the objective of most federal, state, and local initiatives dealing with the educational treatment of minority language students, since it serves to maintain the basic monolingual/monocultural English character of the public school system while seeking change in minority language students themselves. Alternatively, some school authorities and politicians have sought to encourage mainstreaming along with instruction in English as a Second Language instead of bilingual education for similar reasons.

The Canadian immersion programs can also be analyzed in terms of structural-functional equilibrium. Accordingly, French immersion programs represent a modification to the existing public school system that provides majority group, English-speaking Canadian children with the bilingual proficiency they will need in order to maintain their socioeconomic predominance in Quebec and in Canada. The rising tide of French nationalism in Quebec during the 1960s and '70s, along with the growing importance of French as a means of business communication throughout Canada, was threatening to disrupt the established socioeconomic "equilibrium" by favoring French-English bilinguals over monolingual English speakers; French Canadians have traditionally been more bilingual than English Canadians and therefore stood to benefit from this linguistic change.

The structural-functionalist perspective also provides an explanation for the relative success and popularity of the Canadian immersion programs for majority language children in comparison with the ambivalence and mixed results faced by some U.S. bilingual education programs for minority language children. The Canadian programs do not threaten the status quo of the more powerful English Canadian community; to the contrary, they serve to maintain their socioeconomic status. Therefore, immersion programs are supported by the community at large and by the educational sector in particular. U.S. bilingual programs, however, especially those that seek to develop full bilingual proficiency, threaten the status quo because they promote the institutionalization of non-English languages and cultures in the public school system. As a result, they lack general support and are particularly susceptible to sociocultural factors that could undermine their goals.

Conflict Paradigm.   In contrast to the equilibrium paradigm, the conflict paradigm emphasizes conflicts over values, resources, and power inherent in complex social systems. Conflict and the instability resulting from it are viewed as natural, inherent characteristics of complex societies, and radical or disruptive change is accepted as necessary in some cases if real change is to occur. The problem faced by minority language groups is not defined in terms of "unequal opportunity" but rather in terms of "social inequity," that is, the unequal distribution of power, rewards, advantages, and resources along ethnolinguistic lines.

Proponents of the conflict paradigm argue further that society and its constituent parts, including schools, reflect the characteristics, values, and goals of the majority group, and therefore society functions to serve the majority group, sometimes by maintaining minority language groups in disadvantaged and subordinate positions:

> The schools are but a mirror of the larger society. In the United States today language minorities occupy the lowest educational and occupational levels; they are largely excluded from the political process; and they are discriminated against linguistically and culturally by the major institutions. The educational system plays a central role in the perpetuation of this social stratification that is based on class and race distinctions. . . . The educational problems of language minorities are thus revealed to be a result of inherent

and systematic inequalities in the schools, which reflect the prevailing political and economic philosophies of society. Historically, every educational
approach used with language minority populations has operated within this
paradigm of structured inequality. (Hernandez-Chavez, 1984, p. 178)

Thus, schools, including transitional bilingual education, reflect and perpetuate
the inequities of society at large and thereby function to maintain low academic
performance and ultimately low socioeconomic status among members of minority ethnolinguistic groups.

According to the conflict paradigm, bilingual education should attempt to
cope with such inequities or social injustices. The long range goals of bilingual
education should be to maximize equity in the distribution of wealth, power, and
other social advantages rather than simply enhancing the effectiveness or efficiency of second language teaching to minority language students, as proposed
by proponents of the equilibrium paradigm. This means that from the conflict
perspective the factors that influence the success or failure of bilingual education
will not necessarily be found in educational programs themselves, but rather can
also be found outside the school setting. As well, indices of program effectiveness
should not be limited to student learning outcomes, as measured by standardized
tests, as is recommended by the equilibrium paradigm, but rather should include
nontraditional measures, such as employment figures following graduation, delin-
quency, social mobility, and other indices of inequity. To use Paulston's (1980)
characterization, the conflict paradigm views bilingual education itself as influenced by certain socioeconomic-political forces and, more technically, as an
intervening process mediating the effects of societal processes on student outcomes (see Figure 6). In contrast, the equilibrium paradigm views bilingual
education as the primary causal factor effecting certain academic and linguistic
outcomes.

Proponents of the conflict perspective argue that the consequences of transitional bilingual education are inherently circumscribed because these programs overlook important causal factors outside the school setting. They argue,
moreover, that transitional bilingual education is likely to produce only limited
change because it actually perpetuates social inequity or inequality by maintaining the predominance of English over other languages for instructional and

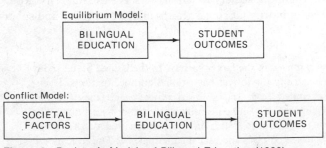

Figure 6   Paulston's Models of Bilingual Education (1980)

evaluative purposes. At the very least, bilingual education should aim for maintenance of the students' home language and culture. Maintenance of bilingual education can better redress social inequity by, among other things, 1) institutionalizing minority languages, thereby according them social status; 2) providing a basis for ethnic diversity, thereby reducing the chances of assimilation; and 3) representing minority language group members at all levels of the educational hierarchy, thereby providing minority language students with high-status, professional models.

Thus, proponents of the conflict position define the problem in terms that go beyond language proficiency and cognitive development. This is not to say that transitional bilingual education programs ignore the sociocultural dimension altogether; in fact, an explicit bicultural component is built into many programs. For example, the use of teachers from the students' ethnolinguistic group as well as culturally appropriate instructional materials address these issues to a certain extent. However, such practices could just as easily be counterproductive if minority instructional staff members indicate to their students, either directly through their predominant use of English or indirectly through differential attitudes they express toward the value of English and other languages, that even in bilingual education programs English is accorded more status than the home language. This perspective thus identifies limitations in the overall structure and orientation of transitional bilingual education.

Summary.   The sociocultural perspectives presented by Paulston and Hernandez-Chavez redefine the nexus of the problem faced by bilingual educators to focus on societal factors as well as the linguistic, cognitive, and cultural characteristics of minority language children as primary causal determinants of their academic performance. These perspectives also provide a basis for explaining the apparently contradictory fact that immersion programs that aim for maintenance bilingualism are popular and successful in Canada, whereas bilingual education in the United States, even of the transitional type, has received relatively little public support.

AN INTERGROUP PERSPECTIVE

The general implication of the theses of Paulston and Hernandez-Chavez is that, other things being equal, educational programs for minority language students in North America, even bilingual education, are likely to perpetuate the socioeconomic disadvantages that minority groups experience in society by re-creating in school the psycho-educational disadvantages associated with ethnolinguistic differences. However, as noted earlier, not all minority groups do poorly in school. A comprehensive description of education for minority language groups must take such group differences into account. In this section, a framework is presented that describes group differences in reaction to sociocultural factors in society at large and the implications of such differences for the educational success or failure of some minority groups.

This framework draws on Tajfel's theoretical notions of intergroup relations. Along with a number of other social psychologists, Tajfel holds that individuals feel compelled to define themselves and significant others in their community (Tajfel, 1974; Tajfel & Turner, 1979). One way in which this can be achieved is through categorization of oneself as a member of a specific social group. The recognition and acknowledgement of one's membership in a specific group along with the value associated with group membership are important aspects of a person's social definition, which in turn forms part of one's definition of self, or one's self-concept. Social identity acquires meaning and significance only as a result of comparisons with other relevant social groups. Comparisons can be based on material possessions, social power, abilities, personal attributes, and the like. According to social comparison theory, individuals are motivated to belong to groups that are positively valued and psychologically distinct from other groups with which they are compared. Group comparisons that result in positive valuation and distinctiveness are more satisfying than those with negative valuation or lack of distinctiveness. Group members who experience an unsatisfactory identity will seek to change the group comparisons on which their negative identity is based and thereby attempt to develop a more satisfactory social identity. Groups that experience an adequate or satisfactory social identity will not seek change.

On the one hand, dominant or majority social groups usually possess considerable material goods, social power, and status. Consequently, members of these groups enjoy positive, distinctive group identities and are not likely to seek a change in group comparisons. To the contrary, majority groups generally try to maintain the status quo on which their positive group identity is based. On the other hand, minority social groups usually lack material possessions, social power, and status and thus experience a negative and unsatisfactory social identity. They will seek to improve their social identity by changing group comparisons, but only if they are aware that alternatives are possible and only if they perceive their current status to be unstable and unjust. Otherwise, they will accept, perhaps reluctantly, their social inferiority. Traditionally, women and blacks in North America have been in this situation, although this has changed considerably. Even within groups that accept their negative social identity, *individual members* of the group may seek social change in their individual status by "passing" or assimilating into the dominant group or, if this is not possible, by changing their basis of comparison from members of the advantaged, majority group to more disadvantaged members within their own group.

A number of different strategies for establishing and maintaining a positive and satisfactory social identity are available to groups that have a negative social identity and seek to change it. They can 1) assimilate; 2) create new positive, distinctive group characteristics; 3) redefine previously negatively valued group characteristics; or 4) compete directly with the majority group. While these strategies have wide-ranging implications, their possible impact on educationally relevant aspects of minority group behavior is particularly pertinent to the present chapter and will be the focus of discussion in the following sections. The characterizations that follow are generalizations intended to identify some common patterns in the ways that different minority groups react to their sociocultural circumstances. However, it must be recognized that all generalizations are inaccurate in some respects, and furthermore generalizations that describe group processes represent modal or average reactions derived from a sample of individuals who vary widely from one another.

Assimilation. As commonly defined, assimilation means abandoning those distinctive, often socially stigmatized characteristics of the minority group for characteristics of the dominant group that are viewed more positively. Assimilation in the direction of the dominant group can often be the initial strategy of minority groups when faced with a negative social identity. In any case, it often occurs "naturally" over generations as a result of gradual attrition of the heritage language and culture. On the one hand, assimilation can be adaptive in the long run to the extent that the minority group involved successfully adopts important majority group characteristics and to the extent that they are accepted by the majority group. In the North American context, this process is likely to be most successful among minority groups that share a European, Caucasian background and therefore are "assimilatable."

On the other hand, assimilation can be maladaptive, at least in the short term, for a number of reasons. First, it can entail implicit, if not explicit, denigration of fundamental and distinctive group characteristics so that, contrary to its intended goal of improving the group's status, it can actually reduce it further, thereby promoting feelings of even greater social inferiority. As we will see in the next section, inferior social status can lead in turn to negative academic expectations and through self-fulfilling prophecies to academic underachievement.

Second, members of a minority group may be frustrated in their efforts to seek a satisfactory social identity through assimilation by a majority group that is unwilling to accept them. This is likely to be especially true for minority groups that are visually, culturally, and linguistically distinct from the majority group. This can create an anomic and/or subtractive bilingual/cultural context whereby members of the minority group give up what is distinctive to their group but fail to gain valued outgroup acceptance. Lambert (1980a) and others (Hernandez-Chavez, 1984; Cummins, 1985) have argued that this "subtractive" state is not conducive to academic achievement because the possible positive incentive associated with academic success can be offset by negative incentive associated with rejection of or dissociation from the in-group.

Third, in the short term, assimilation may lead to the adoption of behaviors and values that are superficially similar to those of the majority group while other fundamental differences remain unchanged. Heath (1986), for example, has described ways in which language use (or genres) can differ among social groups and how the genres characteristic of some groups may differ from those used and needed in school. It is likely that such complex, abstract language patterns, which are often firmly rooted in community life-styles, can be changed only slowly as a result of fundamental alterations in the group's social and cultural characteristics. It is unlikely that such changes can be achieved quickly or easily. Heath argues further that minority groups seeking to promote proficiency in the dominant group's language by using that language at home may unwittingly be depriving their children of valuable language experiences that could be furnished more effectively using their more proficient home language. In other words, minority parents' use of limited English with their children at home may restrict the range and types of language genres that they acquire and subsequently bring to school (see also Cummins, 1981).

Creation of New Group Characteristics.   In contrast to total assimilation to the dominant group as a means of establishing a positive group identity, this strategy implicates selective adoption of certain dominant group characteristics while retaining other characteristics distinctive to the minority group. In this regard, Ogbu and Matute-Bianchi (1986) suggest that the characteristics, values, and behaviors that a particular minority group will adopt depend in important ways on their folk theory of "getting ahead." More specifically, they contend that schools are structured to train students to become active and productive members of the economic system and that all social groups develop folk theories of the relationship between schooling and socioeconomic status and advancement. Groups that perceive a link between school achievement and socioeconomic success will come to believe that the way to get ahead is through schooling. Parents in these groups, therefore, will value schooling and going to school and they will encourage and adopt behaviors that support academic success. Parental values and behaviors will be passed on to children through socialization—in effect, children in these groups will "learn how to go to school and how to succeed."

Many minority groups experience discrepancies between their academic qualifications and the socioeconomic rewards they enjoy; that is to say, they may be excluded from certain desirable jobs and limited to certain low-paying ones no matter what their educational qualifications. Ogbu and Matute-Bianchi contend that, despite such discrepancies, certain minority groups see an economic value to schooling because they expect to be rewarded for their educational achievements either "back home" in their country of origin or within their immediate ethnic community where they are not subject to out-group economic exploitation. In many cases, these are groups that have emigrated more or less voluntarily and/or hope to return home at some future date when their American education will be valuable. Alternatively, they could reemigrate to a new country where their academic qualifications would bring socioeconomic benefits. Examples of such groups include Chinese-, Japanese-, and Cuban-Americans.

In effect then, these groups do not adopt the norms and behaviors of the dominant majority group as their only culture frame of reference. Rather they retain the basic cultural characteristics and values of the in-group. At the same time, they adopt and promote those behaviors and values that are instrumental for academic success. Ogbu and Matute-Bianchi have referred to this as an *alternation model of behavior:* "The essence of the alternation model is that it is possible and acceptable to participate in two different cultures or two different languages, perhaps for different purposes, by alternating one's behavior according to the situation" (1986, p. 23). In this way, the group members are able to maintain a positive and distinctive group identity while promoting behaviors and values that are associated with success in school settings that are dominated by the majority group and by majority group values.

Redefinition.   This strategy entails redefining previously negatively valued group characteristics to make them more positive. The redefined characteristics are usually distinct to the minority group and distinguish it in unique and obvious ways from the majority group (e.g., skin color, language, origin, etc.). The most celebrated example of a group that has used this strategy are black Americans, whose slogan "Black Is Beautiful" became a call for ethnic pride encompassing not only skin color but also language, culture, and their African origins. In a different vein, Amerindians have promoted their aboriginal status as true Native Americans as a basis for positive group distinctiveness. The positive distinctiveness ascribed to specific in-group characteristics may be generalized to most aspects of the group. Conversely, any or all behaviors and values associated with the dominant group may be rejected and disdained because they represent assimilation and loss of cultural distinctiveness. Ogbu and Matute-Bianchi (1986) have proposed a similar strategy of identity development which they refer to as an *oppositional cultural frame of reference.* According to Ogbu and Matute-Bianchi, these "minorities tend to form a sense of peoplehood or collective social identity in opposition to the collective social identity of the dominant group" (1986, p. 29). Psycho-educationally, these groups differ from those that create new dimensions of identity in that they may reject, or at least do not endorse, those values and behaviors needed for academic success within the mainstream educational system.

Ogbu and Matute-Bianchi use the concept of a folk theory of schooling once again to explain this reaction. In contrast to groups that perceive a link between schooling and socioeconomic success despite economic exploitation, other minority groups may develop folk theories of schooling in which there is no strong link between performance in school and success in the job market. In fact, they perceive and believe that academic success is not a means to socioeconomic advancement—no matter how well they do in school, they will be relegated to low-status jobs. Ogbu and Matute-Bianchi attribute this reaction to the historical fact that such groups have usually been incorporated into the new society more or less *involuntarily* and permanently, through slavery, conquest, or colonization. Consequently, they have no homeland to return to or they are subordinated in their own homeland (e.g., black Americans and Mexican-Americans). Thus, unlike some minority groups, they have no alternative frame of reference and no expectations of benefiting from academic achievement elsewhere. At the same time, all of the evidence available to them indicates that they will not be treated equitably in the job market and that sociocultural assimilation into the dominant group as a means of attaining equity cannot be achieved readily, owing to evident and immutable differences between them and the dominant group. Consequently, they seek a positive cultural identity in their distinctive group characteristics.

Redefinition may be adaptive to the extent that the group is able to control and tailor the educational system to correspond to their distinctive cultural characteristics and, in particular, to the distinct learning and interactional styles of their children. However, to the extent that their children must attend public schools that reflect majority group values and goals, then they may be disadvantaged, since they have not been socialized in ways that prepare them for mainstream schooling. In fact, they may subconsciously resist mainstream education because they perceive it as a threat to their cultural identity. Unless there is a discernible change in their status in the job market, their orientation toward schooling may be passed on from generation to generation and thereby become part of their cultural identity.

Direct Competition.   An additional strategy for establishing positive group identity is direct competition with the majority group for power, status, or scarce resources. Direct competition may be undertaken by groups that have been incorporated into society voluntarily or involuntarily. Only those groups that have sufficient *ethnolinguistic vitality,* however, are likely to adopt such a strategy. Giles, Bourhis, and Taylor (1977) define ethnolinguistic vitality as "that which makes a group likely to behave as a distinctive and active collective entity in intergroup situations" (p. 308). It comprises three major factors—status, demographic, and institutional support, each of which are composed of a number of subfactors. *Status* factors refer to a number of prestige variables associated with the group (e.g., economic status, social status); *demographic* factors are related to the sheer number of group members and to their geo-political distribution; and *institutional support* factors refer to a group's representation in the various institutions of a nation, community, or territory. Relative strength in each domain is associated with vitality.

Thus, a minority group that is dissatisfied with its social identity and has some measure of ethnic vitality may seek to enhance the group's status through direct competition with the majority group if it views its social inferiority as unstable and unjust. Direct competition between minority and majority groups over power or scarce resources can ameliorate the group's status and prestige by establishing its superiority over or equality with the dominant group.

A case in point is French Canadians in Quebec, who enjoyed considerable demographic and institutional support within the province but lacked prestige and status on linguistic and economic dimensions—English Canadians controlled the economy of the province and the country, and the English language enjoyed prestige because it was associated with socioeconomic power. French Canadians sought to change this social situation by using the political power available to them as a result of their demographic strength (they comprised 5 million residents in a province of 6 million) and their institutional support (they held considerable political power). More specifically, laws were passed by the largely French-controlled provincial government to establish French as the working language of the province and to prevent job discrimination on the basis of lack of English proficiency. As well, educational reform was sought—there was a shift in focus from "classical education" with an emphasis on training in the humanities and the arts to education with an emphasis on science, business, and technology.

While the long-term outcomes are not yet in, preliminary evidence suggests that some measure of improvement in French Canadian status has been achieved. For example, language surveys in Quebec indicate that French and not English is increasingly the *lingua franca* in communication involving members of both ethnolinguistic groups (Bourhis, 1983), and language attitude studies indicate some change in French Canadians' perceptions of the French language (Maurice, Genesee, Holobow, & Chartrand, 1984). Moreover, major industrial achievements, such as Hydro Quebec and Bombardier, have served to change French Canadians' image of themselves as "hewers of wood and drawers of water" to that of world-class entrepreneurs. Of particular interest is the fact that in 1978 French Canadians living in the province of Quebec rejected a referendum seeking to separate Quebec from the rest of Canada in order to ensure their ethnolinguistic integrity and survival. Their vote could be interpreted as an indication that their social status had improved to the point where such an option was no longer necessary or desirable.

In contrast to the preceding sociocultural reactions, which entail the creation of new bases of identity formation, redefinitions of old ones, or the assimilation of out-group ones, direct competition entails primarily the forceful assertion of existing ones. With regard to education, in particular, the minority group may reorient or modify its educational priorities somewhat (that is, redefine them), but the consequences of this are likely to be secondary to those that derive from their vigorous application of existing educational values and goals as part of a competitive strategy to upgrade their status. Competition between the minority group and the majority group may be specific and circumscribed, implicating education in some cases (for example, the provision of minority language schools) and not in others (for example, the provision of minority language telecommunications media). Clearly, the psycho-educational implications of this strategy will depend upon the bases of competition and the changes that ensue from competition.

Summary.   In the same vein as Paulston and Hernandez-Chavez, the present intergroup perspective seeks to understand bilingual education within the sociocultural context of which it is a part. At the same time, it attempts to describe and account for some of the different ways minority groups react to sociocultural forces and ultimately to schooling. Viewed from the present perspective, changes in and by both minority groups and the majority group are called for if the educational performance of minority language students is to be optimized. Clearly, changes in society at large are not easy to achieve and are likely to be gradual and small. In the next section, we will consider how sociocultural processes of the sort discussed in this section can influence educational processes and outcomes within the school setting itself, since it is in schools that change is most likely to be effected.

SOCIOCULTURAL FACTORS IN SCHOOL

Cleghorn and Genesee's (1984) ethnographic study of teacher interaction in a Montreal French immersion school indicated that, unless systematic and concerted strategies are implemented to counteract the effects of societally based intergroup relations, bilingual/mixed ethnic schools will tend to perpetuate the social patterns characteristic of society at large. It will be recalled that they found that French Canadian and English Canadian teachers tended to interact and use language in ways that reflected patterns of interaction that prevailed when English was predominant over French. Similarly, Legaretta (1977) has reported that the use of English predominated over the use of Spanish in bilingual classes in the United States; this was especially true in situations marked by displays of social power. Thus, contrary to their stated objective of promoting minority languages and cultures, immersion and bilingual programs may reinforce the very social patterns they seek to alter. This point has also been made forcefully in research on school desegregation. It has been noted by a number of researchers that, contrary to their intention of equalizing status relationships between black and white students and thereby enhancing the academic performance of black students, desegregated schools tend to recreate the same patterns of social inequity and differential expectations that characterize segregated settings (Cohen, 1980).

Status Differentials and Performance Expectations.   Key elements in understanding bilingual and other mixed ethnic school groups are the status and power relationships among the participants within the school itself and the ways in which these relationships can affect student performance. Cohen (1980) identifies four ways in which status differentials can manifest themselves in mixed ethnic schools: 1) status problems between the students themselves; 2) power and authority relationships within the formal organization of the school; 3) the social structure of classrooms; and 4) student and teacher norms for social interaction outside instructional periods.

Briefly, status problems among students refer to any expected or manifest differences between students from different ethnolinguistic groups that are associated with differential status attribution; for example, being from the high-prestige, and often higher socioeconomic majority group versus a low-prestige, often lower socioeconomic minority group. Power and authority relationships can also entail status differences insofar as there is an inequitable representation of minority and majority group members in positions of power and authority in the school (e.g., principals, vice-principals, and department heads are majority group members whereas members of the minority group are limited to instructional or service positions). Patterns of social interaction between school participants outside instructional periods that are biased or conflictual can also engender status differentials—the predominant use of English over non-English languages in informal interaction will reinforce the status of majority group students over minority group students (see also Cleghorn & Genesee, 1984); or open conflict between students from different ethnolinguistic groups in the hallways or school-yard can be misinterpreted in "racial" terms when the real basis of the problem could be socioeconomic. Such misattributions can falsely reinforce status-loaded ethnic stereotypes.

Classroom procedures and norms that favor one group over another can also foster status differentials and influence students' classroom performance in significant ways. A number of researchers have shown that students from high social status groups will be more active and influential than students from low-status groups when working together on collective tasks (Webster & Driskell, 1978). This has been shown in comparisons of black versus white students, Chicano versus Anglo students, and Western versus Middle Eastern Jewish students (Cohen, 1980). Status attributions in school may be based on such *diffuse characteristics* as race, ethnicity, or gender, or they may be based on more *specific characteristics,* such as reading ability. It has been found, for example, that junior high school students who were perceived by their classmates to be good readers were more active during instructional time than students who were perceived to be poor readers. It has also been found that there is a high degree of agreement among teachers and students on the ranking of students according to reading ability (Rosenholz, and Rosenholz & Wilson, in Cohen, 1980). The same results have been found for overall academic ability (Cohen, 1972; Hoffman & Cohen, 1972, in Cohen, 1980).

These findings have been explained in terms of status generalization theory, or what is more commonly called self-fulfilling prophecy. Individuals who are perceived to rank low on status characteristics, either of the specific or diffuse type, are often viewed to be relatively incompetent and therefore are called on to perform less often in a variety of situations, even when nonacademic competence may be called for. This generalization process is not one-sided, however, so that individuals who are perceived by others to have low status and low competence can come to see themselves in this way and behave accordingly.

The most straightforward illustration of this effect involves reading ability. To the extent that classroom performance calls for reading ability, then those students who are perceived to be good readers would be expected to dominate the activity because they will be called upon to perform. In contrast, those with poor reading ability would not be called upon and therefore would be relatively inactive. Students who demonstrate reading ability in one set of activities are often expected to possess similarly high levels of competence in other domains, even if reading ability is not called for. As a result, they may be called upon to perform major roles in other activities. In turn, high-status students come to see themselves as competent and are ready to assume dominant, influential roles in a variety of activities.

A similar chain of events can be invoked to describe the effect of diffuse status characteristics on performance. Diffuse status characteristics, such as ethnicity, are often associated with a set of negative social evaluations that depict the minority group member as incompetent and lacking in ambition and/or ability. Research using the matched-guise technique as a means of determining social evaluations associated with language variation attest to such perceptions (Ryan & Giles, 1982). Thus, in lieu of information to the contrary, students with low-status social characteristics are often expected to possess less competence and therefore may be called upon to perform less than students with high-status social characteristics.

Expectations concerning minority language students' academic competence may also be based on actual differences in school-related abilities. Many minority language students, in fact, have lower levels of reading achievement (Carter & Segura, 1979) and therefore will be disadvantaged and seen to be disadvantaged by their peers in tasks that require reading. Or some minority students may not have been socialized to use certain language genres that are prevalent in school (Heath, 1986) and therefore may be withdrawn and inactive during activities that require these genres. This may give the false impression to others, students and teachers alike, that they are academically inferior or unmotivated. This kind of social information may then influence the students' and teachers' performance expectations of minority students' competence in other situations. Thus, minority students may be called upon less frequently to participate in a variety of classroom activities, even those that are not specifically related to their reading ability or general language proficiency, because the expectation of incompetence or low motivation has been generalized.

Research has shown that teacher interactions with students who are perceived as low- and high-achieving are different in a number of respects (Good & Brophy, 1978; Kerman, 1979). In general, teacher interaction with students who are perceived as high achievers is more motivating and more supportive than that with students perceived as low achievers. High achievers receive more time to respond to questions and, when they have difficulty, teachers tend to delve, give clues, or rephrase questions more frequently than with low achievers. Teachers give more affirmative and corrective feedback, and they give more praise and more reasons for praise to high achievers than to low achievers. They also show more personal interest in, are more complimentary and courteous to, and maintain closer physical proximity with high achievers (Good & Brophy, 1978; Kerman, 1979).

"Single ability classrooms" that emphasize reading ability throughout the curriculum can exacerbate performance differentials to the extent that they give an advantage to majority language students who are often better readers (Cohen, 1980). Classrooms that are competitive in nature and call for public displays of competence can also engender performance differentials insofar as they provide occasions for performance evaluation and call on abilities and learning styles that minority language students may not have. It is performance evaluations that form the basis for performance expectations and ultimately performance differentials.

Assessment procedures, both formal and informal, that seek to identify the cause of the students' performance in the students themselves can also exacerbate differential expectations and thereby put minority language students at a disadvantage (Cummins, 1985). More specifically, most assessment procedures, and certainly norm-referenced ones, focus attention on the psychological or intellectual functioning of the student and are biased in favor of majority group standards of performance. To the extent that minority language students do poorly on such "tests," performance expectations will be maintained at a low level. Furthermore, any problems the student might be facing because of social norms or performance expectations in the classroom will be ignored if standardized tests are the primary basis for assessing performance.

Ethnographic studies of ethnolinguistically mixed classes have found that, indeed, minority students are less active and less influential and they receive less supportive attention than Anglo students. For example, the U.S. Commission on Civil Rights (1973) examined student–teacher interactions in over 400 classrooms in California, New Mexico, and Texas and found that, compared to Anglo-American students, Mexican-American students were praised 36 percent less often; had their ideas developed 40 percent less often; were responded to positively 40 percent less often; had questions directed to them 21 percent less often; and generally received less attention. Kagan (1986) reports that "In traditionally structured bilingual classrooms, compared to other students Limited English Proficient students are the recipients of less teacher and peer communication, and communication at a lower cognitive and linguistic level (Long, 1980; Schinke-Llano, 1983)."

Summary

The intent here has been to show how sociocultural factors in society at large might be used to describe interaction patterns in mixed ethnolinguistic classrooms. In particular, status and power differentials have been used to explain differences in the academic performance of minority and majority group students. The sociocultural effects discussed in this section are mediated by the social structure of classrooms. It is not difficult to imagine how the three other domains of school life identified by Cohen—power relationships in the formal organization of the school, status differences between the students, and norms for social interaction outside the classroom, could reinforce and contribute to these effects. The school described by Cleghorn and Genesee is an example of how the formal organization of a mixed language school can play an important part in establishing status differentials. In the immersion school under investigation, the school administration (i.e., the principal) as well as the district administration were dominated by English-speaking Quebecers—even the French consultant for this immersion school was a native English-speaker. While there are sound pedagogical and historical reasons for these personnel placements, the fact still remains that, from a sociocultural point of view, the school and district were dominated by, and seen by the students to be dominated by, English Canadians. This is undoubtedly a frequent situation in the case of bilingual programs in the United States.

Clearly the picture presented here is incomplete. The dynamics of classroom interaction and its effect on student performance are much more complex than this brief exposition would indicate. We have ignored the possible effects of other mitigating factors, such as cognitive, affective, and pedagogical. Moreover, we have not considered individual student differences or the possibility of subgroup differences. The present perspective, with its emphasis on status and power, has been used to describe the dynamics of classroom interaction and its possible effects on student performance and achievement because it links societal factors, as described in the preceding two sections, with classroom processes, and, moreover, it enjoys some empirical support.

A SYNTHESIS

An integration of the three sociocultural perspectives presented in the preceding sections is illustrated in Figure 7. This model recognizes societal factors (sector "A") as primary causal variables in explaining the nature of schooling for minority language students and their performance in public schools. In particular, it has been suggested that the history of minority groups' incorporation into the host society, their strategies for developing a positive and distinctive cultural identity, and their ethnolinguistic vitality, along with the sociocultural characteristics of schools themselves, can each play a significant role in influencing academic performance. It has been proposed that the effects of societal factors on school performance are mediated by two sets of intervening variables—one set implicates minority groups themselves (sectors "B" and "C") and the other public schooling and schools (sectors "D" and "E").

On the one hand then, intergroup relations in society at large shape the cultural identities of minority groups and their orientations and values toward schooling (sector "B"). Depending upon the history of a particular group's incorporation into society, its ethnolinguistic characteristics and vitality, it may or may not adopt a cultural identity that supports behaviors and values that promote academic success in public schools. The development of cultural identity was

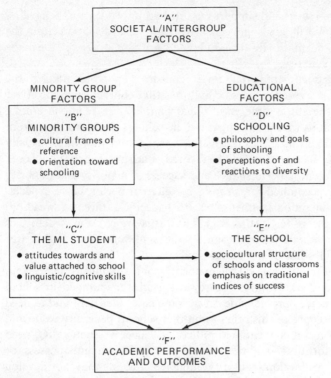

Figure 7 Sociocultural Model of Minority Group Education

characterized in terms of assimilation, creation of new dimensions of cultural identity, and redefinition of old ones. Yet other groups will promote academic success as part of a strategy of upgrading their cultural identity by competing directly with the majority group for status and power.

The cultural orientation of each minority group along with its specific orientations and attitudes toward schooling are passed on to their children through socialization (sector "C"). The linguistic and cognitive factors discussed by Cummins (chapter nine) and Heath (1986) would figure in this causal chain, since they are influenced in important ways by processes within the family and thereby come to exert significant intervening effects on school performance. From the perspective of the minority language child then, one could conceptualize the consequences of these sociocultural effects in terms of *socialization* and *cognitive/linguistic training*.

At the same time, societal factors at large will also influence the philosophy of schooling (sector "D"), as proposed by Hernandez-Chavez and Paulston, and, in turn, the very structure and pedagogical processes of schools (sector "E"). It is widely held that the goals of public schooling in North America are to train students to assume the social, economic, and political responsibilities of society and that they therefore reflect and support majority group values and behaviors. Differences from the majority group are generally regarded as deviations from the norm and therefore problematic. Radical differences are discouraged in the name of maintaining social stability.

It has been widely documented that, unless concerted efforts are made to the contrary, schools will recreate the social conditions that charactertize society at large. In particular, the status differentials that characterize relations among groups in the community are often mirrored in schools with students from different ethnolinguistic groups. This means that certain student groups, usually those from the majority social group, will be favored or advantaged in school over other groups. The differential performance and success of majority and minority group students can be accounted for, in part, by different performance expectations based on status differentials, either of a school-specific nature (e.g., reading) or of a more general nature (e.g., ethnicity). Thus, it is argued, the structure of mixed ethnolinguistic schools often promotes the achievement of high-status students while impeding that of low-status students.

The orientation of schools toward the majority group also means that certain behaviors, attitudes, and motivations are rewarded and encouraged in school while others are regarded as problematic or, in some cases, deficient and in need of remediation. It is because of this orientation that schools generally value and base important decisions on conventional indices of "success" such as IQ, need achievement, and conformity—qualities that most majority students possess, or at least are socialized to develop. Minority language students may not develop these qualities to the same extent as majority group children, or they may not exhibit them in the same ways owing to sociocultural differences. Therefore, they may be disadvantaged or appear disadvantaged in school. As well, educators may often overlook or even denigrate the unique skills, behavioral styles, or social orientations that minority language children bring to school, either because they are not familiar with such culturally distinct characteristics or because they rigidly uphold majority group characteristics. In so doing, they may impede some students' academic progress.

Strategies for Change.   Certain approaches to changing the sociocultural fabric of schools in order to upgrade the status of minority language students and optimize their academic performance are indicated by the present framework. It follows from this framework that it is not sufficient to merely use the students' home language in bilingual programs; nor is it sufficient to employ members of the minority group in the school only as teachers and support personnel. What is called for is the use of the students' home language and the employment of minority language group members in ways that upgrade their status and power relative to that of English and English-speaking people. This might mean "over-using" the minority language or "over-representing" the minority group in the administrative hierarchy of the school, relative to their predominance in the community at large, in order to offset the inferior social status otherwise associated with the group. The San Diego two-way bilingual program for both Spanish-speaking and English-speaking students, for example, stressed the use of Spanish during the early years of the program in order to overcome the tendency for English to dominate and in order to give Spanish the status needed to promote its acquisition. Iadicola (1979) has found that the tendency for Anglo students to be more active and dominating than minority students was markedly reduced in schools where there were more minority group members in the student body, the faculty, and the administration.

Suggestions for fundamental change in the curriculum are also indicated by this framework. Insofar as competitive, single-ability classes, with frequent opportunities for public displays of competence, tend to favor high-status majority group students, the curriculum needs to be structured to reduce or eliminate this effect. One way of achieving this is through the use of cooperative learning tasks that reduce competitiveness among students (see Kagan, 1986, for a detailed discussion of this). Cooperative learning tasks have the added advantage that they are thought to be more compatible with the cooperative learning styles of many minority students in contrast to the competitive styles of many majority students (Kagan, 1986). Cohen (1980), is careful to point out, however, that the mere use of cooperative learning tasks is not sufficient to reduce status differentials, since many such tasks entail differential status effects. This is likely to occur in tasks in which individual students are evaluated on the basis of how much their performance contributes in absolute terms to group performance, or, conversely, the group is evaluated on the basis of how much each student contributes in absolute terms to the accomplishment of the task. In these cases, low-achieving students who contribute relatively little to group performance will come to be seen as weak members of the group by other group members, thereby perpetuating differential performance expectations. "Improvement point scoring," according to which student progress is evaluated on the basis of their improvement from previous performance and, likewise, group performance is based on improvement from past performance, can reduce the problems inherent in evaluating absolute performance levels. In short, cooperative learning tasks must be chosen carefully if they are to upgrade the status of minority language students and maximize their achievement gains.

An additional curricular innovation suggested by the present framework is the use of multiple-ability classes that allow minority students to demonstrate and be given credit for their particular competencies. Individualization of instruction, along with improvement point methods of evaluation, is one way in which heterogeneous abilities can be recognized. The reader is referred to Cohen (1980), Cummins (1985), Kagan (1986), and Ogbu and Matute-Bianchi (1986) for additional suggestions regarding changes in mixed ethnolinguistic schools that are compatible with the present framework.

An important feature of the intergroup model is that it recognizes the roles and responsibilities of both minority and majority groups in the academic success or failure of minority language students. In other words, the processes associated with academic success/failure are not defined in a one-sided way, with minority groups being depicted as victims of consciously oppressive majority groups. Rather, minority groups and minority group members are recognized as dynamic and adaptive social entities that react to and in turn create social forces (see also Cortes, 1986). Cleghorn and Genesee's (1984) ethnographic study of teacher interaction in an early French immersion program in Montreal illustrates this conceptualization in some detail. It will be recalled that the interaction patterns identified in that school were seen to be the product of both English teachers' attempts to maintain the status quo and French teachers' attempts to maintain professional harmony. Their shared social reality included complex social interaction patterns that both groups of teachers had developed and tacitly accepted. Thus, if significant change is to occur, it will have to implicate both the minority group and the majority group (see also Ogbu & Matute-Bianchi, 1986).

A sociocultural framework of the type outlined here is an important adjunct to the cognitive/linguistic perspectives presented by others (Baker & de Kanter, 1983; Cummins, 1981; Epstein, 1977). As long as our conceptualization of the educational problems of minority language students emphasizes linguistic and cognitive factors, our responses to these problems will be cognitive and linguistic in nature. As the preceding proposals imply, such responses may not be optimal.

11

Bilingual Education: Teaching and Learning English

⌐Since its beginning some 20 years ago, bilingual education programs for minority language children in the United States have been the subject of heated debate. As we have seen in chapter nine, the most controversial feature of these programs has been their use of non-English languages for a substantial part of curricular instruction. On the one side are those who argue in favor of this practice for pedagogical, social, and economic reasons (Cummins, 1981; Hernandez-Chavez, 1984), and on the other side are those who argue against such a practice largely on economic and ideological grounds (Bethell, 1979; Edwards, 1981). The debate has been long-standing and far-reaching, drawing in academics, researchers, public policy makers, government officials, media editorialists, and even "the common man and woman in the street." It is far from being resolved. ⌐

At the same time, there would appear to be a consensus concerning the other side of the bilingual education coin, that is, the English side. Even the most ardent supporters of bilingual education recognize the primary importance of English language proficiency for minority language students: "for minority language children in the United States, strong English proficiency in all domains is essential" (Hernandez-Chavez, 1984, p. 171). Furthermore, the available evidence indicates that most minority language students are not in bilingual programs and that those who are often receive most of their academic instruction through the medium of English (Waggoner & O'Malley, 1985). Thus, there is an evident need to ensure that minority language students both in bilingual programs and in non-bilingual programs receive the best quality English language instruction possible.

In this chapter we will address the question of teaching and learning English in programs for minority language students. In particular, a number of significant features that characterize successful second language programs, as exemplified by immersion, will be identified and applied to the case of minority language students. Before proceeding to the discussion of these features, let us examine the debate over bilingual education versus immersion in English for minority language students.

IMMERSION VERSUS BILINGUAL EDUCATION

Despite their common interests in language education, immersion and bilingual education have been uncomfortable allies. In fact, as often as not, immersion programs and their very success have been depicted as "enemies" of bilingual education, or at best as an approach to be avoided. Thus, for example, Paulston (1980), in a discussion of theoretical issues in bilingual education, opines "I consider the St. Lambert study one of the most potentially dangerous studies I know, as its findings are so often cited as a rationale against bilingual education for minority group members" (p. 25). Paulston clearly acknowledges that it is not the immersion programs themselves that are to be mistrusted, but rather the interpretations that are often made of them. Hernandez-Chavez (1984), along with a number of other writers, have pointed out important sociocultural differences between majority language students and minority language students that caution against the application of immersion for minority language students (Cohen & Swain, 1976; McLaughlin, 1984):

> For majority language students enrichment education (i.e., immersion) is aligned with the Canadian cultural and social condition. It is unreasonable in the extreme to expect the Canadian enrichment model to be directly transferable to language minority contexts in the United States. This model is appropriate and effective in Quebec and now in other parts of Canada, because the program was designed under specific educational conditions by and for a middle class majority population and with the guidance of dedicated researchers backed by sound psycholinguistic theories. The Canadian enrichment model is not appropriate for language minority children in the United States because the requisite sociopolitical, sociolinguistic, and educational conditions for the successful conduct of an enrichment program are completely different. (p 168)

In 1984 the California State Department of Education published a volume entitled *Studies on Immersion Education: A Collection for United States Educators.* (see California . . . , 1984). The purpose of this collection of invited papers was to describe in detail the Canadian immersion programs and to consider their implications for public education in the United States. The volume was intended to rectify some of the prevailing misperceptions and myths that surround the Canadian programs so that their points of relevance and nonrelevance for American educators could be better discerned. Such discussion was deemed to be especially important in the case of minority language students, in view of recent suggestions that "immersion programs" be implemented as educational treatments alternative to bilingual education (e.g., Baker & de Kanter, 1983).

Two major conclusions emerged from the California collection. First, immersion programs are a feasible and effective means of achieving high levels of functional proficiency in a second language among majority group, English-speaking students, one that does not jeopardize their native-language, academic, sociocultural, or cognitive development; the evidence in support of this conclusion was reviewed in chapters three and four. Second, it was concluded that "the Canadian immersion models cannot simply be accepted in toto" when considering the education of minority language children, that is to say limited- or non-English proficient children (Hernandez-Chavez, 1984, p. 170).

The conclusion regarding the use of the immersion approach for educating minority language students was based on concerns over what might be thought of as the programmatic or structural features of the Canadian immersion programs and especially the early total immersion option. In particular, the use of a second language as the primary language of instruction prior to use of the native language, as is the case in immersion programs, runs counter to the bilingual education approach which advocates use of the students' native language for instructional purposes before English is used. A conceptual rationale for, and empirical evidence in favor of, the latter sequence in educational programs for minority language students were discussed in chapter nine.

Reservations about the relevance of the immersion approach for educating minority language students are appropriate and well founded because of the sequence-of-language-of-instruction issue. There is no logical or empirical basis on which to justify the application of this feature of immersion to the education of such students. Very simply, it does not follow from the success of the immersion programs with majority language students that minority language students will be educated through the medium of the majority group language. Even within the Canadian context itself, immersion programs in which minority French-speaking Canadians would receive their primary instruction through English have been disfavored by experts in the field for fear of the detrimental effects that might result from use of this approach with minority group children (Lambert, 1980b; Tucker, 1980).

The principal argument behind the position in favor of English immersion for minority language students is that it provides maximum exposure to English and therefore expedites English language development. In fact, there is ample evidence from a number of research studies that, when it comes to learning English in North America, more exposure to English in school is not necessarily better. The extensive evaluation results of the Canadian immersion programs certainly support this conclusion. Additional corroboration comes from yet other studies in Canada that have looked at French-speaking Canadian students who attend French-medium schools located in English-dominant communities (Hebert, 1976). These studies have found that the French students attending the French-medium schools achieve the same levels of proficiency in English as do comparable French-speaking students attending English-medium schools in the same communities. The findings of recent evaluations of bilingual programs also indicate that more instruction in English does not necessarily result in higher levels of English language proficiency than less instruction. It seems likely that reduced use of English in bilingual and immersion programs is more than compensated for by the extensive exposure that North American children have to English outside school.

Examining the relevance of immersion for educating minority language students exclusively in terms of the sequencing-of-language feature risks throwing the baby out with the bathwater because it ignores other aspects of immersion programs of possible relevance. One would be surprised if the Canadian immersion programs were totally irrelevant to considerations concerning the education of minority language students. After all, the evaluations of immersion programs indicate that they provide effective general education and, more specifically, effective second language education, both of concern to bilingual educators. The relevance of immersion to minority language student education is likely to be found at the level of pedagogical approach or methodology rather than at the level of program structure which, as just noted, might be expected to take quite different forms in the case of majority language students versus minority language students.

A consideration of immersion programs suggests three general pedagogical features of relevance to the design of second language programs for minority language students. They are: 1) an integrated approach to language and academic instruction, 2) an interactional basis for second language learning, and 3) an emphasis on intrinsic motivation to learn academic material. The potential relevance of each feature to programs intended to teach English to minority language students will be examined in this chapter (see also Dolson, 1985b).

LANGUAGE IN SCHOOL

It seems reasonable to begin a discussion of significant features of effective second language learning programs with a consideration of the nature of language proficiency and its development. In recent years there have been a substantial number of important studies and theoretical positions on the nature of language learning and use both in the home and in school settings (Cummins, 1981; Heath, 1983; Snow, 1983; Wells, 1981). Although differing in a number of respects, scholars concur on a number of important points. All agree that language usage and, therefore, proficiency in school differs in some important respects from language usage in home settings. Hence, students who learn patterns of language usage characteristic of school prior to or quickly upon entering school are likely to succeed, whereas students who do not are likely to experience academic difficulty.

As noted earlier, Cummins has characterized language usage in school as context-reduced and cognitively demanding. Snow (1985) has also characterized language usage on a continuum ranging from *contextualized* to *decontextualized,* with the latter emphasized in school settings. Wells (1981) and his colleagues have carried out a longitudinal study of language development and use in the home and in primary school. Wells concludes, on the one hand, that

> there is little in the nature of interactional demands which will be made of children in school that they will not already have become familiar with at home at the level of conversational structure. (p. 237)

He believes, on the other hand, that language usage in the home and in school differ in other important respects: 1) the relative frequency of certain types of conversational structures; 2) the asymmetry of the participants' contributions to interactions; and 3) the significance or meaning attached to certain conversational structures. In contrast to the fairly general characterizations of language usage offered by Snow, Cummins, and Wells, Heath (1986) has described a number of specific patterns of language usage characteristic of mainstream schools. They include, for example, label quests (i.e., requests for the names of items), meaning quests (i.e., requests for the meaning of words, pictures, events, or behavior), and eventcasts (i.e., a running narrative on events currently in the attention of the teller and the audience).

There is also consensus among language researchers that language experiences of an essentially interactional nature provide the basis for development of language proficiency. While language experiences involving literacy (i.e., reading and writing) are generally regarded as important for the development of school-relevant language skills (Heath, 1986), experiences with oral language that has features of decontextualized or literacy-type language are also regarded as important. Snow (1983) has identified some of the features of oral language that make it like literacy: an informational distance between the sender and receiver (or information-gap), explicitness of referencing, complexity of syntax, and a high degree of cohesion. Wells points out the importance of experiences with oral language in everyday life for the development of school-relevant language skills:

> . . . whilst part of the facilitating experience of the more successful children involved the shared activities of being read to, and looking at and talking about books, equally important was the way in which everyday events were picked up in talk, and meanings developed and made more coherent through extended conversation. (1981 p. 263).

Cummins has also argued that the way minority language parents use oral language with their children in the home has an important influence on their development of language for academic purposes.

Thus, recent research has provided us with valuable insights about the development and use of language in the home and in school. There have been serious and systematic attempts to identify those features of language usage in school settings that distinguish it from other settings. In view of the putative differences between language usage in school and in the home, there is an evident need in instructional programs for minority language students to emphasize the attainment of language for academic purposes. This point has been made before, most notably by Cummins (1981). At the same time, the task of identifying specific categories of language usage in school is proving to be very difficult. This poses a serious dilemma for traditional approaches to second language pedagogy that have been largely "analytic" in nature in that they presuppose a finite set of language units that are analyzable and, therefore, teachable; thus, for example structural linguistics gave us grammatical units to teach. From a practical, instructional point of view, how does one teach something that cannot be identified and described clearly?

In lieu of an analytic approach to second language pedagogy, a process approach is suggested. In other words, the essential conditions that are thought to underlie language learning are incorporated into the school curriculum. In particular, certain interactional processes of a discoursal nature, as identified by language researchers, are instantiated in the academic tasks or activities of the classroom. These conditions effectively define the pedagogical approach of the curriculum. The precise units of language to be learned are defined by the communication requirements of the academic tasks that comprise the curriculum and not by some *a priori* theory of language or language learning. It follows that second language learning will then proceed in response to the communication demands of academic work, given certain motivational conditions. In this approach, there is an emphasis on the attainment of language proficiency for academic purposes. Students' demonstrated language proficiency or lack of proficiency during the performance of academic work provides an empirical basis for conscious and systematic language instruction. Key features of such a process approach will be discussed in the following three sections.

AN INTEGRATED APPROACH TO SECOND LANGUAGE TEACHING

In immersion programs, there is an emphasis on academic instruction as a basis for second language teaching and learning. Indeed, the success of the immersion programs has been judged in large part in terms of their academic outcomes—IM students achieve the same levels of academic knowledge and skill as majority language students instructed entirely through English. From a language learning point of view, this means that the programs are successful at enabling students to learn the second language skills they need in order to attain normal levels of academic achievement. That the primary focus of immersion programs is academic achievement is evidenced by the fact that the programs are deemed highly successful despite the evident linguistic weaknesses of IM students. More nativelike levels of second language proficiency at the expense of normal academic achievement would not have been regarded by Canadian educators or parents as success. What is important about the students' level of second language development is that it does not limit their academic development.

The documented effectiveness of the immersion programs indicates that an approach in which second language instruction is integrated with academic instruction is an effective way to teach the language skills needed for educational purposes. It is evident that an isolated second language approach of the FSL type would not have permitted students to benefit from academic instruction through the second language to the same extent that immersion did, nor would an FSL approach have resulted in the same high levels of functional proficiency in the second language. Given minority language students' need to acquire proficiency in English for academic purposes, and given the success of the immersion approach in this regard, it is suggested that English language instruction to minority language students be integrated judiciously with academic instruction. Viewed differently, having to teach curriculum material through English to minority language students need not be viewed as impossible or disadvantageous. Rather, content instruction through a second language can provide a powerful means for promoting second language learning. Integration of language instruction with academic instruction is an essential condition of the process approach to second language teaching being proposed here.

In an integrated second language program, the primary basis of instruction is not language, as is the case in most second language programs. In fact, language is secondary and, from the students' point of view, it is often incidental—language is taught and learned to serve communication needs in the pursuit of academic goals. This is not to say that language learning is always incidental, either from an instructional or from a learning point of view. To the contrary, conscious, intentional teaching and learning of language is probably essential for the achievement of literacy skills and higher-order oral language skills, the kinds of context-reduced or decontextualized language proficiency referred to previously (Snow, 1985; Ellis, 1984).

The primary basis of instruction in an integrated second language program is defined in academic terms. If second language instruction is to be truly and naturally integrated with academic instruction, then it should be integrated with the instructional practices normally used by teachers. Research on teacher planning has found that *task* is the basic unit of planning used by teachers and the basis for most instructional activities in the classroom (Shavelson & Stern, 1981). In other words, the notion of task is commonly used by teachers to think about and plan their instructional time. The notion of task has also been used widely in research on the nature of academic work in schools. Doyle (1983) conceptualizes the curricula of elementary and secondary schools as a collection of academic tasks. The notion of task focuses attention on three aspects of students' work: 1) the products students are to formulate, 2) the operations that are used to generate products, and 3) the resources available to students in generating a given product.

Student *resources* can be defined in terms of students' language, cognitive, and social skills as well as their interests and needs (to be discussed later). The resources available to students determine the limiting conditions on task performance and therefore on task selection by the instructor. Doyle defines task *operations* in terms of the cognitive operations involved in task accomplishment. Four general task types are 1) memory tasks, in which students are asked to recognize or reproduce information encountered previously; 2) procedural tasks, in which students are expected to apply a standardized or predictable formula to generate answers (e.g., subtraction problems); 3) comprehension tasks, in which students might be asked to recognize transformed versions of previously encountered information, to apply procedures to new problems, or to draw inferences from previously encountered information; and 4) opinion tasks, in which students are asked to state a preference or give an evaluation of something. Academic tasks can be further described in terms of their degree of complexity and their degree of abstractness or concreteness.

What is important about tasks is that students will learn what tasks lead them to do—students learn by doing tasks. In general then, task selection by the instructor is the way by which he/she directs and influences student learning. Tasks should be selected in accordance with general curriculum guidelines and objectives. While it may be necessary to select simplified academic tasks at the outset for minority language students, continued selection of simplified tasks is not advisable. Rather, in general, the same tasks prescribed for English-proficient students should be expected of minority language students (Chamot, 1985). Indeed, IM students are expected to complete the same academic tasks and demonstrate the same level of achievement in the performance of these tasks as students in the regular program.

Language figures in a task-based approach because it is an integral part of many task products and a prerequisite for successful task performance and as such needs to be learned. Requisite language skills may include discourse features or language functions demanded by the task or simply vocabulary or technical terminology associated with task content. It is not possible at present to provide generic descriptions of the language needed to perform academic tasks (cf. Heath, 1986). At the same time, careful examination by instructors of the tasks they are using and the way they are using them should make it possible to consciously and formally teach some of the requisite language skills involved in specific tasks either as part of or preliminary to academic instruction. In any case, proficiency in the language associated with academic tasks is not presumed in an integrated program. An advantage of a task-based approach is that language required of specific academic tasks is taught in context. Transference of the language skills needed to perform one task do not have to be transferred from another task. In contrast, independent language instruction, of the pull-out ESL type, presupposes transference of skills from the language arts class to the math class, the social studies class, and so on. In fact, we do not know whether such transfer occurs effectively or efficiently.

Evaluation of student performance in an integrated second language program is based on accomplishment of academic tasks, taking into account all resources, both language and nonlanguage, available to the student. Language is included as part of performance evaluation to the extent that explicit language requirements are included in the definition of task products; otherwise, language is not necessarily an integral part of formal performance evaluation. In other words, students should be given due credit for having accomplished academic tasks using any means possible. Teachers of minority language students should be encouraged to recognize the academic accomplishments of their students independently of their language competence, unless language is an explicit product of the task (e.g., an essay). This is necessary if students' self-esteem and motivation for academic learning is to be sustained. There is the danger that minority language students will become discouraged and unmotivated because of their non-native competence in English if language is overemphasized when evaluating their academic performance. The results from immersion programs demonstrate quite convincingly that students can achieve noteworthy academic accomplishments without complete, nativelike mastery of the language of instruction. IM students are undaunted in their pursuit of academic goals despite nonnativelike competence in the target language because they are not penalized for non-nativelike use of language.

While it was pointed out in chapter four that IM students seldom achieve nativelike mastery of the second language, there are a number of reasons for thinking that minority language students in American schools would not experience the same "linguistic ceiling" effect. Minority language students have considerably more exposure to English in school than IM students do to their target second language. Bilingual education programs are part of an otherwise English language school system that provides much English language exposure, whereas immersion schools provide relatively little target language exposure outside the classroom. Minority language students attending bilingual programs in the United States also have considerably more exposure to English outside school, with peers and adults, and through the media, than IM students do to the second language. As noted in chapter seven, Genesee (1978b, 1981a) found that even IM students in the bilingual city of Montreal do not actively seek out situations in which they can use French, and they appear to have relatively little direct contact with French speakers except for public service encounters. Moreover, it seems likely that minority language students are motivated to acquire nativelike English language skills in order to become American, whereas the evidence suggests that neither IM students, their parents, nor the educational system want them to become French Canadian. Thus, there is probably more tolerance toward IM students' imperfect use of French, for example, than toward minority language students' imperfect use of English.

As noted earlier, not all language learning in an integrated program need be incidental. Intentional, systematic learning guided by explicit instruction is also needed. Ongoing informal assessment of students' language proficiency during task performance can provide useful input for explicit language instruction. In other words, the content of language arts instruction should be derived from an informal assessment of the students' language proficiency as demonstrated in their other subjects. In this way, language arts instruction can be integrated with academic instruction. In some cases this may mean modifying language arts materials to better teach the language skills needed by the students in their regular classes. In other cases, it may mean using regular academic material for language arts instruction. In either case, this may mean that the language arts instructor, if he/she is not the regular classroom teacher, will need to monitor content classes in order to better ascertain the kinds of language required in these classes.

In sum, an integrated instructional approach to second language teaching for minority language students entails the following implications: 1) language learning is not a pre-requisite or precusor to academic learning; rather, they co-occur; 2) academic achievement is the primary incentive for second language learning; 3) English language learning and teaching are organized according to the communicative and cognitive requirements of academic tasks; 4) evaluation of students' academic performance does not overemphasize language competence, unless the goal of the lesson is explicitly language-related; 5) teachers charged with academic instruction through English (i.e., regular teachers) should recognize and assume some responsibility for satisfying their minority language students' English language learning needs; and 6) ESL instruction should be coordinated with the language requirements of academic instruction.

AN INTERACTIONAL BASIS OF SECOND LANGUAGE LEARNING

It is not mere use of the target language for academic instruction that accounts for the effectiveness of immersion programs; nor is this approach likely to work well with minority language students, as history has shown us. The effectiveness of immersion undoubtedly depends very much on the quality of the interaction between the teacher and the students. In fact, little systematic examination of interaction patterns in immersion classes has been undertaken so that we do not know precisely how language is used by immersion teachers. As a result, the following description is largely speculative and awaits empirical validation.

The scant data that are available (Cleghorn, 1985), along with anecdotal observations, suggest an instructional style in immersion classes that could be characterized in terms of Wells's notion of "negotiation of meaning" (Wells, 1979). Negotiation of meaning involves a set of interaction strategies that promotes mutual understanding among the participants. In particular, these strategies promote the learners' comprehension of what the teacher is intending to mean, what the situation means, and therefore what the language means and how it works. Comprehension is important because immersion programs aim for normal levels of academic achievement. Comprehension is also important because it is through comprehension of the total communicative situation, including both verbal messages and the nonverbal significance of events, that the student comes to learn how to decode the target language and ultimately how to use it effectively.

This aspect of negotiation of meaning resembles Krashen's Input Hypothesis, or what is more commonly known as comprehensible input. According to Krashen's input hypothesis,

> We acquire language by understanding input that is a little beyond our current level of competence. . . . Listening comprehension and reading are of primary importance in the second language program, and . . . the ability to

speak (or write) fluently in a second language will come on its own with time. Speaking fluency is thus not "taught" directly; rather, speaking ability "emerges" after the acquirer has built up competence through comprehending input. (1983, p. 32)

In other words, acquisition of a second language depends upon input that is comprehensible and just slightly ahead of the learner's current level of proficiency. That comprehensible input is achieved successfully in immersion classes is attested to by the results of academic achievement testing.

But, how can input be made comprehensible? A number of obvious and simple strategies come to mind. The first five that follow are strategies used by the teacher; three of them are explicitly linguistic in nature while two are nonlinguistic:

1.   Modifications of teacher talk is a primary strategy. In particular, the use of simplified, redundant and slower speech can serve to facilitate comprehension by second language learners in much the same way that it is thought to do in the case of first language learners (Snow & Ferguson, 1978). It has been found that the language used by native speakers with nonnative speakers in non-school settings has these same characteristics (Long, 1980). Simplified teacher talk can help the second language learner identify the constituent parts of speech, which in turn can facilitate learning the language. Slower, redundant speech gives the learner more time to process language input and at the same time decreases memory load by reducing the amount of language that has to be stored in memory. It is not advisable that simplified speech always be used by teachers with minority language students, since it is likely that this would lead to simplified learner competence, or pidgin. As was pointed out in chapter four, students probably need progressively more complex language models and communication demands made on them in the classroom if their proficiency is to continue to develop. As well, it is important that the conceptual or academic content not be simplified, except perhaps during the early stages of language learning (Wong-Fillmore, Ammon, McLaughlin, & Ammon, 1985).

2.   Direct questioning by the teacher of previously presented material is another obvious strategy. Here teachers must be prepared to assume considerable responsibility for communication breakdown; they must be prepared to reformulate misunderstood messages or to try other means of conveying the same thing.

3.   Another strategy entails providing explanations of new or unfamiliar concepts that will cause confusion if they are not clarified before instruction begins. Similarly, definitions or clarification of language that is new to the students is useful. This strategy is akin to a needs analysis of the learners' conceptual and linguistic needs prior to each lesson. It is in this sense that language and academic learning are integrated.

4.   Meaning can also be made comprehensible through the provision of contextual support, that is, the use of nonverbal frames of reference, such as physical objects or realia, or experiences familiar to the students. Cummins (1981)

has emphasized the progression from context-embedded to context-reduced language in educating minority language students; Parker (1985b) has made a similar proposal in describing sheltered English programs for minority language students.

5.   Teachers of minority language students must also demonstrate general sensitivity to nonverbal feedback from the learners that they are confused or do not understand. Here the teacher needs to be able to detect and interpret feedback that may be culturally different from what he/she is used to—silence may denote confusion in one culture but comprehension in another.

Other strategies involve the learner:

6.   Direct questioning of the teacher or demands for clarification, simplification, or repetition. The teacher must make it clear to the students that such demands are legitimate and she/he may need to teach students how to ask such questions or make such demands.

7.   Nonverbal gestures that indicate a lack of comprehension.

8.   Use of the native language. There is no reason why students should not use their native language to communicate with their teachers, provided they are bilingual, especially when the students' proficiency in English is insufficient to allow communication to take place. As noted earlier, students use their native language in the early stages of immersion programs. This strategy can serve not only to encourage communication and therefore facilitate negotiation of meaning when the students' English language skills are rudimentary, but it can also engender a sense of well-being and belongingness. Likewise, there is no reason why bilingual teachers might not also use the students' native language to help clarify their message when all else fails. Teachers, however, should avoid overuse of both languages, as in the case of the so-called concurrent method. The success of second language learning ultimately depends on the learner having to rely exclusively on the target language for communication.

Student–student interaction can also provide much valuable comprehensible input. If academic tasks are selected and structured carefully, then those students who have already acquired the language skills necessary for task performance, be they native speakers or proficient non-native speakers, can serve as language models and teachers for non-proficient speakers. Cooperative learning tasks have been suggested as effective means for capitalizing on student–student interaction (Kagan, 1986). An obvious advantage of utilizing student–student interaction is the opportunity it gives students to use language productively. In comparison, there are real limitations on how much students can talk if their interactions are restricted to the teacher. This brings us to a discussion of the importance of language output or production as part of negotiation of meaning.

As noted in the previous quotation, Krashen contends that the only role of output on the part of the learner is to generate more comprehensible input. He has argued that language production skills, i.e., speaking and writing, proceed naturally from comprehending input; production skills do not have to be taught or practiced directly. There are a number of reasons to think that active production of language in communicative interaction is important for second language learning—not only in order to generate more comprehensible input, but also in order to generate language itself (see also Swain, 1985). First of all, there is the obvious argument that language comprehension does not by itself constitute total language proficiency. There is ample anecdotal evidence of children of immigrant parents who have learned to decode their parents' secret messages in the mother tongue but who are incapable of actually speaking the language because they have never practiced using it. The evidence from the immersion programs themselves attest to the limitations of extensive comprehensible input in the absence of comparable output. More specifically, it is clear that IM students receive extensive comprehensible input in class, but they do not attain nativelike levels of productive proficiency, especially when it comes to speaking.

Expressed more technically, language production is important because it serves as a means whereby the learner can test out hypotheses about the elements and rules of language *use*. It is a way of trying out rules of expression to see if they work. Knowing the specific rules of a language is not always necessary for accurate comprehension because many rules are strictly grammatical and serve no real semantic purpose. For example, one does not have to know and understand the rule for forming third person singular verbs in English in order to understand the sentence "He hates onions." The pronoun "he" carries the important semantic information of who hates onions in an easier and phonologically more salient way than the third person singular "s" marker.

Furthermore, the meaning of many verbal messages can be gotten from contextual cues and does not depend on a precise grammatical analysis of the message. For example, it is not necessary to comprehend the precise grammatical rules that make up the sentence "Do you want some chocolate cake?" in order to comprehend this request and to respond to it appropriately when one is made a direct offer of cake. But, for the second language speaker to make a similar nativelike offer depends upon his/her mastery of the grammatical rules that underlie formation of interrogatives. Thus, opportunities for language production provide the learner with practice in stringing together linguistic elements in correct grammatical form in order to try out his/her production skills. It is difficult to imagine how any amount of comprehensible input would suffice to make one nativelike in speaking a second language. Lacking nativelike proficiency will mark the individual as a non-native speaker, which in turn can have negative social connotations (Ryan, 1983).

There are neurophysiological reasons for believing that language comprehension and language production depend upon different neurophysiological subsystems in the brain. It has been well established that damage to certain areas of the brain will impair language comprehension and leave production skills relatively in tact, while damage to other areas of the brain will have the opposite effects (Penfield & Roberts, 1959). That language production and language comprehension have different locuses of neurological control suggests that they develop somewhat independently. It is also interesting to observe here that second language fossilization has always been described in terms of output performance and not comprehension, again suggesting a linguistic di-morphism. In any event, the implication is that one learns to speak by speaking and to write by writing. This is not to say that comprehension of spoken and written language is irrelevant to mastery of speaking and writing skills, but they are not the same.

It could also be argued that using language productively is particularly important when studying academic material because talking about such material gives the learner an opportunity to analyze, manipulate, and evaluate it. Such linguistico-cognitive activities may be important for acquiring new information and skills (Piaget, 1959). Passive comprehension is probably insufficient for true assimilation and retention of new information.

Finally, it has been suggested by many language researchers that language is learned by taking part in discourse "which gives due weight to the contribution of both parties, and emphasizes mutuality and reciprocity in the meanings that are constructed and negotiated through talk" (Wells, 1981, p. 115). The available evidence suggests that this is equally true for classroom second language learning (Ellis, 1984). In terms of the integrated approach discussed in the preceding section, it follows that academic tasks that allow students to *"do discourse"* are probably beneficial for second language learning. Ellis has suggested five features of instructional materials, and one could add academic tasks, that characterize real discourse in the classroom:

1. There must be a communicative purpose, not merely a pedagogic one.
2. There must be a focus on the message or on meaning rather than on how the message is conveyed.
3. There must be an information-gap—one speaker must not know what the other speaker is going to say.
4. Communication must be negotiated rather than predetermined. In particular, there must not be rigid control over the language to be used.
5. The learners must be allowed to use whatever resources, verbal or nonverbal, are at their disposal.

In summary, it is being suggested here that negotiation of meaning which entails both comprehensible *input* and *output* provides an interactional strategy by which students and teachers can actively pursue both second language learning and academic achievement. Negotiation of meaning serves academic achievement since academic content provides the substance for negotiation and a reason for negotiation. At the same time, it is through active negotiation of the meaning of academic instruction that the new language is decoded and ultimately mastered.

Evaluation research on immersion, both in Canada and in the United States, has been almost entirely product or summative in orientation. As a result, there is a virtual absence of information concerning the pedagogical and linguistic strategies used by immersion teachers. Consequently, it cannot be asserted with any certainty that the strategies described here are actually used commonly or consistently in immersion classes. Lacking such information, we are poorly prepared to train teachers in the most effective instructional strategies. A program of research to investigate how immersion teachers integrate academic and language instruction is called for. In this regard, a number of characteristics of social interaction that are thought to facilitate acquisition of decontextualized skills and specifically literacy-related language skills have been suggested by language researchers: semantic contingency (Cross, 1978; Wells, 1980), scaffolding (Bruner, 1978), and accountability procedures (Dore, 1985). These strategies of social interaction could be primary focuses of research centering on interaction patterns in immersion classrooms. Heath's (1986) school-related language genres would also be likely candidates for investigation. The information collected in such research would be doubly useful, since it could be used to optimize the effectiveness of instruction for both minority language students in English classes and majority language students in immersion.

MOTIVATION AND SECOND LANGUAGE LEARNING

No discussion of effective second language learning environments would be complete without a consideration of student motivation. The importance of motivational factors in bilingual education can be considered from two different perspectives—one that focuses on the minority language child as a member of society and one that focuses on the individual learner.

According to the societal view, the academic and linguistic development of minority language students can be impeded by their minority group status and, in particular, by the differential and even discriminatory treatment they sometimes receive in otherwise majority language schools that make no special provisions for their special language needs or that give no special recognition to their distinctive cultural backgrounds. The poor academic performance of many minority language students in this situation can be viewed in motivational terms— they do not do well because to succeed in traditional majority language schools requires that they give up or reject their home language and culture, a sociolinguistic doublebind. In many cases they cannot or will not do this and, hence, they experience academic difficulties. Accordingly, educational programs for minority language students need to provide positive role models in the form of highly trained teachers who speak their native language and who represent their culture. Similarly, the use of native language and culturally sensitive educational materials can serve to complement minority language students' ethnic identity. A case was made in the preceding chapter for modifying classroom organizations and instructional strategies in order to offset the differential and disadvantaging kinds of treatment that can occur in classes with mixed ethnolinguistic student groups. It has even been argued that real improvements in employment opportunities and social advancement for minority language group members are needed in order to provide incentives for academic achievement (Ogbu & Matute-Bianchi, 1986). Since these perspectives have been discussed in some detail in the preceding chapter and elsewhere by others (e.g., Cummins, 1985; Hernandez-Chavez, 1984), they will not be repeated at this time.

Rather attention will focus on the second aspect of motivation, namely the minority language child as an individual learner. A number of research studies that have investigated the characteristics of successful second language learners have reported that students' attitudes and feelings about the immediate learning experiences provided in the classroom and by instructional materials and approaches can have significant effects on second language achievement (Genesee & Hamayan, 1980; Naiman, Frohlich, & Stern, 1975). It might be expected that this aspect of motivation could be just as important in some cases as the societal one. It is possible to imagine, for example, minority language students who do not feel alienated from the school environment and who do not feel pressure to abandon their home language and culture in exchange for fitting in to a predominantly English-speaking society, but who nevertheless are still not motivated to learn in school because of largely pedagogical factors.

At the outset, it can be assumed that there are probably few individuals who are motivated to learn second or foreign languages for their own sake; certainly there are few school-aged children who are so motivated. However, most existing ESL methods suppose such motivation, or they make thinly disguised attempts to present language learning as something else. In contrast, the premise of the immersion approach or an integrated approach is that students will be motivated to learn the second language to the extent that they are motivated academically. Language according to this approach is merely a tool to be learned in order to attain the real goal, that of academic success. Viewed from this perspective, the issue of motivation is not unique to bilingual education. It is fundamental to all education. The question can then be reformulated to ask what types of school environments best motivate students. This is basically a question of the nature and quality of the educational curriculum.

Social-psychological research has shown that the social environment can have a strong effect on the type of motivation that underlies people's actions (Deci, 1985). More specifically, environments that control behavior engender predominantly *extrinsic motivation* while environments that support automony engender *intrinsic motivation*. Intrinsic motivation is having the desire to be effective, while extrinsic motivation is feeling pushed by external rewards and punishments to achieve. Research on motivation in school settings has found that students in the classrooms of control-oriented teachers showed less intrinsic motivation, perceived themselves as less competent, and felt less good about themselves than other students. In terms of actual learning, it was found that intrinsically motivated students demonstrated greater conceptual learning than extrinsically motivated students, although both types of students were equally good at rote memorization tasks. The importance of intrinsic motivation for second language learning is that it is a better means of tapping those individualistic and personal reasons that would motivate someone to learn a second language to a high level of proficiency. In contrast, a learning environment that works on extrinsic motivation presupposes a common agenda for learning. As well, intrinsic motivation is more likely than extrinsic motivation to sustain the learners' interest and effort in second language learning.

The importance of intrinsic motivation has been emphasized in a somewhat different way in Piaget's theory of development. According to Piaget (1959), cognitive development can be characterized as a sequence of mutually interrelated stages. Individuals advance through these stages as a result of their interactions with the environment, be it defined in physical, cognitive, or social terms. It is the individual's attempt to assimilate increasingly complex and abstract aspects of his/her environment that promotes development. It is implicit in Piaget's theory that cognitive development and learning are based on the individual's intrinsic motivation to understand and master salient and significant aspects of his or her environment. Although Piaget tends to view these forces as biological or cognitive in nature rather than social-psychological, his conceptualization has evident implications for classroom organization and management in that it emphasizes an interactive learning environment and intrinsic motivation as the primary bases for learning.

The application of these principles to curriculum design and the impact they can have on student motivation and second language achievement can be illustrated by reference to immersion once again. The immersion program of relevance here is the activity-centered program that was discussed in chapter five. It will be recalled that this program was designed to capitalize on individual students' motivation to learn academic topics of their own choosing as a basis for second language learning. Programmatically, it was a grade 7 partial immersion program in which half of the school day was spent in English and half was spent in French. The French half of the curriculum was activity-based and included language arts, science, and social studies. The students worked individually or in small groups on a number of different social studies and science projects throughout the year. Many of the projects provided hands-on experiences that provided rich contextual support for second language learning. The projects often required that the students go beyond the classroom to complete their projects, e.g., extensive library work or the collection of information in the community or neighborhood (see Stevens, 1983, for a discussion of some of these projects).

The program also emphasized individualization in that each student was actively involved in defining the goals and means of attaining the goals of his/her projects. This allowed the students to work at their own pace and according to their own personal learning styles, with the condition that a certain number of projects had to be completed in each subject area by the end of the year. Each project was accompanied by a variety of language-related activities, such as written reports to the teacher and oral reports to fellow students. All of this was done in French, their second language, so that the students had to learn a considerable amount of new language in order to complete their projects. Thus, language was an essential but often incidental component of each project. In this type of classroom the role of the teacher is quite different from that of traditional classrooms. The teacher serves as a resource and counselor for learning, not as an authority who dispenses information. Students are free to seek alternative sources of information in pursuing their own goals.

The second language proficiency of students who participated in this program was compared to that of comparable students participating in a teacher-centered French immersion program (Stevens, 1976). In this case, the curriculum was made up of regular course work and procedures, and it was largely teacher-centered and group-oriented so that all students worked on the same topics, at the same time, and for the same length of time. Student participation generally involved reacting to teacher-led instructional activities and classroom routines.

Another point of contrast between the two programs was time. Whereas the activity-centered program involved approximately 40 percent of the school day, the teacher-centered program involved approximately 80 percent of the school day, the remaining 20 percent being devoted to English language arts. Thus, the time factor favored the teacher-centered group. Despite this, research results, gathered at the end of grade 7, showed that the students in the activity-centered program had achieved the same level of proficiency as the regular immersion students in the interpersonal communication skills of speaking and listening comprehension, and almost the same levels of proficiency in reading and writing. Stevens attributed the success of the program to 1) the high level of motivation created when students participate in decision-making about learning, 2) the opportunity to use language in personally meaningful situations, and 3) the possibility of interacting with peers and their teacher in an informal, supportive environment.

While there are undoubtedly other innovative ways of designing educational programs that will motivate students intrinsically, the activity-centered approach described here is particularly suitable and effective for promoting second language learning because it incorporates the two other conditions that have been identified with successful language learning environments: 1) it provided a highly integrated academic/language learning classroom environment; and 2) negotiation of meaning was an integral feature of the curriculum by virtue of the opportunities it provided the students to interact with one another and with the instructional materials, many of which were concrete or experiential in nature.

SUMMARY

Three pedagogical aspects of second language immersion programs of possible relevance to teaching English as a Second Language to minority language students have been identified and discussed. They are 1) the integration of second language teaching and academic teaching; 2) classroom interaction characterized by negotiation of meaning; and 3) a curriculum of study that is intrinsically motivating. The importance of these instructional features for second language learning is supported by others. Three of the five features identified by the Significant Bilingual Instructional Features Study are directly related to the "immersion features" described here; they are 1) use of both the students' native language and English for instruction; 2) integration of English language development with basic skills instruction; and 3) use of active teaching behaviors (from Fisher & Guthrie, 1983). Parker (p. 7, 1985b) has recently outlined a proposal for a sheltered-English program for minority language students that contains most of the essential elements of feature 2 (i.e., negotiation of meaning):

> Sheltered-English refers to instruction which is designed for the non-native speaker of English who has some English language proficiency. The subject matter and the delivery of the lessons are done using as many extra-linguistic clues and modifications as possible. Teachers change their speech register by slowing down, limiting their vocabulary and sentence length, by repeating, emphasizing, and explaining key concepts, and by using examples, props, visual clues and body language to convey and reinforce meaning.

The importance of this teacher–student interactional style is further corroborated in a study by Ramirez and Stromquist (1978) on effective ESL methodology in bilingual elementary schools. They identified five teacher behaviors that had significant positive associations with second language achievement. Three of these behaviors are concerned with negotiation of meaning in the classroom: 1) requiring the students to manipulate objects or aids so that the teacher can check their comprehension; 2) asking students questions based on information previously presented in order to reduce ambiguity; and 3) clarifying the meaning of new words using synonyms and antonyms or Spanish equivalents. Ramirez and Stromquist also identified a number of teacher behaviors that had significant *negative* associations with second language learning. All three are incompatible with negotiation of meaning: inappropriate or ambiguous use of visual aids, the use of repetition or imitation as a means of teaching language structures, and a concern for linguistic errors in the students' spoken messages irrespective of the messages' communicative effectiveness. Finally, the instructional features reviewed here are also compatible with Ellis's discourse features, as discussed in the preceding section.

Since many minority language children probably come to school lacking native language proficiency in the kinds of skills that are required for academic performance, the instructional approach described here would also be appropriate for native language development in bilingual programs. Indeed, these same suggestions probably apply to some majority language children as well.

The concern for English language pedagogy expressed in this chapter is not a call for reducing the use of minority language students' home language and extending the use of English. The preceding comments need to be reconciled with the importance of developing minority language students' native language both in school and in the home. As noted repeatedly, a number of researchers (including Cummins, 1981; Heath, 1985; Snow, 1986; and Wells, 1979) have pointed out that an important precursor of academic success is the nature of language development in the home. Minority language parents should be encouraged to provide their children with a full range of language experiences in whatever language they are most able to; in many cases, this is probably the home language, not English (see Dolson, 1985, for a study of the effects of using non-English languages in the home on academic achievement). Minority language parents who are enthusiastic about their children learning English may be prompted to use English themselves with their children even though their proficiency is limited. They may unwittingly be depriving their children of valuable language experiences that could be provided were the parents to use their more proficient home language.

Genesee, along with the other contributors to the California collection of papers on immersion education, pointed out that

> successful implementation of an immersion program for a particular group of children requires knowing more than when to teach students using a second language. More importantly, it involves knowing which sociocultural conditions and educational approaches will facilitate their learning. (Genesee, 1984b, p. 53)

The suggestions contained in the present chapter are intended to contribute to the formulation of an effective pedagogical approach for the education of minority language students by drawing on the experiences and approaches of what is generally regarded as one of the most successful experiments in second language teaching. The instructional features identified here are implicit in immersion programs and in the reports that describe these programs; they have not always been examined explicitly by immersion researchers. In proposing these specific features, a call for further research into their actual prevalence in immersion and their relevance to teaching English to minority language students is also being proposed.

CHAPTER 12

Conclusions

IMMERSION

Second language immersion programs in Canada and the United States have been found to be feasible and effective forms of education for majority group, English-speaking students. The results of numerous longitudinal evaluations in Canada have consistently indicated that majority language students participating in these programs do not experience any long-term deficits in native language development or academic achievement. This has been found to be the case even in "super immersion" programs where English language arts instruction is delayed until the middle elementary grades and then limited to less than three hours a week (Genesee, Holobow, Lambert, Cleghorn, & Walling, 1985). At the same time, students in immersion programs achieve functional proficiency in the second language that is markedly better than that of students in core second language programs. Although not truly nativelike in all aspects, their second language skills are rated very high even by native speakers of the target language. Double immersion programs in which two non-native languages are used as major media of curricular instruction during the elementary grades have been found to be similarly effective.

Comparisons of alternative forms of immersion—early, delayed, late, partial, and total—support the following generalizations: second language proficiency tends to increase the earlier immersion begins and the more second language exposure the learner has. Thus, early total immersion generally yields higher levels of second language proficiency than early partial immersion, delayed immersion, or late immersion. Notwithstanding this general trend, there is also evidence that older students are faster second language learners than younger students, other things being equal, and that intensity of second language exposure may be as important as cumulative exposure. *Post hoc* comparisons between two-year late immersion students attending programs in Montreal and Ottawa suggest that the ultimate level of second language proficiency attained in a particular alternative may depend to a significant extent upon the follow-up component of the program. There are indications from Genesee's results in Montreal, as well as from other sources, that the follow-up component of some immersion programs may not be promoting the students' second language skills fully (see Adiv, 1980b, for example). Even feedback from IM students to surveys concerning their perceptions of the program indicates some dissatisfaction with the follow-up component relative to the immersion component (Cziko, Lambert, Sidoti, & Tucker, 1980). The students often feel that the follow-up is not sufficiently challenging.

Genesee's comparative evaluations of the Montreal programs suggest that the follow-up to early immersion should provide extensive second language exposure and that English should not be introduced too soon or too quickly if the students' second language proficiency is to continue to develop fully. An additional factor to be considered is the nature of language use in immersion classrooms. Immersion programs probably cannot be expected to stimulate continuous growth in the second language if the students' linguistic needs in the classroom are not expanded progressively. What is being suggested here is that there may be a finite set of linguistic skills that are absolutely required to perform the communicative demands characteristic of most immersion classrooms and that this set of skills can be acquired relatively early in the program and does not advance much in the higher grades. It follows then that continuous second language development is likely to be achieved only if increased demands are made on the students' use of the second language.

Related to this issue, it was suggested that immersion classes may only realize their full language teaching potential when they exploit the role of discourse in language learning. Classes that are teacher-dominated, as many immersion classes are, are likely to be rich in comprehensible input but poor in discourse. Research on language acquisition in school and non-school settings indicates that language is learned by engaging in discourse, and, moreover, that the development of language proficiency needed for school work is associated with particular discourse features (Ellis, 1984). Hence, modifications to classroom organizations are recommended to allow IM students more opportunities to "do discourse" of the type associated with the development of academic language proficiency so that they can maximize their second language development. The activity-centered immersion program discussed in chapter five is an example of such a classroom. At the same time, the importance of explicit language teaching for literacy development and other academic language skills of a largely oral nature must be recognized. At present, there is a dearth of research on the precise nature of language use by teachers and students in immersion classes. Identification of particularly successful immersion classes with subsequent in-depth investigation of language use and other pedagogical practices in these classes could be informative in delineating effective instructional practices.

Majority language students with characteristics that normally limit their achievement in conventional school programs have been shown to attain the same levels of achievement in basic academic subjects in immersion programs as do comparable students in regular native language school programs. The characteristics that have been examined systematically are general academic ability, first language ability, and socioeconomic status. At the same time, these "disadvantaged" students achieve much higher levels of second language proficiency than they would were they receiving core second language instruction. Thus, the empirical evidence indicates that these traditional correlates of academic success are not justifiable bases for excluding children from participating in immersion. At present, there exists no single or simple criterion that can validly be used to determine the admissibility of individual children to immersion. Such a determination should be based on multiple criteria and should probably be made only once the child's actual performance in immersion can be judged. As Bruck's research indicates, the true underlying causes of difficulty in immersion are not always readily discernible (Bruck, 1985a, 1985b). The decision to withdraw a student from an immersion program because of difficulties entails important social, pedagogical, and ethical considerations. Moreover, the question of how best to treat students who decide to stay in immersion programs despite difficulties has been largely unexplored and remains unanswered.

Investigations of some of the social-psychological aspects of immersion indicate that the participating students develop the same identity with and positive attitudes toward the English Canadian culture and language as do students attending English language programs. At the same time, IM students have been found to perceive English Canadians in general and themselves in particular as being more similar to French Canadians. IM students' attitudes toward French Canadians tend to be more positive than those of non-immersion students during the early years of the program and then come to resemble those of their non-immersion compatriots in later years. It was suggested that lack of ongoing contact with French Canadians as well as the general sociopolitical climate between French and English Canadians may account for this developmental shift.

Students express positive attitudes toward learning French in immersion programs. In fact, many of their comments indicate that they are in favor of more French, especially during the follow-up years. Non-immersion students, in contrast, often express relatively negative attitudes toward their French program and toward learning French in general. Notwithstanding certain reservations that immersion students appear to have concerning the use of French at the expense of English, they generally express a willingness to use French when called upon to do so, and, in fact, students in Montreal report using French in face-to-face encounters much more often than do non-immersion students. It is likely that the social consequences of second language learning in immersion are influenced in important ways by general sociocultural factors and events.

Since immersion programs are optional, the results reviewed here necessarily reflect the performance of students who have chosen, or whose parents have chosen on their behalf, to attend the program instead of a "regular" English school. Therefore, these findings cannot be generalized to programs that do not allow freedom of choice. Nevertheless, since this is an inherent characteristic of immersion, the available evidence can be said to be valid as a description of the performance of those types of students who typically attend immersion programs. As the findings of research concerning the suitability of immersion for all students indicate, immersion appears to be effective with students with diverse learner characteristics. Research from across Canada and in the United States attests to the effectiveness of immersion for majority language children living in communities with diverse social, linguistic, and political characteristics.

BILINGUAL EDUCATION

At about the same time that immersion programs were being developed in Canada, American educators were beginning to experiment with bilingual education programs for minority language students. In contrast to the immersion approach, which advocates initial instruction through the medium of the students' second language, bilingual education advocates primary instruction through their home language. The rationale for bilingual education rests, in part, on a conceptualization of language proficiency as multidimensional with a certain subset of language skills being essential for academic performance. Viewed from this perspective, bilingual education is intended to be an extension of minority language students' psycholinguistic development. That their development of language skills needed for school work could be extended as a result of instruction through English is arguable. Some researchers contend that it is the nature and quality of the linguistic interaction outside of school that is critical for school-related language development and not whether these interactions take place in the home language or in the language of school instruction (e.g., Heath, 1986). In fact, there is some evidence from national surveys of academic achievement testing that students from certain ethnolinguistic minority groups do well in school, higher in some skills areas even than majority group students. That the school-related language skills of minority language children can be developed more readily through their native language because their initial schooling is based on existing language proficiency is an important argument in favor of bilingual education.

Also critical to an understanding of bilingual education is the notion of linguistic interdependence, according to which development of proficiency in the home language, especially as this pertains to literacy or other school-related language skills, will facilitate development of corresponding skills in a second language. Evidence for this has been proffered by a number of researchers. Linguistic interdependence also serves to explain the rapid native language development that majority language students in immersion programs make despite greatly reduced exposure to English language instruction.

It is widely recognized that the success of any educational program for minority language students, including bilingual education, will depend on sociocultural factors. Lambert has described the general sociocultural conditions in which minority language children learn English in regular English schools as *subtractive* in contrast to the *additive* conditions in which majority language children learn a second language in immersion programs. In this regard, it was suggested that status relations between minority groups and the majority group, along with the historical background and ethnolinguistic vitality of specific minority groups, can shape their cultural identity and in turn their orientation toward schooling and the value of academic achievement. In some cases, this may lead to successful school performance, while in other cases it may lead to lack of success or failure. Status relations between minority and majority group students can also be associated with differential treatment and behavior in class and ultimately to differential levels of academic success. Some curriculum innovations and classroom organizations were suggested as ways to mitigate these kinds of effects. Advocates of bilingual education contend, with some justification, that use of the students' home language, along with culturally sensitive curricular materials and instructional approaches, can offset some of the sociocultural disadvantages that minority language students are likely to experience in all-English schools.

U.S. bilingual programs have encountered resistance and opposition in some quarters because they run counter to the common-sense, albeit largely invalid, expectation that more exposure to English in school is associated with higher levels of English language proficiency. Empirical evidence testifies against this view. Opposition to bilingual education has also run afoul of ideological positions that identify linguistic diversity with divisiveness and even un-American attitudes (Bethell, 1979). Efforts to validate the bilingual approach through empirical evaluation have been fraught with problems. A considerable number of research studies of bilingual education have not met basic research standards and therefore have led to inconclusive results. In comparison with evaluations of immersion programs, evaluations of bilingual education programs are inherently more complex and troublesome (see also McLaughlin, 1985). For example, unlike majority English-speaking children attending second language immersion programs, minority language children in bilingual programs have widely varied levels of proficiency in both their home language and in the second language, English. As a result, classification of students for research purposes is difficult. As well, students in bilingual programs are "exited" from the program once they have met specified, locally-set language proficiency levels. This practice, along with the generally high geographical mobility of many minority language children, creates an unstable student population that impedes longitudinal research efforts. Evaluation of bilingual education programs is further complicated by the lack of uniform program designs. Consequently, there is often little generalizability of research findings. As was seen in the case of the Canadian evaluations, it has been largely as a result of systematic, longitudinal research that immersion programs have established their validity among Canadian educators and parents. The lack of comparable research in the United States has hampered acceptance of bilingual education both among educational professionals and the lay public.

Notwithstanding myriad research problems, evidence from primary evaluations of individual bilingual programs indicates that bilingual education can work (see Baker & de Kanter, 1983; Cummins, 1981; and Troike, 1978; for examples). It has also been shown, using statistically appropriate procedures to control for variation in both programs and research design, that *in general* students in bilingual programs outperform students in non-bilingual programs on measures of language and academic development administered in English or in the native language (Willig, 1985). Preliminary results from a national study comparing the relative effectiveness of immersion in English versus bilingual education favor students in bilingual programs over students in immersion (Ramirez et al., 1985).

Serious discussions regarding the suitability of immersion for minority language students in the United States are currently underway and have provoked much controversy. If immersion in English is to be effective with minority language students, it will require more than simply providing basic curricular instruction through the medium of English, an approach that has been referred to as "submersion." Effective application of the immersion approach with minority language students will require an understanding of the pedagogical and linguistic strategies embodied in immersion programs. The exact instructional practices and linguistic strategies employed by immersion teachers that might account for the programs' success with majority language students have not yet been examined adequately to be described in detail. In lieu of a precise description, a general characterization of significant immersion instructional features of possible relevance to educational programs for minority language students was offered in chapter eleven. Immersion classrooms were characterized as interactive learning environments in which academic and language learning are integrated using a curriculum that is intrinsically motivating. The implications of these features for teaching English to minority language students was considered in some detail.

Taken together, studies of immersion and bilingual education have indicated some of the potential and some of the limits of education through a second language. The debate over bilingual education for minority language students, along with the experiments in second language immersion for majority language students, have been instrumental in focusing educators' attention on the nature of language and its relationship to academic performance and achievement. Although these issues have been considered by others interested in language, such as sociologists and anthropologists, the present discussions mark a milestone in educational thinking as educational professionals turn away from the simplistic conceptualizations of language that were the hallmark of earlier times to a more variegated and probably more valid perspective. Immersion and bilingual classrooms provide unique settings in which these issues can be explored and elucidated further to the benefit not only of second language education but of all education.

References

Adiv, E. 1977. The significance of language in social identity. *The Canadian Zionist* (Nov.): 18–22.

Adiv, E. 1980a. *A comparative evaluation of three immersion programs: grades 10 and 11.* Unpublished manuscript, Protestant School Board of Greater Montreal, Quebec.

Adiv, E. 1980b. *An analysis of second language performance in two types of immersion programs.* Ph.D. thesis, Department of Education, McGill University, Montreal.

Adiv, E. 1983. *Jewish day school programs: an assessment of linguistic proficiency and academic achievement in multilingual educational settings.* Unpublished manuscript, Hebrew University, Jerusalem.

Aguirre, E., & R. Cepeda. 1981. *Hispanics and Education in the 1980s.* Oakland, CA: The National Hispanic Center for Advanced Studies and Policy Analysis.

Amir, Y. 1976. The role of intergroup contact in change of prejudice and ethnic relations. In P.A. Katz (ed.), *Towards the Elimination of Racism.* New York: Pergamon Press, 245–308.

Andersson, T., & M. Boyer. 1970. *Bilingual Schooling in the United States* (2d ed.). Austin, TX: National Educational Laboratory Publishers.

Anisfeld, E., & W.E. Lambert. 1964. Evaluational reactions of bilingual and monolingual children to spoken languages. *Journal of Abnormal and Social Psychology* 69: 89–97.

Arnopoulos, S.M., & D. Clift. 1980. *The English Fact in Quebec.* Montreal: McGill-Queens University Press.

Asher, J.J., & R. Garcia. 1969. The optimal age to learn a foreign language. *Modern Language Journal* 8: 334–341.

Asher, J.J., & B.S. Price. 1967. The learning strategy of the total physical response. *Child Development* 38: 1219–1227.

Baker, K., & A. de Kanter. 1983. Federal policy and the effectiveness of bilingual education. In K. Baker & A. de Kanter (eds.), *Bilingual Education.* Lexington, MA: D.C. Heath, 33–86.

Barik. H. 1976. *French Comprehension Test.* Toronto: Ontario Institute for Studies in Education.

Barik, H., M. Swain, & V.A. Gaudino. 1975. *A Canadian experiment in bilingual schooling in the senior grades: the Peel study through grade ten.* Unpublished manuscript, Ontario Institute for Studies in Education, Toronto.

Barth, F. 1969. *Ethnic Groups and Boundaries.* Boston: Little, Brown.

Ben-Zeev, S. 1977. The influence of bilingualism on cognitive development and cognitive strategy. *Child Development* 48: 1009–1018.

Bethell, T. 1979. Against bilingual education. *Harper's* 258: 30–33.

Bloom, P., L. Hood, & P. Lightbown. 1974. Imitation in language development: if, when, and why. *Cognitive Psychology* 6: 380–420.

Bourhis, R.Y. 1983. Language attitudes and self-reports of French-English language usage in Quebec. *Journal of Multilingual and Multicultural Development* 4: 163–179.

Bourhis, R.Y. 1985. *Language Conflict and Language Planning in Quebec.* Clevedon, England: Multilingual Matters.

Brown, R., C. Cazden, & U. Bellugi. 1970. The child's grammar from I to III. In R. Brown (ed.), *Psycholinguistics.* New York: The Free Press.

Bruck, M. 1978. The suitability of early French immersion programs for the language disabled child. *Canadian Journal of Education* 3: 51–72.

Bruck, M. 1982. Language disabled children: performance in an additive bilingual education program. *Applied Psycholinguistics* 3: 45–60.

Bruck, M. 1985a. Predictors of transfer out of early French immersion programs. *Applied Psycholinguistics* 6: 39–61.

Bruck, M. 1985b. Consequences of transfer out of early French immersion programs. *Applied Psycholinguistics* 6: 101–120.

Bruck, M., W.E. Lambert, & G.R. Tucker. 1976. *Cognitive consequences of bilingual schooling: the St. Lambert project through grade 6.* Unpublished manuscript, Psychology Department, McGill University, Montreal.

Bruck, M., G.R. Tucker, & J. Jakimik. 1975. Are French immersion programs suitable for working class children? A follow-up investigation. *Word* 27: 311–341.

Bruner, J. 1964. The course of cognitive development. *American Psychologist* 19: 1–15.

Bruner, J.S. 1978. Learning how to do things with words. In J.S. Bruner & R.A. Garton (eds.), *Human Growth and Development.* Oxford, UK: Oxford University Press.

Burstall, C. 1974. *Primary French in the Balance.* Windsor, England: NFER Publishing.

California State Department of Education. 1981. *Schooling and Language Minority Students: A Theoretical Framework.* Los Angeles: Evaluation, Dissemination, and Assessment Center.

California State Department of Education. 1984. *Studies on Immersion Education: A Collection for United States Educators.* Sacramento: California State Department of Education.

Campbell, R. 1984. The immersion education approach to foreign language teaching. In California State Department of Education (ed.), *Studies on Immersion Education: A Collection for United States Educators.* Sacramento: California State Department of Education, 114–143.

Canadian Parents for French. 1985. *Remedial and enrichment instruction in French immersion programs: a survey.* Unpublished report, 309 Cooper St., Ottawa, Ont., K2P 0G5.

Carroll, J.B. 1975. *The Teaching of French as a Foreign Language in Eight Countries.* New York: John Wiley.

Carter, T.P., & R.D. Segura. 1979. *Mexican Americans in School.* New York: College Entrance Examination Board.

Castellanos, D. 1983. *The Best of Two Worlds.* Trenton, NJ: New Jersey State Department of Education.

Chamot, A.U. 1985. Guidelines for implementing a content-based English language development program. *NCBE Forum* 8: 2.

Chomsky, N. 1972. *Language and Mind.* New York: Harcourt & Brace.

Christophersen, P. 1948. *Bilingualism.* London: Methuen.

Cleghorn, A. 1985. *An observational study of teaching strategies in mixed language classrooms.* Manuscript in preparation, Psychology Department, McGill University, Montreal.

Cleghorn, A., and F. Genesee. 1984. Languages in contact: an ethnographic study of interaction in an immersion school. *TESOL Quarterly* 18: 595–625.

Cohen, A. 1974. The Culver City Spanish immersion program: the first two years. *Modern Language Review* 58: 95–103.

Cohen, A. 1975. *A Sociolinguistic Approach to Bilingual Education.* Rowley, MA: Newbury House.

Cohen, A., & M. Swain. 1976. Bilingual education: the "immersion" model in the North American context. *TESOL Quarterly* 10: 45–54.

Cohen, E. 1972. Interracial interaction disability. *Human Relations* 25: 9–24.

Cohen, E. 1980. Design and redesign of the desegregated school. In W.G. Stephan & J.R. Feagan (eds.), *School Desegregation: Past, Present and Future.* New York: Plenum, 251–280.

Coleman, J.S. 1966. *Equality of Educational Opportunity.* Washington, DC: U.S. Government Printing Office.

Cook, R., J. Saywell, & J. Ricker. 1977. *Canada: A Modern Study.* Toronto: Clarke, Irwin.

Cortes, C.E. 1986. The education of language minority students: a contextual interaction model. In *Social and Cultural Factors in Schooling Language Minority Students.* Sacramento: California State Department of Education.

Cowan, J.R., & Z. Sarmed. 1976. Reading performance of bilingual children according to type of school and home language. *Working Papers on Bilingualism* 11: 74–114.

Cronbach, L.J. 1984. *Essentials of Psychological Testing* (4th ed.). New York: Harper & Row.

Cross, T.G. 1978. Mother's speech and its association with rate of linguistic development in young children. In N. Waterson & C. Snow (eds.), *The Development of Communication.* London: John Wiley.

Cummins, J. 1976. The influence of bilingualism on cognitive growth: a synthesis of research findings and explanatory hypotheses. *Working Papers on Bilingualism* 9: 1–43.

Cummins, J. 1979. Should the child who is experiencing difficulties in early immersion be switched to the regular English program? A reinterpretation of Trites' data. *Canadian Modern Language Review* 36: 139–143.

Cummins, J. 1981. The role of primary language development in promoting educational success for language minority students. In *Schooling and Language Minority Students: A Theoretical Framework.* Los Angeles: Evaluation, Dissemination, and Assessment Center, 1–50.

Cummins, J. 1984. Wanted: a theoretical framework for relating language proficiency to academic achievement among bilingual students. In C. Rivera (ed.), *Language Proficiency and Academic Achievement.* Clevedon, England: Multilingual Matters, 2–19.

Cummins, J. 1985. *Disabling minority students: power, programs and pedagogy.* Unpublished manuscript, Ontario Institute for Studies in Education, Toronto.

Cummins, J., M. Swain, K. Nakajima, J. Handscombe, & D. Greene. 1981. *Linguistic interdependence among Japanese immigrant students.* In C. Rivera (ed.), *Communication Competence Approaches to Language Proficiency Assessment: Research and Application.* Clevedon, Eng.: Multilingual Matters, 60–81.

Cziko, G. 1975. *The effects of different French immersion programs on the language and academic skills of children from various socioeconomic backgrounds.* M.A. thesis, Psychology Department, McGill University, Montreal.

Cziko, G., N. Holobow, & W.E. Lambert. 1977. *A comparison of three elementary school alternatives for learning French: children at grades four and five.* Psychology Department, McGill University, Montreal.

Cziko, G., N. Holobow, W.E. Lambert, & G.R. Tucker. 1977. *A comparison of three elementary school alternatives for learning French: children at grades 5 and 6.* Psychology Department, McGill University, Montreal.

Cziko, G., W.E. Lambert, & J. Gutter. 1980. The impact of immersion-in-a-foreign-language on pupils' social attitudes. *Working Papers on Bilingualism* 19: 13–28.

Cziko, G., W.E. Lambert, N. Sidoti, & G.R. Tucker. 1980. Graduates of early immersion: retrospective views of grade 11 students and their parents. In R.N. St. Clair & H. Giles (eds.), *The Social and Psychological Contexts of Language.* Hillsdale, NJ: Lawrence Erlbaum.

d'Anglejan, A., & G.R. Tucker. 1973. Sociolinguistic correlates of speech style in Quebec. In R.W. Shuy & R.W. Fasold (eds.), *Language Attitudes: Current Trends and Prospects.* Washington, DC: Georgetown University Press.

Danoff, M.N., G.J. Coles, D.H. McLaughlin, & D.J. Reynolds. 1977a. *Evaluation of the Impact of ESEA Title VII Spanish/English Bilingual Education Programs, Vol. I: Study Design and Interim Findings.* Palo Alto, CA: American Institute for Research.

Danoff, M.N., G.J. Coles, D.H. McLaughlin, & D.J. Reynolds. 1977b. *Evaluation of the Impact of ESEA Title VII Spanish/English Bilingual Education Programs, Vol. II: Project Descriptions.* Palo Alto, CA: American Institute for Research.

Danoff, M.N., G.J. Coles, D.H. McLaughlin, & D.J. Reynolds. 1978. *Evaluation of the Impact of ESEA Title VII Spanish/English Bilingual Education Programs, Vol. III: Year Two Impact Data, Educational Process, and In-depth Analysis.* Palo Alto, CA: American Institute for Research.

Day, R.R. 1982. Children's attitudes toward language. In E. Ryan (ed.), *Attitudes Toward Language Variation: Social and Applied Contexts.* London: Edward Arnold.

Deci, E.L. 1985. The well-tempered classroom. *Psychology Today* 19: 42–43.

de Vos, G.A. 1973. Japan's outcastes: the problem of the Burakumin. In B. Whitaker (ed.), *The Fourth World: Victims of Group Oppression.* New York: Schocken, 307–327.

Diaz, R. 1983. Thought and two languages: the impact of bilingualism on cognitive development. In E. Norbeck, D. Price-Williams, & W. McCord (eds.), *Review of Research in Education* (vol. 10). Washington, DC: American Educational Research Association, 23–54.

Diebold, A.R. 1968. The consequences of bilingualism on cognitive development and personality formation. In E. Norbeck, D. Price-Williams, & W. McCord (eds.), *The Study of Personality: An Interdisciplinary Appraisal.* New York: Holt, Rinehart & Winston, 218–245.

Dolson, D. 1985a. The effects of Spanish home language use on the scholastic performance of Hispanic pupils. *Journal of Multilingual and Multicultural Development* 6: 135–155.

Dolson, D. 1985b. *The Applications of Immersion Education in the United States.* Rosslyn, VA: National Clearinghouse for Bilingual Education.

Dore, J. 1985. Intentionality, accountability, and play: the intersubjective basis for language development. In R. Golinkoff (ed.), *The Transition from Prelinguistic to Linguistic Communication.* Hillsdale, NJ: Lawrence Erlbaum.

Doyle, W. 1983. Academic work. *Review of Educational Research* 53: 159–199.

Dulay, H.C., & M. Burt. 1978a. Some remarks on creativity in language acquisition. In

W.C. Ritchie (ed.), *Second Language Acquisition Research: Issues and Implications.*
New York: Academic Press, 65–89.

Dulay, H.C., & M. Burt. 1978b. *Why bilingual education? A summary of research findings*
(2d ed.). San Francisco: Bloomsbury West.

Edwards, H.P., S. Colletta, L. Fu, & H.A. McCarrey. 1979. *Evaluation of the Federally
and Provincially Funded Extensions of the Second Language Programs in the Schools
of the Ottawa Roman Catholic Separate School Board: Annual Report 1978–1979.*
Toronto: Ministry of Education, Ontario.

Edwards, H.P., H.A. McCarrey, & L. Fu. 1980. *Evaluation of Second Language Program
Extensions Offered in Grades 3, 4 and 5: Final Report 1979–80.* Ottawa: Ottawa
Roman Catholic Separate School Board.

Edwards, J. 1981. The context of bilingual education. *Journal of Multilingual and Multicultural Development:* 2: 25–44.

Ellis, R. 1984. *Classroom Second Language Development.* Oxford: Pergamon Press.

Epstein, N. 1977. *Language, Ethnicity and the Schools: Policy Alternatives for Bilingual-
Bicultural Education.* Washington, DC: Institute for Educational Leadership.

Fathman, A. 1975. The relationship between age and second language productive ability.
Language Learning 25: 245–253.

Ferguson, C.A., C. Houghton, & M.H. Wells. 1977. Bilingual education: an international
perspective. In B. Spolsky & R. Cooper (eds.), *Frontiers of Bilingual Education.*
Rowley, MA: Newbury House.

Fisher, C.W., & L. Guthrie. 1983. *Executive Summary: The Significant Bilingual Instructional Features Study.* San Francisco: Far West Laboratory for Educational Research
and Development.

Fishman, J. 1972. The sociology of language. In P.P. Giglioli (ed.), *Language and Social
Context.* Middlesex, England: Harmondsworth.

Fishman, J., & J. Lovas. 1970. Bilingual education in sociolinguistic perspective. *TESOL
Quarterly* 4: 215–222.

Fletcher, A. 1976. *An enquiry into the educational experience of children who discontinue
participation in an elementary French immersion program.* M.A. thesis, Concordia
University, Montreal.

Foidart, D. 1981. *Research and evaluation of French immersion programmes in Manitoba:
preliminary report.* Winnipeg, Manitoba: Centre for Research and Consultation.

Gardner, R.C. 1979. Social psychological aspects of second language acquisition. In H.
Giles & R. St. Clair (eds.), *Language and Social Psychology.* Oxford: Basil Blackwell,
193–220.

Gardner, R.C. 1982. Language attitudes and language learning. In E. Ryan & H.
Giles (eds.), *Attitudes Toward Language Variation.* London: Edward Arnold, 132–
147.

Gardner, R.C. 1986. *Social Psychological Aspects of Second Language Learning.* London:
Edward Arnold.

Gardner, R.C., L. Gliksman, & P.C. Smythe. 1978. Second language learning: a social
psychological perspective. *Canadian Modern Language Review* 32: 198–213.

Gardner, R.C., & W.E. Lambert. 1972. *Attitudes and Motivation in Second Language
Learning.* Rowley, MA: Newbury House.

Gendron, J.D. 1972. *Commission of Inquiry on the Position of the French Language and
on Language Rights in Quebec: Language of Work.* Quebec: L'editeur officiel du
Quebec.

Genesee, F. 1976a. *Evaluation of the 1975–76 grade 11 French immersion class: addendum.* Report submitted to the Protestant School Board of Greater Montreal, Quebec.

Genesee, F. 1976b. The role of intelligence in second language learning. *Language Learning* 26: 267–280.

Genesee, F. 1977a. *Departmental leaving examination results: June 1977.* Report submitted to the Protestant School Board of Greater Montreal, Quebec.

Genesee, F. 1977b. *French immersion students' perceptions of themselves and others: an ethnolinguistic perspective.* Protestant School Board of Greater Montreal, Quebec.

Genesee, F. 1978a. A longitudinal evaluation of an early immersion school program. *Canadian Journal of Education* 3: 31–50.

Genesee, F. 1978b. Second language learning and language attitudes. *Working Papers on Bilingualism* 16: 19–42.

Genesee, F. 1978c. Scholastic effects of French immersion: an overview after ten years. *Interchange* 9: 20–29.

Genesee, F. 1981a. Bilingualism and biliteracy: a study of cross-cultural contact in a bilingual community. In J. Edwards (ed.), *The Social Psychology of Reading.* Silver Spring, MD: Institute of Modern Languages, 147–172.

Genesee, F. 1981b. A comparison of early and late second language learning. *Canadian Journal of Behavioral Sciences* 13: 115–128.

Genesee, F. 1981c. *Evaluation of the Laurenval early partial and early total immersion programs.* Psychology Department, McGill University, Montreal.

Genesee, F. 1981d. Response to M. Swain: linguistic environment as a factor in the acquisition of target language skills. In R. Andersen (ed.), *Second Language Acquisition and Use Under Different Circumstances.* Rowley, MA: Newbury House.

Genesee, F. 1983. Bilingual education of majority language children: the immersion experiments in review. *Applied Psycholinguistics* 4: 1-46.

Genesee, F. 1984a. *The social psychological significance of bilingual code switching revisited.* Unpublished manuscript, Psychology Department, McGill University, Montreal.

Genesee, F. 1984b. Historical and theoretical foundations of immersion. In *Studies on Immersion Education: A Collection for United States Educators.* Sacramento: California State Department of Education.

Genesee, F. 1987. Neuropsychological perspectives. In L. Beebe (ed.), *Issues on second language acquisition.* Cambridge, MA: Newbury House.

Genesee, F., & R. Bourhis. 1982. The social psychological significance of code switching in cross-cultural communication. *Journal of Language and Social Psychology* 1: 1–27.

Genesee, F., & S. Chaplin. 1976. *Evaluation of the 1974–75 grade 11 French immersion class.* Report submitted to the Protestant School Board of Greater Montreal, Quebec.

Genesee, F., & E. Hamayan. 1980. Individual differences in second language learning. *Applied Psycholinguistics* 1: 95–110.

Genesee, F., N. Holobow, W. E. Lambert, A. Cleghorn, & R. Walling. 1985. The linguistic and academic development of English-speaking children in French schools: grade 4 outcomes. *Canadian Modern Language Review* 41: 669–685.

Genesee, F., & W.E. Lambert. 1980. *Evaluation of the Hebrew-French double immersion program: year 5.* Unpublished manuscript, Psychology Department, McGill University, Montreal.

Genesee, F., & W.E. Lambert. 1983. Trilingual education for majority language children. *Child Development* 54: 105–114.

Genesee, F., N. Holobow, W.E. Lambert, A. Cleghorn, & R. Walling. 1985. The linguistic and academic development of English-speaking children in French schools: grade 4 outcomes. *Canadian Modern Language Review* 41: 669–685.

Genesee, F., S. Morin & T. Allister. 1974. *Evaluation of the 1973–74 grade 7 French immersion class.* Report submitted to the Protestant School Board of Greater Montreal, Quebec.

Genesee, F., E. Polich, & M. Stanley. 1977. An experimental French immersion program at the secondary school level. *Canadian Modern Language Review* 33: 318–332.

Genesee, F., P. Rogers, & N. Holobow. 1983. The social psychology of second language learning: another point of view. *Language Learning* 33: 209–224.

Genesee, F., & M. Stanley. 1976. The development of English writing skills in French immersion programs. *Canadian Journal of Education* 3: 1–18.

Genesee, F., & B. Stefanovic. 1976. *Evaluation of the 1975–76 grade 11 French immersion class.* Report submitted to the Protestant School Board of Greater Montreal, Quebec.

Genesee, F., G.R. Tucker, & W.E. Lambert. 1975. Communication skills of bilingual children. *Child Development* 46: 1010–1014.

Genesee, F., G.R. Tucker, & W.E. Lambert. 1978. The development of ethnic identity and ethnic role-taking skills in children from different school settings. *International Journal of Psychology* 13: 39–57.

Gibson, M.A. 1983. *Home-School-Community Linkages: A Study of Educational Equity for Punjabi Youths.* Final Report. Washington, DC: The National Institute of Education.

Giles, H., R. Bourhis, & D. Taylor. 1977. Towards a theory of language in ethnic group relations. In H. Giles (ed.), *Languages, Ethnicity and Intergroup Relations.* London: Academic Press, 307–348.

Good, T., & J. Brophy. 1978. *Looking Inside Classrooms* (2d ed.). New York: Harper & Row.

Gould, S. 1981. *The Mismeasure of Man.* New York: W.W. Norton.

Gray, V. 1980. *Evaluation of the French immersion programme in Fredericton, N.B.: Grades 5 and 6.* Psychology Department, University of New Brunswick, Fredericton.

Gray, V. 1981. *Evaluation of the grade 6 French immersion programme in Fredericton, N.B.* Psychology Department, University of New Brunswick, Fredericton.

Gray, V., R.N. Campbell, N.C. Rhodes, & M.A. Snow. 1984. *Comparative evaluation of elementary school foreign language programs.* Final report to Hazen Foundation. Washington, DC: Center for Applied Linguistics. ED No. 238255.

Greer, C. 1972. *The Great School Legend: A Revisionist Interpretation of American Public Education.* New York: Penguin Books.

Hakuta, K. 1986. *Mirror of Language: The Debate on Bilingualism.* New York: Basic Books, 14–44.

Harley, B. 1976. Alternative programs for teaching French as a second language in the schools of the Carleton and Ottawa school boards. *Canadian Modern Language Review* 33.

Harley, B. In press. Transfer in the written compositions of French immersion students. In H.W. Dechert & M. Raupach (eds.), *Transfer in Production.* New York: Ablex.

Harley, B., & M. Swain. 1984. *The interlanguage of immersion students and its implications for second language teaching.* Paper presented at the Interlanguage Seminar in Honour of Pit Corder, Edinburgh, April 1984.

Heath, S.B. 1983. *Ways with Words.* Cambridge, England: Cambridge University Press.

Heath, S.B. 1986. Sociocultural contexts of language development. In *Social and Cultural Factors in Schooling Language Minority Students.* Sacramento: California State Department of Education.

Hébert, R. 1976. *Rendement academique et langue d'enseignement chez les eleves francomanitobains.* Saint-Boniface, Manitoba: Centre de recherches du College Universitaire de Saint-Boniface.

Hernandez-Chavez, E. 1984. The inadequacy of English immersion education as an educational approach for language minority students in the United States. In *Studies on Immersion Education: A Collection for United States Educators.* Sacramento: California State Department of Education, 144–183.

Hohn, R.L. 1973. Perceptual training and its effect on racial preferences of kindergarten children. *Psychological Reports* 32: 435–441.

Holobow, N., L. Chartrand., & W.E. Lambert. 1985. *A comparative evaluation of French language skills of secondary V students in various programs of study.* Psychology Department, McGill University, Montreal.

Holobow, N., F. Genesee, W.E. Lambert, M. Met, & J. Gasright. 1987. Effectiveness of partial French immersion for children from different social class and ethnic backgrounds. *Applied Psycholinguishes,* in press.

Iadicola, P. 1979. *Schooling and social power: a presentation of a Weberian conflict model of the school.* Ph.D. dissertation, University of California, Riverside.

Ireland, D., K. Gunnell, & L. Santerre. 1980. *A Study of the Teaching and Learning of Aural/Oral French in Immersion Classes.* Ottawa: Ottawa Valley Learning Centre, Ontario Institute for Studies in Education.

Irujo, S. 1984. *Evaluation of the French immersion program in Holliston Public Schools.* Unpublished manuscript, Bedford, Mass.

Kagan, S. 1986. Cooperative learning and sociocultural factors in schooling. In *Beyond Language: Social and Cultural Factors in Schooling Language Minority Students.* Sacramento: California State Department of Education.

Kamin, J. 1980. *Difficulties in Early French Immersion: A Transfer Study.* Toronto: Ontario Institute for Studies in Education.

Kamin, L. 1974. *The Science and Politics of IQ.* Potomac, MD: Erlbaum.

Katz, P. 1973. Stimulus predifferentiation and modification of children's racial attitudes. *Child Development* 44: 232–237.

Katz, P. 1976. *Towards the Elimination of Racism.* New York: Pergamon Press.

Katz, P., J. Johnson, & D. Parker. 1970. *Racial attitudes and perception in black and white urban school children.* Paper presented at the American Psychological Association Meeting, Sept. 1970.

Kerman, S. 1979. Teacher expectations and student achievement. *Phi Delta Kappan* (June).

Kloss, H. 1977. *The American Bilingual Tradition.* Rowley, MA: Newbury House.

Krashen, S. 1974. The critical period for language acquisition and its possible bases. *Annals of the New York Academy of Sciences* 263: 211–224.

Krashen, S. 1981. Bilingual education and second language acquisition theory. In *Schooling and Language Minority Students: A Theoretical Framework.* Sacramento: California State Department of Education.

Lambert, W.E. 1980a. The social psychology of language: a perspective for the 1980s. In H. Giles, W.P. Robinson, & P.M. Smith (eds.), *Language: Social Psychological Perspectives.* Oxford: Pergamon Press, 415–424.

Lambert, W.E. 1980b. The two faces of bilingual education. *NCBE Forum* 3.

Lambert, W.E., R.C. Hodgson, R.C. Gardner, & S. Fillenbaum. 1960. Evaluational reactions to spoken languages. *Journal of Abnormal and Social Psychology* 60: 44–51.

Lambert, W.E., & G.R. Tucker. 1972. *The Bilingual Education of Children: The St. Lambert Experiment.* Rowley, MA: Newbury House.

Lamont, D., W. Penner, T. Blowers, H. Mosychuk, & J. Jones. 1976. *Evaluation of the second year of a bilingual (English-Ukrainian) program.* Report submitted to the Edmonton Public Schools, Alberta.

Lamy, P. 1979. Language and ethnolinguistic identity: the bilingualism question. *International Journal of the Sociology of Language* 20: 23–36.

Lapkin, S. 1982. The English writing skills of French immersion pupils at grade 5. *Canadian Modern Language Review* 39: 24–33.

Lapkin, S. 1983. *How well do immersion students speak and write French?* Paper presented at the Conference of Canadian Parents for French, Calgary, Alberta, Jan. 1983.

Lapkin, S., C.M. Andrew, B. Harley, M. Swain, & J. Kamin. 1981. The immersion centre and the dual-track school: a study of the relationship between school environment and achievement in a French immersion program. *Canadian Journal of Education* 2: 1–23.

Lapkin, S., & J. Cummins. 1984. Canadian French immersion education: Current administrative and instructional practices. In *Studies on Immersion Education: A Collection for United States Educators.* Sacramento: California State Department of Education, 87–112.

Lapkin, S., M. Swain, J. Kamin, & G. Hanna. 1982. Late immersion in perspective: the Peel study. *Canadian Modern Language Review* 39: 182–206.

Legaretta, D. 1977. Language choice in bilingual classrooms. *TESOL Quarterly* 11: 9–16.

Lenneberg, E. 1967. *Biological Foundations of Language.* New York: John Wiley.

Lewis, G. 1977. Bilingualism and bilingual education: the ancient world to the Renaissance. In B. Spolsky & R. Cooper (eds.), *Frontiers of Bilingual Education.* Rowley, MA: Newbury House.

Long, M.H. 1980. Linguistic and conversational adjustments to non-native speakers. *Studies in Second Language Acquisition* 2: 177–193.

Long, M.H. 1983. Does instruction make a difference? A review of research. *TESOL Quarterly* 17: 359–382.

Mackey, W. 1972. *Bilingual Education in a Binational School.* Rowley, MA: Newbury House.

Mackey, W. 1978. The importation of bilingual education models. In J. Alatis (ed.), *Georgetown University Roundtable—International Dimensions of Bilingual Education,* 1–18.

MacLennan, H. 1945. *Two Solitudes.* Toronto: Duell, Sloan & Pearce.

Macnamara, J. 1973. Nurseries, streets and classrooms. *Modern Language Journal* 57: 250–254.

Malherbe, E.G. 1946. *The Bilingual School.* London: Longmans Green.

Maurice, S., F. Genesee, N. Holobow, & L. Chartrand. 1984. *Evaluational reactions to spoken language: a twenty year follow-up study.* Unpublished manuscript, Psychology Department, McGill University, Montreal.

McLaughlin, B. 1984. Review of children's second language learning. *Modern Language Journal* 68: 158.

McLaughlin, B. 1985. Chapter 10: evaluation. In B. McLaughlin (ed.), *Second-Language Acquisition in Childhood: Volume 2, School-Age Children.* Hillsdale, NJ: Lawrence Erlbaum, 224–245.

McNeill, D. 1970. *The Acquisition of Language: The Study of Developmental Psycholinguistics.* New York: Harper & Row.

Melikoff, O. 1972. Parents as change agents in education. The St. Lambert experiment. In W.E. Lambert & G.R. Tucker (eds.), *Bilingual Education of Children: The St. Lambert Experiment.* Rowley, MA: Newbury House, 219–236.

Montgomery County Public Schools. 1976. *End of the second year report on the French immersion program at Four Corners.* Unpublished report submitted to the Montgomery County Board of Education, Maryland.

Morrison, F. 1981. *Longitudinal and Cross-Sectional Studies of French Proficiency in Ottawa and Carleton Schools.* Ottawa: Research Centre, The Ottawa Board of Education, Ontario.

Morrison, F. 1982. *After Immersion: Ottawa and Carleton Students at the Secondary and Post-Secondary Level.* Ottawa: Research Centre, The Ottawa Board of Education, Ontario.

Morrison, F., C. Pawley, & R. Bonyun. 1979. *Reasons for Student Transfer from Late-Entry Immersion and High School Bilingual Programs: Grades 9 and 12.* Ottawa: Research Centre, The Ottawa Board of Education, Ontario.

Muller, L.J., W.J. Penner, T.A. Blowers, J.P. Jones, & H. Mosychuk. 1975. *Evaluation of a bilingual (English-Ukrainian) program.* Edmonton Public School Board, Edmonton, Alberta.

Naiman, N., M. Frohlich, & H.H. Stern. 1975. *The Good Language Learner.* Toronto: Ontario Institute for Studies in Education.

Nelson, K. 1981. Individual differences in language development: implications for development and language. *Developmental Psychology* 17: 170–187.

Ogbu, J. 1978. *Minority Education and Caste: The American System in Cross-Cultural Perspective.* New York: Academic Press.

Ogbu, J., & M.E. Matute-Bianchi. 1986. Understanding sociocultural factors: knowledge, identity and school adjustment. In *Social and Cultural Factors in Schooling Language Minority Students.* Sacramento: California State Department of Education.

Olson, D.R. 1977. From utterance to text: the bias of language in speech and writing. *Harvard Educational Review* 47: 257–281.

Oyama, S. 1976. A sensitive period for the acquisition of a non-native phonological system. *Journal of Psycholinguistic Research* 5: 261–285.

Oyama, S. 1978. The sensitive period and comprehension of speech. *Working Papers on Bilingualism* 16: 1–17.

Parker, D. 1985a. *The great school myth: everybody's grandfather made it . . . and without bilingual education.* Unpublished manuscript, Bilingual Education Office, Sacramento, California State Department of Education,

Parker, D. 1985b. *Sheltered English: theory to practice.* Paper presented at the National Association for Bilingual Education Conference, San Francisco, California.

Paulston, C.B. 1977. Theoretical perspectives on bilingual education. *Working Papers on Bilingualism* 13: 130–180.

Paulston, C.B. 1980. *Bilingual Education: Theories and Issues.* Rowley, MA: Newbury House.

Peal, E., & W.E. Lambert. 1962. The relation of bilingualism to intelligence. *Psychological Monographs* 76.

Penfield, W., & L. Roberts. 1959. *Speech and Brain Mechanisms.* New York: Atheneum.

Piaget, J. 1959. *The Language and Thought of the Child* (3d ed.). London: Routledge & Kegan Paul.

Polich, E. 1974. *Report on the evaluation of the lower elementary French immersion program through grade 3.* Protestant School Board of Greater Montreal, Quebec.

Price, E. 1978. *Bilingual Education in Wales: 5–11.* London: Evans/Methuen Educational.

Pycock, C.J. 1977. *The effectiveness of two approaches used to introduce English in grade two bilingual classes.* Unpublished manuscript, South Shore Protestant Regional School Board, St. Lambert, Quebec.

Ramirez, A.G., & N.P. Stromquist. 1978. *ESL Methodology and Student Learning in Bilingual Elementary Schools.* Stanford, CA: Center for Educational Research at Stanford.

Ramirez, J.D. 1985. *Summary Results of Pre/Post Achievement Test Comparisons for Matched Groups of Target Students, FY 1984–1985.* Memorandum. Mountain View, CA: SRA Technologies.

Ramirez, J.D., S.D. Yuen, D.R. Ramey, & B. Merino. 1986. *First Year Report: Longitudinal Study of Immersion Programs for Language-Minority Children.* Washington, DC: U.S. Department of Education.

Richards, J.C. 1985. *Planning for proficiency.* Paper given at CATESOL Convention, San Diego, California.

Rivera, C. 1984. *Language Proficiency and Academic Achievement.* Clevedon, England: Multilingual Matters.

Rosansky, E. 1975. The critical period for the acquisition of language: some cognitive developmental considerations. *Working Papers on Bilingualism* 6: 92–102.

Rosenholz, S.J. 1985. Modifying status expectations in the traditional classroom. In J. Berger & M. Zelditch (eds.), *Status, Attributions and Influence.* San Francisco: Jossey-Bass, 445–470.

Rosenholz, S.J., & B. Wilson. 1980. The effect of classroom structure on shared perceptions of ability. *American Educational Research Journal* 17: 75–82.

Ryan, E.B. 1983. Social psychological mechanisms underlying native speaker evaluations of non-native speech. *Studies in Second Language Acquisition* 5: 148–161.

Ryan, E.B., & H. Giles. 1982. *Attitudes Toward Language Variation: Social and Applied Contexts.* London: Edward Arnold.

San Diego City Schools. 1982. *Bilingual Demonstration Project.* San Diego, CA: San Diego Unified School District.

Schinke-Llano, L.A. 1983. Foreigner talk in content classrooms. In H.W. Selinger & M.H. Long (eds.), *Classroom Oriented Research in Second Language Acquisition.* Rowley, MA: Newbury House.

Seliger, H., S. Krashen, & P. Ladefoged. 1975. Maturational constraints on the acquisition of second language accent. *Language Sciences* 36: 20–22.

Shapson, S.M., & E.M. Day. 1982. A comparison of three late immersion programs. *The Alberta Journal of Educational Research* 28: 135–148.

Shapson, S.M., & E.M. Day. 1983. *Evaluation studies of bilingual programs in Canada.* Paper presented at the American Educational Research Association Conference, Montreal.

Shapson, S.M., & D. Kaufman. 1977. *Overview of elementary French programs in British Columbia; issues and research.* Paper presented at the Conference on Second Language Learning, College Saint-Jean, Edmonton, Alberta.

Shavelson, R.J., & P. Stern. 1981. Research on teacher's pedagogical thoughts, judgments, decisions, and behavior. *Review of Educational Research* 51: 455–498.

Skutnabb-Kangas, T. 1980. Guest worker or immigrant: different ways of reproducing an underclass. *Rollig Papir* No. 21.

Skutnabb-Kangas, T., & P. Toukomaa. 1976. *Teaching Migrant Children's Mother Tongue and Learning the Language of the Host Country in the Context of the Socio-Cultural Situation of the Migrant Family.* Helsinki: The Finnish National Commission for UNESCO.

Slobin, D.I. 1973. Cognitive prerequisites for the development of grammar. In C.A. Ferguson & D.I. Slobin (eds.), *Studies of Child Language Development.* New York: Holt, Rinehart & Winston, 175–280.

Snow, C.E. 1983. Literacy and language: relationships during the pre-school years. *Harvard Educational Review* 53: No. 2.

Snow, C.E. 1985. *Beyond conversation: second language learners' acquisition of description and explanation.* Unpublished manuscript, Graduate School of Education, Harvard University, Cambridge, Mass.

Snow, C.E., & C.A. Ferguson, 1978. *Talking to Children: Language Input and Acquisition.* Cambridge, Eng.: Cambridge University Press.

Spilka, I. 1976. Assessment of second language performance in immersion programs. *Canadian Modern Language Review* 32: 543–540.

Steinberg, S. 1981. *The Ethnic Myth.* Boston: Beacon Press.

Stern, H.H. 1963. *Foreign Languages in Primary Education.* Paris: UNESCO.

Stern, H.H. 1984. The immersion phenomenon. *Language and Society.* Ottawa: Ministry of Supply and Services, 4–7.

Stevens, F. 1976. *Second Language Learning in an Activity-Centred Program.* M.A. thesis, Department of Educational Technology, Concordia University, Montreal.

Stevens, F. 1983a. Activities to promote learning and communication in the second language classroom. *TESOL Quarterly* 17: 259–272.

Stevens, F. 1983b. *Test linguistique maternelle.* Department of Educational Technology, Concordia University, Montreal.

Swain, M. 1975. Writing skills of grade three French immersion pupils. *Working Papers on Bilingualism* 7: 1–38.

Swain, M. 1978. French immersion: early, late or partial? *Canadian Modern Language Review* 34: 577–585.

Swain, M. 1981. Linguistic environment as a factor in the acquisition of target language skills. In R. Andersen (ed.), *Second Language Acquisition and Use Under Different Circumstances.* Rowley, MA: Newbury House.

Swain, M. 1985. Communicative competence: some roles of comprehensible input and comprehensible output in its development. In S.M. Gass & C.G. Madden (eds.), *Input in Second Language Acquisition.* Rowley, MA: Newbury House, 257–271.

Swain, M., & S. Lapkin. 1982. *Evaluating Bilingual Education: A Canadian Case Study.* Clevedon, England: Multilingual Matters.

Szamosi, M., M. Swain, & S. Lapkin. 1979. Do early immersion pupils 'know' French? *Orbit* 20–23.

Tajfel, H. 1974. Social identity and intergroup behavior. *Social Science Information* 13: 65–93.

Tajfel, H., & J. Turner. 1979. An integrative theory of inter-group conflict. In W.G. Austin & S. Worchel (eds.), *The Social Psychology of Intergroup Relations.* Monterey, CA: Brooks/Cole.

Taylor, D.M., J. Bassili, & F. Aboud. 1973. Dimensions of ethnic identity: an example from Quebec. *Journal of Social Psychology* 89: 185–192.

Terrell, T.D. 1981. The natural approach in bilingual education. In *Schooling and Lan-*

guage Minority Students: A Theoretical Framework. Los Angeles: Evaluation, Dissemination, and Assessment Center, 117–146.

Tikunoff, W.J. 1983. *Compatibility of the SBIF Features with Other Research on Instruction for LEP Students.* San Francisco: Far West Laboratory for Educational Research and Development.

Trites, R. 1981. *Primary French Immersion: Disabilities and Prediction of Success.* Toronto: OISE Press.

Troike, R. 1978. Research evidence for the effectiveness of bilingual education. *NABE Journal* 3: 13–24.

Tucker, G.R. 1980. *Comments on Proposed Rules for Non-Discrimination Under Programs Receiving Federal Financial Assistance Through the Education Department.* Washington, DC: Center for Applied Linguistics.

Tucker, G.R., E. Hamayan, & F. Genesee. 1976. Affective, cognitive and social factors in second language acquisition. *Canadian Modern Language Review* 23: 214–226.

Tucker, G.R., W.E. Lambert, & A. d'Anglejan. 1972. *Are French immersion programs suitable for working class children? A pilot investigation.* Psychology Department, McGill University, Montreal.

UNESCO. 1953. *The Use of Vernacular Languages in Education* (Monograph on fundamental education, No. 6). Paris: UNESCO.

U.S. Commission on Civil Rights. 1973. *The Unfinished Education* (Report II: Mexican American education study). Washington, DC: U.S. Government Printing Office.

Waggoner, R., & J.M. O'Malley. 1985. Teachers of limited-English-proficiency children in the United States. *NABE Journal* 9.

Webster, M.A., & J.E. Driskell, Jr. 1978. Status generalization: a review and some new data. *American Sociological Review* 43: 220–236.

Wells, G. 1979. Describing children's linguistic development at home and at school. *British Educational Research Journal* 5: 75–89.

Wells, G. 1980. *Some antecedents of early educational achievement.* Paper presented at the British Psychological Society, Edinburgh.

Wells, G. 1981. *Learning Through Interaction.* Cambridge, Eng.: Cambridge University Press.

Willig, A. 1985. A meta-analysis of selected studies on the effectiveness of bilingual education. *Review of Educational Research* 55: 269–317.

Wong-Fillmore, L., P. Ammon, B. McLaughlin, & M.S. Ammon. 1985. *Learning English Through Bilingual Instruction: Executive Summary and Conclusions.* Washington, DC: U.S. Department of Education.

Zajonc, R.B. 1968. Attitudinal effects of mere exposure. *Journal of Personality and Social Psychology* (Monograph Supplement 9, Part 2).

Zappert, L., & B.R. Cruz. 1977. *Bilingual Education: An Appraisal of Empirical Research.* Berkeley, CA: Development Associates.

Index